Internet

FOR BUSY PEOPLE

Second Edition

Blueprints for the Internet

On the following pages, we provide blueprints for some of the best ways to use the Internet:

- Shop Around the Clock

- Search for a UseNet Article

- Look for a Long-Lost Friend

- Run a Virtual Meeting

- Make a Web Page

- Track a FedEx Package

- Grab an Image

- Try Out Software

- Have a Visual Chat

Books? Software? T-shirts? Find the site that sells to your heart's delight. No crowds, no waiting. (page 12).

Start by filling in some personal information, as you would for a mail order.

Netscape - [MONSTER T-Shirt Order Form]

File Edit View Go Bookmarks Options Directory Window Help

Back Forward Home Reload Images Open Print Find Stop

Location: http://www.ankiewicz.com/monsters/monsterorder.html

Name: Christian Crumlish

Email Address: xian@pobox.com

Street Address:

City:

State or Province:

Postal Code:

Country:

How many T shirts would you like?

Large: 1 at US $12.00 each.

X-Large: at US $12.00 each.

Document: Done

Start Netscape - [MONSTE... 6:11 PM

Select the product you want, the quantity, and so on. Then submit your order, sit back, and relax. For security, many sites request that you arrange payment by mail or fax.

Visit a search site such as Deja News (http://www.dejanews.com) to get quick hits on newsgroup articles related to your interests (pages 214-218).

Netscape - [Deja News Query Results]

File   Edit   View   Go   Bookmarks   Options   Directory   Window   Help

Back   Forward   Home   Reload   Images   Open   Print   Find   Stop

Location: http://xp2.dejanews.com/dnquery.xp

What's New?   What's Cool?   Destinations   Net Search   People   Software

Hits **1-25** of 1136 for Query: **Sean Connery movies**

Date	Scr	Subject	Newsgroup	Author
1. 96/03/21	044	Re: Sean Connery	rec.arts.movies.mis	ataraxus@beck
2. 96/03/19	044	Sean Connery	rec.arts.movies.mis	cac909@aol.co
3. 95/05/24	043	Re: actors in parts they	rec.arts.movies	kboer@nervm.n
4. 95/09/05	042	Sean Connery films	rec.arts.movies.peo	Max Headroom
5. 96/06/09	041	re:movie	alt.fan.dragonlance	jtreller@kwan
6. 96/05/08	041	sean connery	alt.fan.james-bond	King James <k
7. 96/07/16	039	Re: Really OT: Star Wars	alt.tv.space-a-n-b	Jeff Schlenke
8. 96/07/15	039	Movies with Masonic Cont	alt.masonic.members	cdf <cdf@why.
9. 96/07/05	039	Re: Indy 4, 5, 6 ..	alt.movies.spielber	wakingup@post
10. 96/06/21	039	Re: Most Captivating voi	rec.arts.movies.pas	satterfield@o
11. 96/06/07	039	Re: Sean Connery s recen	rec.arts.movies.pas	llward@primen
12. 96/06/04	039	Re: Dragonheart (was Re	alt.books.m-lackey	hollievirg@ao

http://xp9.dejanews.com/getdoc.xp?recnum=41 1885&server=dnserver.db95q3&CONTEX

Start   Netscape - [Deja Ne...   8:43AM

Whether you're curious about anything from cats to Connery to baseball statistics, your search results in a list of articles with the best, most recent matches first (pages 215-216).

Simply click a Subject link to bring up a specific article. You'll find out what you need to know, fast (page 215).

Is Mary in Missoula or somewhere in Mississippi, and does she have e-mail? Find out by turning to Four11 or other Internet directory services, such as Bigfoot and WhoWhere? (pages 105-110).

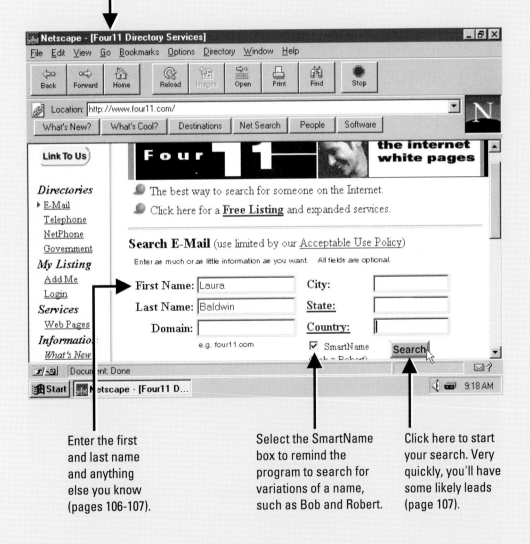

Enter the first and last name and anything else you know (pages 106-107).

Select the SmartName box to remind the program to search for variations of a name, such as Bob and Robert.

Click here to start your search. Very quickly, you'll have some likely leads (page 107).

Like these far-flung folks, you can use Microsoft NetMeeting to have a nice chat (page 241).

Collaborate by sharing applications or working together. Send a file, send private mail, or simply save an address (page 241).

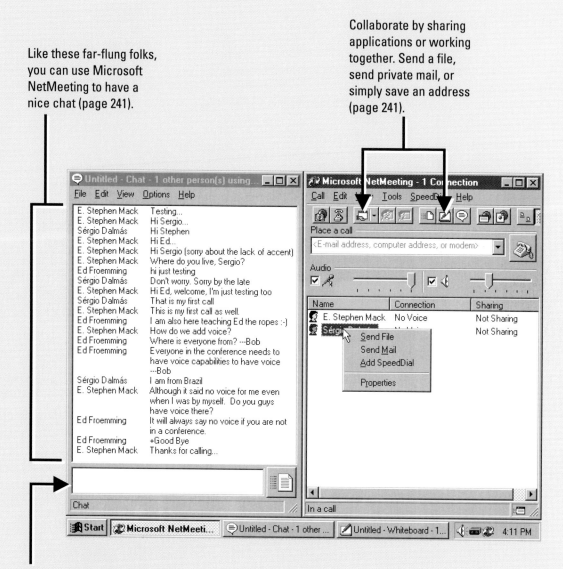

Enter your remarks in this area to communicate with everyone who's present. With the right capabilities, you can even add your voice and hear what's going on.

Alter the look of your page—sizes, styles, and links— with an array of tags, such as this one for a first-level heading (pages 291-292)

Have fun! Create your own web page with an everyday text editor and formatting tags that are easy to learn. (pages 289-295). Or, use a software program that walks you through the process. (pages 295-306).

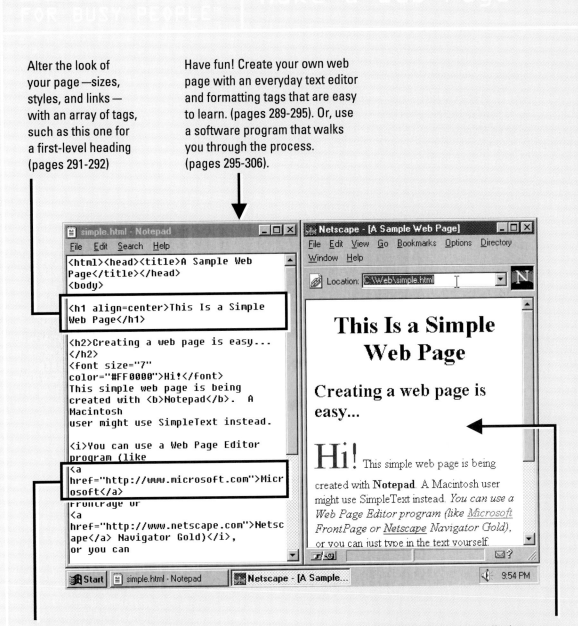

Want to speed your visitors on to other sites? Create a clickable link. (pages 293-294). This HTML tag leads to Microsoft's home page.(HTML stands for HyperText Markup Language.

Any web browser can display your HTML document as an attractive web page. Ask your friends to check out the results of your imagination.

Where oh where can your package be? If you sent it by Federal Express, it's easy to find out online through http://www.fedex.com.

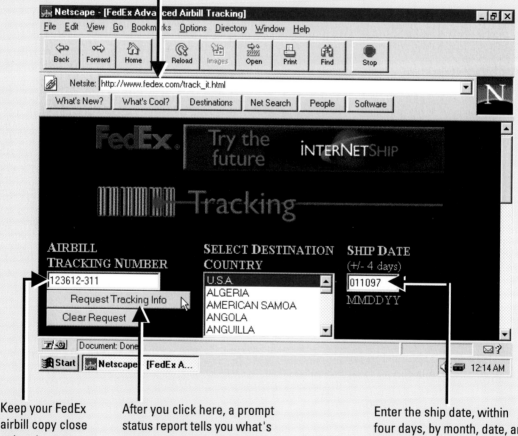

Keep your FedEx airbill copy close at hand so you can enter the airbill number here.

After you click here, a prompt status report tells you what's happening to the package and who signed for it if it has already been delivered.

Enter the ship date, within four days, by month, date, and year. Remember, no slashes or hyphens.

Move over, Monet. The WebMuseum, at http://www.emf.net/wm/net/, offers a rich source of images and information from museums around the world.

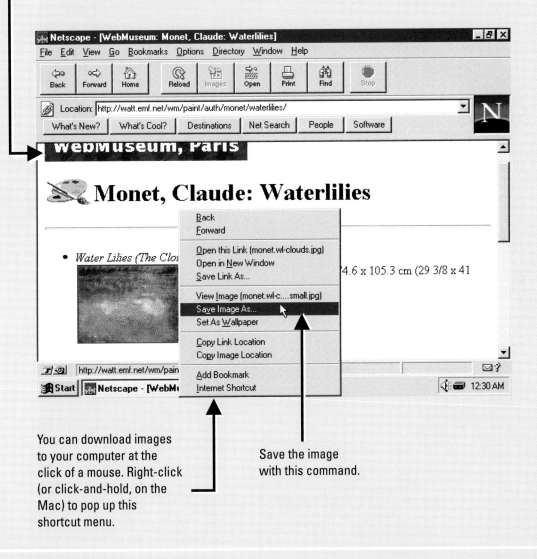

You can download images to your computer at the click of a mouse. Right-click (or click-and-hold, on the Mac) to pop up this shortcut menu.

Save the image with this command.

Visit a great place to browse, search for, and download the best software: http://www.shareware.com. You'll find "fixes" and new versions, too (pages 104-105).

When you find a file you like, try it out. As your browser downloads the file, a dialog box shows you the progress.

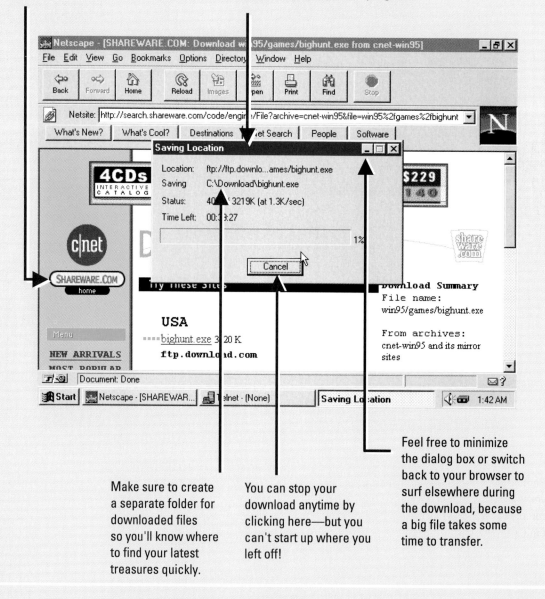

Make sure to create a separate folder for downloaded files so you'll know where to find your latest treasures quickly.

You can stop your download anytime by clicking here—but you can't start up where you left off!

Feel free to minimize the dialog box or switch back to your browser to surf elsewhere during the download, because a big file takes some time to transfer.

Sign on, and see who's there. As people talk, new frames appear, resembling a comic book. It's action packed, and everyone has a starring role (page 236).

See animated conversations come alive with Microsoft Comic Chat, available at http://wwww.microsoft.com/ie/download/. Sorry, not yet available for the Mac (pages 234-236)

A list of participants appears here. Who shall you be (page 236)?

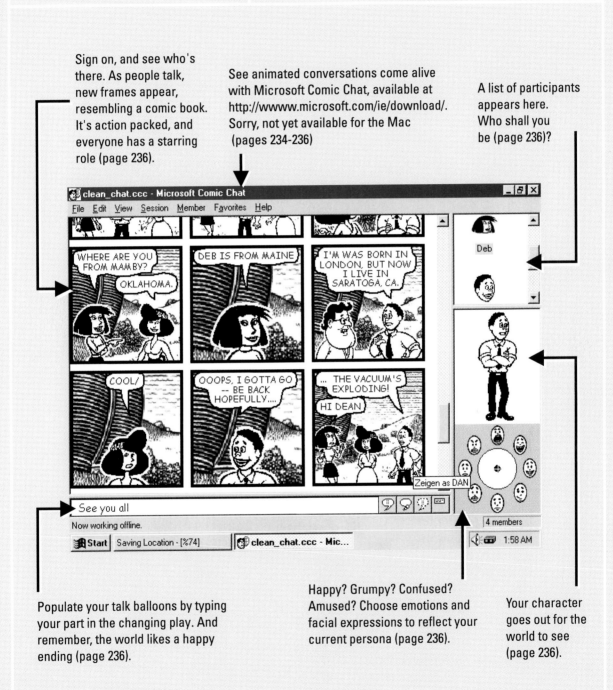

Populate your talk balloons by typing your part in the changing play. And remember, the world likes a happy ending (page 236).

Happy? Grumpy? Confused? Amused? Choose emotions and facial expressions to reflect your current persona (page 236).

Your character goes out for the world to see (page 236).

Internet

FOR BUSY PEOPLE

Second Edition

The Book to Use When There's No Time to Lose!

Christian Crumlish

OSBORNE

Osborne/**McGraw-Hill**

Berkeley / New York / St. Louis / San Francisco / Auckland / Bogotá
Hamburg / London / Madrid / Mexico City / Milan / Montreal / New Delhi
Panama City / Paris / São Paulo / Singapore / Sydney / Tokyo / Toronto

A Division of The **McGraw·Hill** *Companies*

Osborne/McGraw-Hill
2600 Tenth Street
Berkeley, California 94710
U.S.A.

For information on translations or book distributors outside the U.S.A., or to arrange bulk purchase discounts for sales promotions, premiums, or fundraisers, please contact Osborne/**McGraw-Hill** at the above address.

Internet for Busy People, Second Edition

Eudora is a registered trademark of QUALCOMM Incorporated.

1234567890 DOC 9987

ISBN 0-07-882283-1

Publisher: Brandon A. Nordin
Editor in Chief: Scott Rogers
Acquisitions Editor: Joanne Cuthbertson
Project Editor: Emily Rader
Associate Project Editor: Heidi Poulin
Editorial Assistant: Gordon Hurd
Technical Editor: Thomas Powell
Copy Editor: Judy Ziajka
Proofreader: Pat Mannion
Indexer: Valerie Robbins
Computer Designer: Roberta Steele, Leslee Bassin, Peter F. Hancik
Quality Control Specialist: Joe Scuderi
Series and Cover Design: Ted Mader Associates
Series Illustration: Daniel Barbeau

About the Author. . .

Christian Crumlish publishes the online magazine *Enterzone* and writes computer books for people who are as busy as he is. He is the best-selling author of *Word 97 for Busy People™* and coauthor of *Web Publishing with Netscape for Busy People™*.

Dedication

To brooklyn, zeigen, bnisbet, mal, ngm, k9luna, aweilec, annette, bad6, Kcareer, lpellerin, mgoetz, michael, and mijoyce

Contents

ACKNOWLEDGMENTS

First and foremost, let me doff my cap to Stephen Mack, whose yeoman service not only made the second edition of this book possible, but also made it much stronger and richer. Stephen undertook to help me revise this book on a breakneck schedule and helped keep it all together when the going got especially rough. He's to thank for many of the examples and illustrations throughout this book, including the wonderful blueprints.

Thanks to Nick Meriwether and Rich Frankel for timely Macintosh information (and screen shots).

When the whole revision process, with its breakneck writing, editorial, and production pace, really got crazy, I was glad that Emily Rader and Heidi Poulin were there to keep everything under control. Thomas Powell once again proved to be a great technical editor, bringing heavyweight insight and experience to the job. Judy Ziajka's copyedit held my feet to the fire as far as clarity and style are concerned. She also made sure I finished my sentences!

Gordon Hurd coped with his role as liaison extraordinaire with aplomb.

Thanks to for Joanne Cuthbertson for recruiting me to work on this wacky, zany, madcap Busy People series. I'd also especially like to thank Anne Ellingsen, in public relations, as well as the rest of the sales, marketing, and publicity crews at Osborne. You guys deserve a lot of credit for the success of this book so far.

As anyone who's ever been around a publishing house can tell you, it's one thing to plan (or replan) a beautiful design but quite another thing to implement such a design and make it look as good—or better—than the sample pages. The art and production team, headed by Marcela Hancik and including Leslee Bassin,

Peter Hancik, Lance Ravella, and Roberta Steele, has raised my personal standards for design, layout, and typesetting.

Thanks to the military-industrial complex for underwriting the Internet in the early days. Thanks to all of the active citizens of the Net who are busy volunteering their time and information and building communities based on communication. Thanks to Briggs, geebers, my family, the *Enterzone* gang, the antiweb list, the merry punsters, BATG, Nick Meriwether, Meshulam Plaves, and many more.

INTRODUCTION

This book is for people with only a night or a few lunch hours to learn how to explore the Internet. (In the words of radio station 1010 WINS in New York City, "Give us 22 minutes; we'll give you the world.") The digital revolution has given with one hand, creating all kinds of efficient ways to communicate electronically and organize a busy life, and taken away with the other, accelerating everyone's expectations, constantly moving the goalposts. The eruption of the Internet, the Web, and in-house intranets, has, if anything, picked up the pace.

How busy have you become lately? Has your job mushroomed with sprawling layers of responsibility? Do you feel like you have almost no time for anything? How often do you hear people say things like "Fax me that draft," "e-mail me those statistics," "our product release deadline's been moved up due to competitive pressures," or "it took longer than we thought—can you make up the time on your end?"

I Know you're in a Hurry, So...

Let's agree to dispense with the traditional computer book preliminaries. You've probably used a mouse, held down two keys at once, and have heard of this vast global network called the Internet. If you don't yet have Internet access, or if you're not sure what type of connection might already be available to you, start off by flipping to Appendix A, where I explain the different types of connections and how to find and select an Internet service provider (ISP).

So, now lets cut to the chase. After reading the first few chapters, you'll be able to:

- Browse (and search) the World Wide Web
- Send, receive, and reply to e-mail
- Find and join electronic mailing lists
- Subscribe to Usenet newsgroups (discussion groups) and join online IRC chats.

Later chapters will show you how to transfer files from Internet archive sites to your home (or office) computer and how to log into other computers on the Internet. I'll show you how to design, create, and format web pages and what to do when the time comes to publish them on the Internet (or on a local intranet).

As I mentioned, Appendix A is a primer for getting connected to the Internet. Appendix B offers some pointers to starting places and attractions on the Web. Throughout this book, I suggest web addresses (also called URLs) that you can visit for more information or to obtain free Internet programs and other software. All of the web addresses in this book are collected for your easy reference (and kept up-to-date) on the Web at the *Busy People's Bookmarks* (http://syx.com/busy/bookmarks/).

Things You Might Want to Know About This Book

This book uses examples and illustrations showing the Windows 95 versions of most Internet programs and features, but just about all of the information in the book applies equally well to other types of computers and operating systems, including Macintosh and Unix systems and even earlier versions of Windows. Macintosh users will find references for all the most important Mac Internet software in this book.

You can read this book more or less in any order. I suggest cruising Chapter 1 and reading Chapter 2 first, but you can start just as easily with Chapters 4 and 5 (which deal with e-mail) or by jumping directly to Chapter 3 to learn how to search the Web. Use the book as a reference. When you're stuck, not sure how to do something, know there's an answer but not what it is, pick up the book, zero in on the answer to your question, and put the book down again. Besides clear, coherent explanations of this all-over-the-map network of networks, you'll also find some special elements to help you get the most out of the Internet. Here's a quick rundown of the other elements in this book.

Blueprints

Blueprints, in the front of the book, depict and demonstrate key tasks and goals you can accomplish with Word.

Fast Forwards

Each chapter begins with a section called *Fast Forward*. This section should always be your first stop if you are a confident user, or if you are impatient or habitually late. You might find everything you need to get back in stride. Think of Fast Forwards as the *Reader's Digest* version of each chapter. This shorthand may leave you hungry, especially if you are new to the Internet. So, for more complete and leisurely explanations of techniques and shortcuts, read the rest of the chapter.

Expert Advice

Timesaving tips, techniques, and worthwhile addictions are all reported under the rubric of *Expert Advice*. Force yourself to develop some good habits now, while it's still possible! These notes also give you the big picture and help you plan ahead. For example, I'll suggest that you use an "off-line" newsreader program to save on connect-time charges while reading Usenet newsgroups.

Shortcuts

Shortcuts are designed for the busy person: when there's a way to do something that may not be as full-featured as the material in the text, but is *faster*, it will show up in the margin, below the businessman leaping over a fence.

Cautions

Sometimes it's too easy to plunge ahead and fall down a rabbit hole, resulting in hours of extra work just to get you back to where you were before you went astray. *Cautions* will warn you before you commit time-consuming mistakes.

Definitions

Usually, I explain computer or networking jargon in the text, wherever the technobabble first occurs. But if you encounter words you don't recognize, look for this body builder in the margin. *Definitions* point out important terms you might not  know the meaning of. When necessary, they're strict and a little technical, but most of the time they're informal and conversational.

Step by Steps

STEP BY STEP

To help clarify some of the more complicated procedures, blue *Step by Step* boxes will walk you through the necessary steps, using helpful screenshots to guide you.

Netiquette

There are some well-established guidelines for behavior on the Internet, most often referred to as "netiquette," that keep the Net cooperative and help everyone get along. Civility and familiarity with the traditional ways of doing things go a long way in helping you communicate with the total strangers you'll meet online. *Netiquette* boxes will tip you off to standard practices and faux pas to avoid.

Bookmarks

Throughout the book, key web addresses are pulled out into *Bookmark* boxes, so you can find them again easily when you check the book again later. By the way, these addresses, also called URLs, are notoriously long and strangely punctuated. Often, a web address does not fit on a single line of text. To avoid introducing spurious characters that will actually make the addresses incorrect, web addresses are wrapped without hyphens or any other special characters added, usually after a slash (/) or dot (.) character. So, for example, to point your web browser at http://ezone.org/ez/, just type the entire address on one line without any spaces or breaks (and don't type the comma at the end—that's just part of this sentence).

Let's Do It!

Ready? Let's dive into the Internet before the next big thing comes along! Incidentally, I'm always happy to hear your reactions to this or any of my other books. You can reach me through the publisher or on the Net (*xian@syx.com*).

1

See the Net with Your Web Browser

INCLUDES

- Understanding the World Wide Web and the Internet
- Understanding web addresses
- Following hyperlinks
- Understanding Internet jargon
- Saving time on the Web
- Using any web browser
- Making bookmarks

FAST FORWARD

Enter Web Addresses ➤ pp. 5-8

Location: http://www.yahoo.com/News/Daily/

Web addresses (also called URLs), which you can type directly into the address box of any browser, can be long and difficult to remember.

- Whenever possible, avoid typing them by hand.
- When copying by hand, be very careful to copy them exactly.

Browse the Web ➤ p. 8

Most of the time, you'll browse by pointing to and clicking hyperlinks, specially highlighted text or images that lead your web browser to a new destination.

Use the Web Without Wasting Time ➤ pp. 15-17

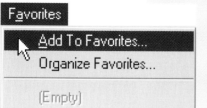

- Keep a goal or destination in mind.
- Save references to interesting destinations for those occasions when you have the leisure to browse freely.

Create a Bookmark ➤ pp. 29-31, 37

- In Netscape, select Bookmarks | Add Bookmark.
- In Internet Explorer, select Favorites | Add To Favorites. (Internet Explorer calls bookmarks *favorites*.)

Go to a Bookmark ➤ pp. 29-31, 37

- In Netscape, select Bookmarks | *bookmarked-item*.
- In Internet Explorer, select Favorites | *favorite-item*.

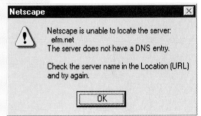

What to Do When Your Browser Fails to Connect to a Site ➤ p. 38

Don't worry about it. The Internet is sometimes "busy." Click the Stop button and try again. If you repeatedly fail to connect, try again later.

It's only recently become possible for a busy person to check out the Internet. Up until just a few years ago, you had to deal with arcane computer-science protocols and, usually, the powerful but willfully obscure Unix operating system. That has all changed in the past few years. First, commercial online services started creating gateways to the Internet, and now direct Internet access—via a network, Internet service provider, or online service—is commonplace and easy to use.

The Web is also fast becoming the easiest and most direct way to buy or sell things on the Internet.

The Web Makes it Easy
to Get Around the Internet

The most important advance in making the Internet easy and convenient to explore has been the development of the World Wide Web (a subset of the Internet) and elegant programs called *web browsers* that enable you to view and thumb through the myriad sources of information, communication, and software out there.

Now, browsing the Internet is a simple matter of running one of these programs and jumping to a destination. Because of the flexibility of the web medium, you can even use a web browser to gain access to items that are out there somewhere on the Internet but not directly on the Web. The web browser acts as a sort of umbrella interface for the entire Internet.

A Network of Networks

We're both too busy to spend all day discussing the history and technology of the Internet and all the fascinating trivia associated with it. You can get those anecdotes anywhere. (For that matter, you can get them for free once you're on the Net.) Suffice it to say that the Internet is not really a coherent network in the same sense as a local area network such as you might find in an office or a wide area network such as you might find on a university campus.

Actually, the Internet is a loosely and redundantly linked collection of smaller networks and individual computers, all of which agree to share (some) information using the various Internet protocols as a *lingua franca*.

When people talk about addresses on the Internet, they usually mean web addresses (URLs) or e-mail addresses (see Chapter 4).

DEFINITION

Protocol: A protocol is an agreed-upon method of communication used by two computers or two programs to interchange information, but don't worry about it.

If you ask what the Internet is like or how it works, you'll get the sort of range of answers obtainable from blind men touching an elephant. The Internet is like a cloud. The Internet is like a web. The Internet is like a tree. I suggest you think of the Internet as a black box. Stuff goes in one end and comes out the other. Forget trying to figure out what happens in the middle. Why did the chicken choose a particular path through the Internet? To get to the other side.

Web Addresses

In a perfect Internet, every interesting destination on the World Wide Web would be accessible via a single click of the mouse. Because the Net evolves so quickly, though, there is no single comprehensive listing anywhere that covers everything you might ever want to see. Sometimes you'll learn about an interesting spot on the Web from a book or newspaper article or even from a friend. In that case, the location on the Web will be expressed in the form of a *URL*.

DEFINITION

URL: *Uniform resource locator. The URL is a standard form of address for any file, object, or resource (any information unit) on the Internet. Pragmatically, a URL is an Internet address expressed in a form that any web browser can understand. Web addresses usually start with http:// (or something else followed by ://) and usually end with .html or just a trailing / to indicate the default file in a folder.*

Here are six sample URLs:

You can leave a trailing "/" off most addresses.

```
http://www.altavista.digital.com/
http://ezone.org/ez/
http://www.emf.net/~mal/antiweb.html
ftp://ftp.cdrom.com/
gopher://garnet.msen.com:70/11/stuff/gutenberg
news:news.announce.newusers
```

The first URL points to the main page (also called the index or default file) on the AltaVista server at the Digital Equipment Corporation site. (Alta Vista is a search engine.)

DEFINITIONS

Search engine: *A large database of Internet addresses that users can visit on the Web and query to search for resources.*

Domain name: *Every computer on the Internet can be identified (and addressed) by a domain name, consisting of, from right to left, a primary domain (such as com, edu, net, mil, or gov), a subdomain (such as gateway2000, princeton, pacbell, or whitehouse), and an optional host, or site, name (such as www, garnet, or grateful), all separated by dots.*

The second URL points to the home page—the primary web document—of a magazine called *Enterzone* on a server called ezone in the domain of not-for-profit organizations (.org). The third URL points to an HTML document describing the Antiweb mailing list, located in the personal directory of the owner of the list (Malcolm Humes) on the web server of his service provider, EMF.

Gopher will be explained in Chapter 9. You'll learn about Usenet in Chapter 6.

The fourth URL points to the public file archive of an online CD-ROM retailer. The fifth URL points to a menu on a Gopher server, which is technically not a web document, but which can be reached via the Web, on a machine on the network of MSEN, an Internet service provider. The last URL is the address of a Usenet newsgroup. Generally, though, a given address corresponds to a specific document somewhere out there on the Internet.

Don't worry about learning the system for URLs. Before long, they'll always be completely hidden. For now, just be sure to spell the URL correctly, carefully copying it character for character (and making sure to duplicate the capitalization as well—parts of URLs are case sensitive), if you plan to use it to reach a destination.

If you *are* forced to copy a web address from paper, beware of some common typographical errors. Web addresses rarely end in periods, for example, so if you see an address printed with a period at the end, it's probably just punctuation in the sentence and not part of the address. Addresses do often end with the letters "html" or with a forward slash (/). Web addresses sometimes have a ~ character (called a tilde) in them, and sometimes newspapers will mess up and leave the symbol out entirely or put it on top of a letter of the alphabet instead of within the address.

CAUTION

If you copy a URL from a newspaper or book, be prepared to deal with typos. Often URLs gain or lose hyphens in key places when typeset in "old-fashioned" publications.

Depending on your mail program, people may be able to send you e-mail with an attached web address so that all you have to do is double-click the attachment and your mail program will start your web browser and go directly to the attached address.

Forget Addresses— Use Hyperlinks to Click and Go

More and more pages these days sport image maps, which are clickable images that connect to different URLs, depending on where they are clicked.

Fortunately, most of the time you'll be able to get around the Web just fine by following links. What are links? Links are parts of a document—sometimes text, sometimes pictures—that lead to other documents, other parts of the same document, or other destinations on the Web. They're really embedded URLs: embedded web addresses that you can click. The organizing structure (such as it is) of the Web is composed of these *hyperlinks*.

Traditionally (on the Web, that means since 1993), link text in web browsers appears in blue (instead of black) and is underlined. Link pictures sometimes have a blue border. Your mouse pointer changes when you place it over a link. More and more web pages are using customized colors, though, so you can't count on blue meaning link. Also, I usually turn off link underlining as I find it often looks ugly, and some link pictures have invisible borders. Ultimately, the only consistent evidence of a link is the appearance of your mouse pointer, which changes (usally to a pointing hand) when you point to a link.

On the Beaten Track

To compare advertisements on the Web with those on television, some people use a pull vs. push metaphor: TV ads are pushed toward you, but web ads pull you toward them, ceding you more control.

The Web is a weird conglomeration of major media outlets, underground or alternative publishing ventures, self-promotion, home movies, and billboards. Amidst all this chaos are some big players, usually tied to major publishing empires and supported by advertising. One nice thing about advertising on the Web is that you can generally avoid it simply by not clicking the links to sponsors' sites. On the other hand, you'll be forced to see (and wait for) the art associated with a link when a web page that includes an ad is loaded.

The web browser you use determines where you start (what home page you start on), and therefore what primary links are available to you and whose list of cool or new sites you see.

Some of the big names or owners of major pages you'll hear about include

- Netscape (makers of the most widely distributed web browser)
- Yahoo! (one of the most comprehensive web directories)
- *HotWired* (the first major commercial web publication)
- PathFinder (Time/Warner's web site)
- CNN (yes, the cable news network)
- clnet (the online publishing network)
- NCSA (distributors of Mosaic, the first graphical browser to really spark the growth of the Web)
- CERN (the lab in Switzerland where the web protocols were designed)

You'll find these sites with no trouble, because all roads lead to them.

Off the Beaten Track

Because the Web is so chaotic and formless, the big boys share shelf space with the works independent web artists, personal confession pages, grass-roots projects, and so on. The links to these sites aren't always well publicized or easy to find, but a lot of them tend to lead to each other in a sort of noncommercial underground Web, or "antiweb," so once you find your way into the boho districts of the Web, you can easily navigate from there.

Other items accessible via the Web, such as Gopher menus, are technically not real web pages, and they therefore lack the facility to fully incorporate links to other web pages. Because of this, they generally function as cul-de-sacs, and you'll need to use your Back button to retreat from them back into the Web proper.

Jargon to Watch For

Just to satisfy your curiosity, Table 1.1 provides a briefing on the jargon you'll encounter on the Web (and the Net), but don't let the terminology get in your way. The point is to sit back and browse, following your own instincts. Let the geeks and gurus yak in the lingo.

Jargon Term	What It Means
Bookmark	A saved link to a web address; also called a hotlist entry or favorite place.
Browser	A program used to connect to sites on the World Wide Web.
Client	A program, such as a web browser, that connects to a centralized server program and obtains information from it.
Client-server model	A method of sharing computer and network resources by centralizing some functions with a server and allowing individual clients to connect to the server to perform those functions.
FTP	File transfer protocol. Used to describe Internet public file archive sites (FTP sites).
Home page	A major or central document at a World Wide Web site, an individual's page, or a web browser's default start-up page.
HTML	Hypertext markup language; the language (consisting mainly of formatting tags) used to describe a document for the World Wide Web, including both structural formatting and hyperlinks.
HTTP	Hypertext transport protocol; the technique used by web servers to dispense information to web browsers.
Hyper	Nonlinear, capable of branching off in many directions; the term can be used alone or as a prefix.
Image map	A clickable image that connects to different URLs depending on which part of the image is clicked.
Information Superhighway, Information Highway, Infoway, Infobahn, Info Highway, and so on	Terms coined to describe a possible information infrastructure, using coaxial or fiber-optic cables, that would upgrade the existing system. These terms correspond to nothing in the real world; the Internet is not a superhighway.

Table 1.1 World Wide Web Jargon

Jargon Term	What It Means
Internet	A collection of networks and computers all over the world, all of which share information, or at least e-mail, using agreed-upon Internet protocols.
Link	A specially designated word or image that, when selected, takes a web browser to a new page or other destination (an embedded web address).
Multimedia	Refers to the incorporation of many different media, often including text, pictures, sounds, video, animation, and so on.
Net	A loosely defined term meant to suggest the loose association of all or most computers on the planet; this term generally refers to a more inclusive set of linked networks than just the Internet, but it also corresponds roughly to the Internet.
Page	On the World Wide Web, an HTML document.
Server	A piece of software or a machine that acts as a centralized source of information or computing resources (such as web sites, Gopher menus, FTP archives, and so on), available to clients.
Site	A location on the Internet, often the host of one or more servers, or a set of related web pages.
Web	The World Wide Web.
World Wide Web	A subset or cross-section of the Internet technically composed of a set of mutually hyperlinked documents and objects stored on web servers, but commonly taken to include any resource on the Net that can be reached with a web browser.

Table 1.1 World Wide Web Jargon (*continued*)

What Can You Use the Web For?

So the Web is the easiest way to get around the Internet, but what can you use it for? What are the practical applications? More and more new services are coming on line all the time, but here are some of the things you can do on the Web right now:

- Shop for products and buy them online.
- Find and download software.

- Join in on ongoing discussions.
- Read some of the wealth of information published on the Web.
- Search for people or information.

The following paragraphs provide examples of applications.

Buying Things

Figure 1.1 shows the Amazon.com online bookstore web site.

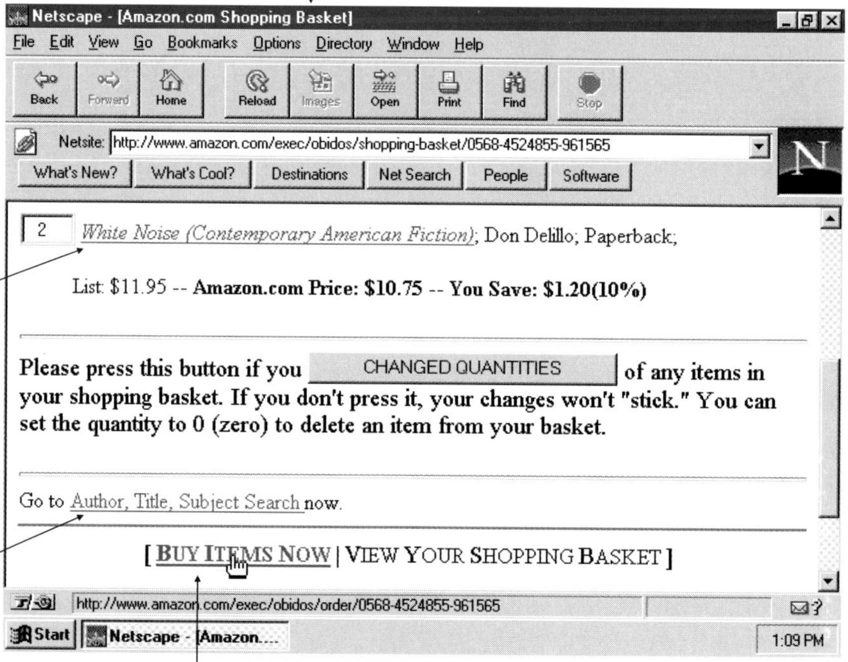

Your purchases are displayed on a page called the Shopping Basket.

To find out about the book *White Noise*, click here.

Click here to search for more books to buy.

Click here to enter your shipping address and other ordering information.

Figure 1.1 Buying books online at Amazon.com

There's more on finding and downloading software in Chapter 3.

Getting Software

Figure 1.2 shows me downloading WinZip from clnet's Shareware.com web site.

I can leave Shareware.com and browse elsewhere while my file downloads

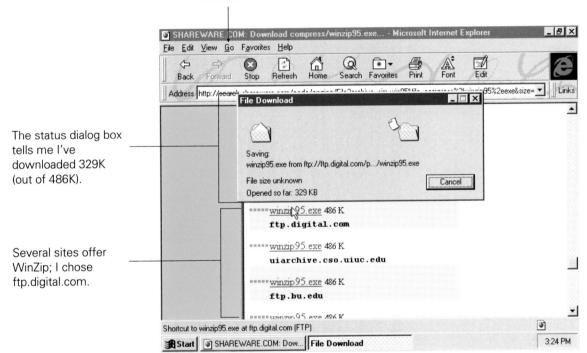

The status dialog box tells me I've downloaded 329K (out of 486K).

Several sites offer WinZip; I chose ftp.digital.com.

Figure 1.2 Downloading WinZip, a shareware compression program

Joining Ongoing Discussions and Chats

The Internet has forums for longstanding ongoing conversations and for live, real-time chatting. Both of these ways of communicating have their own uses, and each of them can help build online communities.

There's more about various forms of online discussion in Chapters 5 through 7.

Figure 1.3 shows a conversation using Netscape's CoolTalk program. If your computer has a sound card and a microphone, you can listen and talk to the other person; otherwise, you can type to each other using the Chat tool, as shown.

This button starts a conference. You need to know the person's username.

You can see who you're talking to.

Both sides of the conversation appear here.

You type what you want to say here.

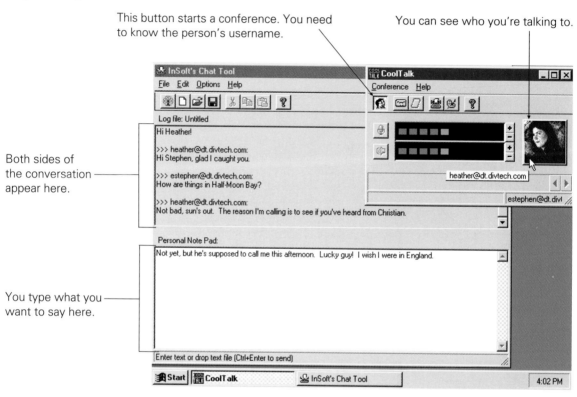

Figure 1.3 Conversing with Heather using CoolTalk

Reading Up

Figure 1.4 shows the contents page of *Slate* (http://www.slate.com), a magazine sponsored by Microsoft and edited by Michael Kinsley.

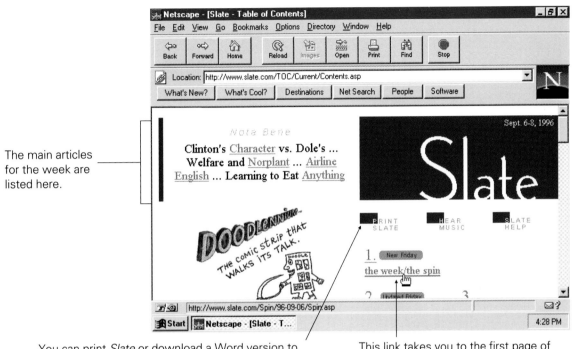

The main articles for the week are listed here.

You can print *Slate* or download a Word version to make reading it easier.

This link takes you to the first page of *Slate*, an update of the week's events.

Figure 1.4 Finding out what's new this week with *Slate*

There's much more about searching in Chapter 3.

Finding Information and People

Figure 1.5 shows the results of a search performed at the AltaVista search-engine site.

Using the Web Without Wasting Time

The biggest impediment to making efficient use of the World Wide Web is that it's essentially a digressive medium, perfectly suited for long asides and fascinating tangents, less well suited for hard-core, finite research.

Click here to have AltaVista search the Web for your text.

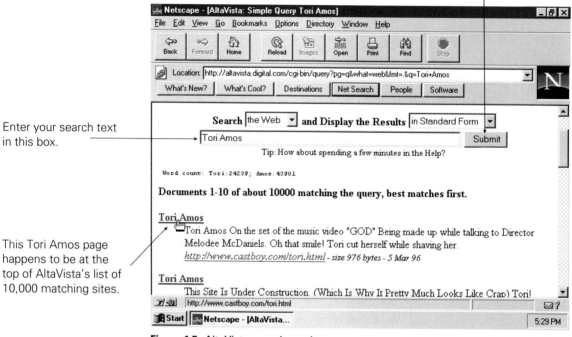

Enter your search text in this box.

This Tori Amos page happens to be at the top of AltaVista's list of 10,000 matching sites.

Figure 1.5 AltaVista search results

CAUTION

With most browsers, once you back up and then head in a new direction, the branch you explored earlier will disappear from your history path. This is one important reason why you should create bookmarks.

There are two things you can do to make more efficient use of your time on the Web. The first is something I cannot emphasize strongly enough: create bookmarks. Create Bookmarks. CREATE BOOKMARKS! The Web is so peripatetic (rambling this way and that) that you're bound to visit interesting sites—and then never see them again, because you won't remember exactly which tangents you followed to get there. You can always remove bookmarks that you end up not needing, so make a bookmark every time you arrive at an interesting-looking site. Later, you'll be glad you did.

EXPERT ADVICE

If any web page takes more than 90 seconds before even beginning to load, stop the browser and try again or come back later. You're too busy to sit there twiddling your thumbs while computers fail to connect to each other.

The other good advice I can offer is to separate out your business or educational use of the Web from your recreational use. To save time on the Web, set yourself a goal and head for it as directly as you can. If, along the way, you are tempted by the siren call of interesting links, note them or make bookmarks for them, but put off visiting them to another time.

Interacting on the Internet

Perhaps the biggest drawback of the Web, or at least of most of its contents, is that it places the user in a passive role. For all its possibilities, at this point using the Web isn't too far removed from watching television. The Internet did not grow in popularity this quickly simply as a venue for personal listings and corporate advertisements. No; much of the culture of the Internet takes place in more interactive formats, such as private e-mail, semi-public mailing lists, and the massive Usenet newsgroup system. Those craving live interaction find their way to the IRC or other *chat* venues.

DEFINITION

IRC: Internet relay chat, a system for real-time (typed) conversation. Some of the newer forms of life communication, such as Internet Phone and video chatting, are based on the IRC protocols. IRC and other forms of chat are explained in Chapter 7

There are already many experiments that incorporate these more interactive features into the web experience, and if and when they become widespread or popular, the Web will absorb yet another aspect of the Internet. For now, though, you should poke your head beyond the web browser and learn a little about e-mail and discussion groups, explained in Chapters 4 through 7.

You've Seen One Web Browser, You've Seen 'Em All

If you need to get, install, or set up Netscape Navigator or Microsoft Internet Explorer, see Chapter 2.

If I've whetted your appetite to check out the World Wide Web for yourself, then it's time for you to fire up a web browser and start exploring. There are quite a few browsers out there, many of which are variations on NCSA Mosaic, the original graphical web browser. By far the most widely distributed browser is Netscape Navigator, usually just referred to as Netscape. By giving away early versions of the browser to individuals (it's still free to educational institutions, nonprofit organizations, and other groups), Netscape established a dominant position in the browser market, so even competing browsers tend to offer the same features as Netscape.

Microsoft's entry in the browser market, Internet Explorer, is widely considered to be Netscape's chief competitor. Between 1995 and 1996, each company released two or three new versions in an ever-escalating features war.

I'll show you how to set up and use both of these browsers, because the odds are that you'll have access to at least one if not both of them. Even if you end up using some other browser, most of the features will be the same. First, I'll give you a basic rundown of how to work with any browser. Then I'll give you the specifics for Netscape and any details that differ for Internet Explorer.

Web Browser Basics

No matter what kind of web browser or even what sort of Internet connection you have, the overall process of running a browser and connecting to the Web is more or less the same. Sometimes the terminology or the actual mechanism varies from program to program, and all browsers don't share the exact same set of capabilities, but the differences are getting smaller all the time. The feature war

If you don't have an Internet connection or don't know whether you are connected, see Appendix A for information on how to shop for and select an Internet service provider (ISP). If you are connected to the Net but you don't have a web browser available, see Chapter 2 for information on how to download and install Netscape Navigator or Microsoft Internet Explorer.

I alluded to earlier means that browsers are squirmy things, changing all the time (so long as you keep upgrading, that is).

With any web browser, you'll need to know how to

- Start the program
- Navigate the Web by following links
- Move backward and forward along your recent path
- Type a web address to go to that location directly
- Turn off graphics for speedy browsing (for graphical browsers only, naturally)
- Create and return to bookmarks
- Assign a favorite web page as your starting page (discussed, along with other customizations options, in Chapter 2)
- Search the Internet (see Chapter 3 for the full lowdown)

EXPERT ADVICE

Another thing you'll have to get used to is updating your software from time to time. If you ever notice that the program in front of you lacks a feature I'm describing in the book, you may need to upgrade your web browser. If so, see Chapter 2.

Once you have these basic techniques down, browsing the Web is simply a matter of starting your program and then following links, visiting bookmarks, entering addresses directly, and searching.

Sure, you'll encounter some variations: pages that are split into frames like a TV dinner, sites that ask you to register and/or enter a password to proceed, secure connections between your browser and a host so you can purchase products online without exposing your credit card to snoops. But the basic routine—the motions: pointing, clicking, going back and forward—doesn't change.

Clicking Links and Going Back and Forward

Most of the time, you'll go from page to page on the Web by clicking hypertext links. These are highlighted words (or images) that, when clicked, jump

Your Internet connection must be up and running for your web browser to work. See Appendix A for more on determining your type of Internet connection.

you to another page or section of a page. Most web browsers also have special links built in. Usually a browser has an icon that leads directly to the browser's own home page and other buttons or menu items that take you to directories, search pages, new site announcements, and so on. Even if you start by visiting one of these built-in destinations, you'll soon be proceeding by clicking links.

Figure 1.6 shows the Netscape screen. This screen features links to the rest of the Netscape site and announcements and news releases. To show you how this screen works, I will click the Net Search button, as shown in the figure.

EXPERT ADVICE

Any time you get tired of waiting for a page to appear, press the Stop button and then either try again (click Reload) or go somewhere else.

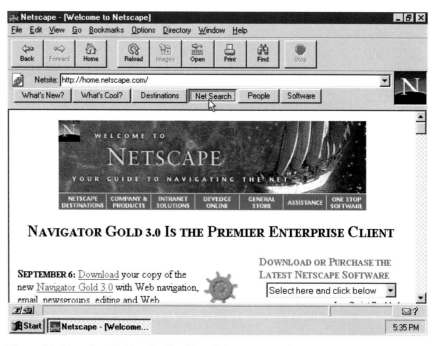

Figure 1.6 Here I'm clicking the Net Search button near the top of the Netscape screen (the same option, labeled Internet Search, is also available on the Directory menu)

Beyond the differences mandated by the operating system (such as the location of the menu bar and aesthetic touches), the program looks and works essentially the same way on every type of computer.

Clicking Net Search takes me to the Destinations part of the Netscape web site, which for me displayed the Yahoo! control panel shown in Figure 1.7. Netscape rotates through a series of different search and directory sites on this page, so you may see a different control panel if you try to follow along.

Next, I'll click the News Headlines link to see what's going on in the world.

Yahoo! offers a number of categorized directory listings as well as a key-word search box. Yahoo! has its own web site (http://www.yahoo.com), as do all other directories and search locations, but Netscape makes the most popular ones available directly through its own site.

Once you find your way to a destination on the Web, you'll still be able to jump elsewhere. Most web sites contain links to other sites in an effort to interconnect themselves. The most important button on any browser is the Back button (or the backward-pointing arrow). It allows you to retrace your steps and follow other paths. Figure 1.8 shows the Yahoo! News and Events page for today

Figure 1.7 The Destinations location; if the control panel of a different directory had appeared, I could have clicked the Yahoo! tab at the top of the search box to display these same options

Click here to retrace your steps.

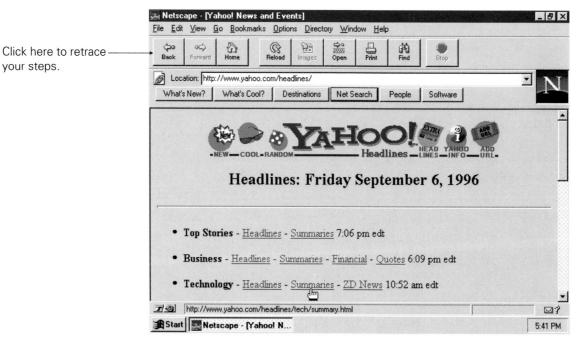

Figure 1.8 The Yahoo! News and Events page; note the Back button

(long in the past by the time you visit for yourself). When exploring a directory such as Yahoo!, you can delve deeply into subcategories and then use the Back button to retrace your steps and explore other nooks and crannies.

EXPERT ADVICE

When you arrive at the home page of a new site on the Web or at any useful central jumping-off point, create a bookmark there so you can find it more easily in the future.

In the example in the preceding paragraphs, I've followed a straight path: Welcome to Netscape | Net Search | Yahoo! News and Events. However, not only can I wander back and forth along that history path, but I can also branch off at any point and pursue a new direction. This is the pleasure and the curse of the Web.

EXPERT ADVICE

If you have to go back many pages in one fell swoop, use the Go menu rather than poking the Back button repeatedly, like (as my technical editor put it) a "hyperactive monkey going for the food pellet button." Seriously, clicking Back repeatedly makes your browser try to reload each of the intermediate pages—a waste of time.

Suppose you change your mind (maybe after looking around the current page a little) and decide you should have gone elsewhere from the previous page. You can do so by returning to the previous page. The command for this action in all the browsers I've ever encountered is called Back (see Figure 1.9).

Click the Forward button to go forward one page.

Pull down the Go menu to go directly to any of the pages you've visited recently.

Click the Back button on the toolbar to go back. Click Back again to go back one more page.

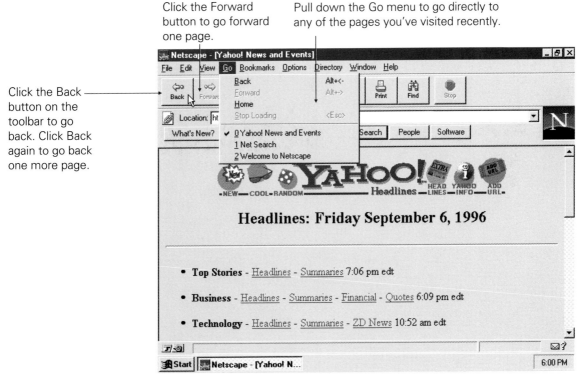

Figure 1.9 Browsing backward and forward on the Web

Typing Addresses Directly

Another way to visit a destination on the Web is to type in its address directly. If you are sent a web address (a URL) via e-mail or some other onscreen medium, then you can select and copy the address and then paste it directly into your browser's address box.

Otherwise, you'll have to click the Location window (it will change its name to the Go To window). The current address will become selected. Type the new address directly over it. For example, type **http://www.cnn.com** as shown here to visit CNN's always-changing web site.

Go to: http://www.cnn.com

CAUTION

Some addresses will take you to one page and then immediately whisk you off to another. If you're ever taken to a page you don't want to be at, just use your Back button or Go menu to head back to familiar territory.

If a web address is sent to you in e-mail or you have it in some other computer file, you can select and cut it in one program and then paste it into the address box of your browser. This saves you the trouble of retyping and the risk of making a typo. In some e-mail programs, you can click or double-click any web address to jump to your browser and visit the page directly.

Fixing an Incorrect Address

If you type an address and receive an error message rather than the web page or resource you were looking for, try trimming the address:

1. Select the final file or directory name in the URL and delete it.
2. Press ENTER.
3. If you still don't get where you want to go, repeat the process until you get down to just the root web address with no path folders or file name (http://*something*).

Figure 1.10 illustrates this process.

Select the final file or
directory name and delete it.

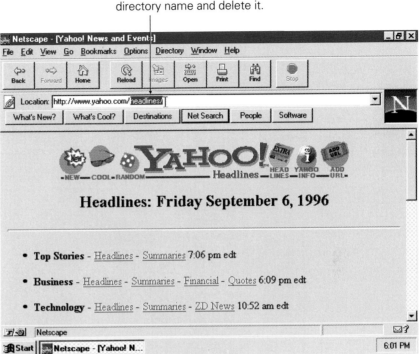

Figure 1.10 Trimming an address to get where you want to go

Printing a Web Page

Print

Even though most people read web pages online, jumping from page to page like a TV-watcher skirting advertisements, you can easily print an interesting page to read at your leisure or to send to someone who lacks Internet access. Just click the Print button (or select File | Print) and then click OK.

EXPERT ADVICE

On a page with multiple frames, your browser will print the current frame (either the one you've clicked or the one that appeared most recently). Background images, even watermark-type images, don't print. (For this reason, you may sometimes want to override the page's color choices when printing.)

Netscape is locked in a tight struggle with Microsoft for dominance of the Web as a new platform, interface, and market. Netscape Navigator is evolving into a program called Netscape Communicator, an interlocking set of tools (including a web browser module) in an attempt to head off Microsoft's plans to incorporate direct web access into its Windows operating system.

Netscape Navigator, the Most Popular Web Browser

So far, I've mostly been showing you examples using Netscape (but just about everything you've seen would look the same in most other browsers, aside from Netscape's built-in buttons, such as Net Search). But what is Netscape?

According to some research, nearly three-quarters of the web browsers in use are versions of Netscape. Suffice it to say that at one time or another, you'll encounter a browser, so Netscape is a good one to start with.

Starting Netscape

To start Netscape, either double-click the Netscape icon or open your computer's Start or Apple menu and select Netscape (or thumb through submenus and *then* select Netscape).

EXPERT ADVICE

See Chapter 2 if you don't have Netscape installed on your computer or you're not sure if you do, or you want to get the most recent version. If you connect to the Internet via an online service such as America Online or CompuServe, visit the Internet area or go directly to the Netscape or web keyword to start Netscape.

Netscape Navigator

(If this is the first time this version of Netscape has been run on your computer, a Netscape License Agreement dialog box will appear. Read the agreement and then click the Accept button.)

Netscape will start and connect you to the Netscape home page, called Welcome to Netscape (see Figure 1.11).

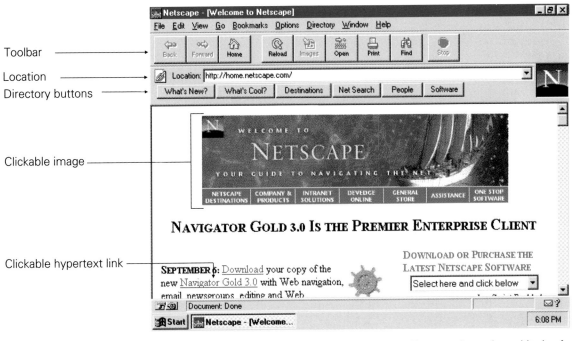

Toolbar

Location

Directory buttons

Clickable image

Clickable hypertext link

Figure 1.11 The Welcome to Netscape page, where Netscape keeps its multitude of customers informed of every little PR move

Figure 1.12 shows the Netscape opening screen on a Macintosh. I'll generally show Windows screens, but I'll always point out differences in the Macintosh version of Navigator (such as shortcuts for commands) as they come up (so don't feel left out, Mac users).

EXPERT ADVICE

If you want to browse quickly, turn off automatic image loading by selecting Options | Auto Load Images. Placeholders will be substituted for images on the pages you browse.

Toolbar —————————

Location —————————

Directory buttons —————————

Clickable image —————————

Clickable
hypertext link —————————

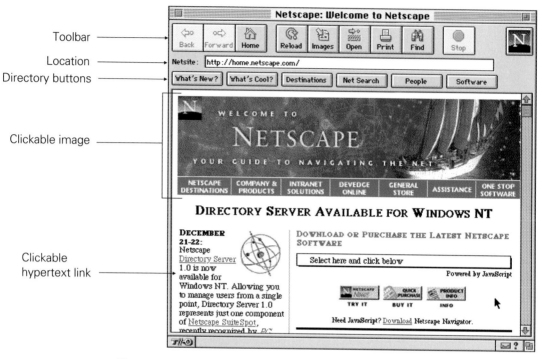

Figure 1.12 The Macintosh version of Netscape has a different characteristic height and width and uses different basic fonts for its display, but it's essentially no different from the Windows (or, for that matter, Unix) version

You can return to your browser's startup page at any point by clicking the Home icon on the toolbar.

Using Your Startup Page as a Starting Point

When you start your browser, it has to open at some location. The lingo is that it starts off "pointing at" some address on the Web. Most browsers come configured to start you on a page maintained by the maker of the browser. Some may come configured to start you at your company's or department's home page on the Web.

DEFINITION

Home page: *1. The primary page of a web site, the front door, the hub. 2. An individual's personal page on the web. 3. The page on which a web browser starts.*

Usually, the startup page will have all kinds of useful jumping-off points for random web "surfing," for specific information resources, and for search utilities that can lead almost anywhere on the Internet.

Netscape's Built-in Directory Links

Your browser may also have some useful links built in to its menus or toolbars. Netscape's Directory menu points to a number of different starting places, some maintained by Netscape, some by independent companies, competing for Netscape's audience. To see Netscape's directory of the Net (still in a primitive stage at this writing), select Directory | Netscape Destinations.

DEFINITIONS

Directory: An Internet directory is a web site that organizes some portion of the contents of the Net into categories.

Search site: Also called a search engine, an Internet search site is a web site that provides an input form you can use to search a database of web resources. (Many directory sites are searchable, and some search sites feature categories.)

To take a look at the leading Internet directories and search sites, select Directory | Internet Search. This takes you to Netscape's Internet Search page (more on this in Chapter 3), which features the dominant "front doors to the Net," with different ones featured (in front) at different times. The first tab (but not necessarily the currently selected one) is for Yahoo!, one of the earliest—and now very thorough—directories.

Creating Bookmarks

If you get to a page you find interesting, but you don't have the time to explore it and all of its links completely in one sitting, create a bookmark for that page. I recommend making bookmarks often. They're easy enough to get rid of, but it can be very difficult to find your way back to a page you vaguely remember from an earlier web session.

bookmark

A saved reference to a web address with which you can return to that address instantly at any time. Also called a hotlist entry or a favorite place.

You can also right-click (click and hold on the Macintosh) on a page to create a bookmark there, or you can right-click (click and hold) on a link to bookmark a page without even visiting it first.

EXPERT ADVICE

To remove an extra bookmark, select Bookmarks > Go to Bookmarks, select the bookmark you want to remove, press DELETE, and then close the bookmark window.

After you add a bookmark, the page will appear at the bottom of the Bookmark menu the next time you pull it down.

STEP BY STEP Create a Bookmark

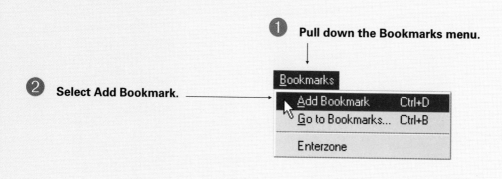

① **Pull down the Bookmarks menu.**

② **Select Add Bookmark.**

Bookmarks

Add Bookmark	Ctrl+D
Go to Bookmarks...	Ctrl+B
Enterzone	

You can continue following other links or backtracking and going off in another direction. When you find another interesting page, bookmark it, too. (Notice that the previous bookmark you added is now on the bookmark list.)

Now you can return instantly to any of your previously bookmarked pages by selecting it from the list.

Saving an Image to Your Computer

If you see an image on a web page that you'd like to save on your own computer, you can snatch it easily with Netscape. Just right-click (on the Macintosh, click and hold) the image you want to save and choose Save Image As.

EXPERT ADVICE

You can save the text contents (as well as the embedded hypertext links) of a web document in the form of an HTML (.html or .htm) file, in much the same way as you save images. Select File | Save As and then save the document.

netiquette

There's nothing wrong with saving other people's images on your computer. Just don't republish the art on the Web or in any other medium without the expressed permission of the artist and original publisher.

A Save As dialog box will appear. Change the name if you want or the location where the image will be saved. Then click the Save button.

Previewing a Page Before Printing

If you want to preview a page before printing, don't click the Print button or select File | Print. Instead follow these steps:

1. Select File | Print Preview. This changes Netscape to a Print Preview mode similar to that of a word processing program.

2. Click the magnifying glass icon anywhere to zoom in to that place, to see how well Netscape renders the page for printing. (Some web pages won't look good or won't be legible when printed.)

3. Repeat step 2 to zoom in closer and then, after three clicks, zoom back out again.

4. If everything looks OK, click the Print button.

Figure 1.13 shows pages in Print Preview mode.

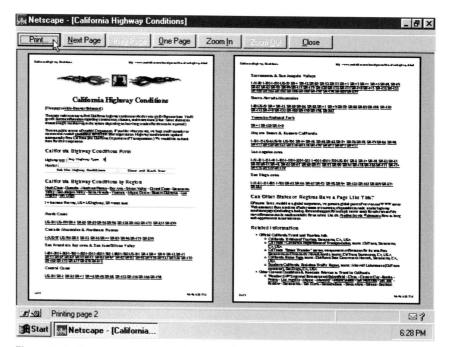

Figure 1.13 You can preview a web page before printing it

*See Chapter 4 for an
explanation of Internet e-mail.*

Sending E-Mail from Netscape

There are two ways to send e-mail while browsing the Web, but each of
them uses the exact same mechanism in Netscape. Some web pages have e-mail
links, also referred to as mailto links (because the name of the protocol for the
URL of such a link is mailto, as in mailto:xian@pobox.com). Click one of these
links, and Netscape will open up a mail dialog box with the e-mail of the recipient
automatically in place, drawn from the link URL. These links allow web publishers
to invite easy interaction from the audience.

However, you don't need a mailto link to send e-mail from within Netscape.
You can also select File | Mail Document (to send a copy of the page you're viewing
to someone) or File | New Mail Message (CTRL-M or COMMAND-M). This brings
up a mail message window (see Figure 1.14). Netscape suggests a subject (the title
of the page) and, if you chose to mail the document, pastes the current URL into
the first line of the message window and includes the document itself as an
attachment.

Click Send to send
your e-mail.

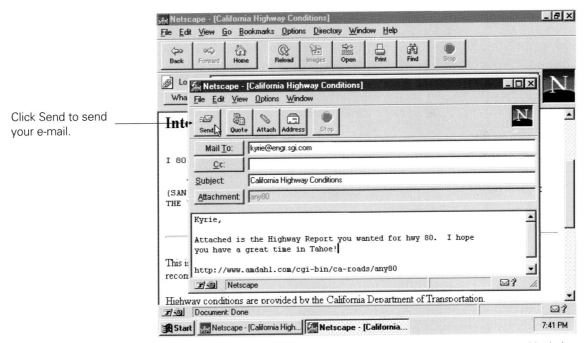

Figure 1.14 Send e-mail to anyone on the Internet from within Netscape and include
the text contents of your current web page, if you like

Quitting Netscape

When you're finished browsing and have created bookmarks to all the tantalizing loose ends that you plan to pursue later, quit Netscape by selecting File | Exit. Then get back to work!

Microsoft Internet Explorer, the Challenger

If you need help obtaining a copy of Microsoft Internet Explorer, see Chapter 2.

Gaining rapidly on Netscape's dominance of the web-browser market is Microsoft's Internet Explorer, which can be downloaded for free from its web site (http://www.microsoft.com/ie). Internet Explorer's close ties to the Windows platform might slow its acceptance among Macintosh and Unix users, but these ties will inevitably help it prosper if Microsoft succeeds in integrating the web interface into the company's dominant operating system product.

Microsoft Terminology

Partly as a consequence of Internet Explorer's compliance with Windows 95 standards, some of the terminology it uses differs from that used elsewhere on the Internet. To save yourself from embarrassing faux pas in front of Internet purists, Table 1.2 provides you with some translations.

What Everyone Else on the Web Calls	Microsoft Calls
A link	A shortcut
Bookmarks (or hotlist)	Favorites
Images	Pictures
Reloading a page	Refreshing a page

Table 1.2 Microsoft Terminology vs. Common Internet Terminology

Starting Internet Explorer

To start Internet Explorer, double-click the Microsoft Internet Explorer icon. In Windows 95, the Internet Explorer somewhat presumptuously creates on your desktop an icon called the Internet. It does the same thing as the Internet Explorer icon.

Internet Explorer

If you run some versions of Internet Explorer for the first time, the program will attempt to connect to a startup page that no longer exists and will alert you to this fact with a dialog box, as shown here:

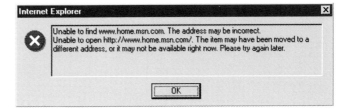

If you have an older installation, you may be started off at a page called Welcome to MSN! If so, go to http://home.microsoft.com to get with the program.

Just click OK to dismiss the dialog box.

Internet Explorer starts you at a page called Your Internet Start Page (see Figure 1.15). This page may change, and as with any browser, you can assign a different page as your startup page.

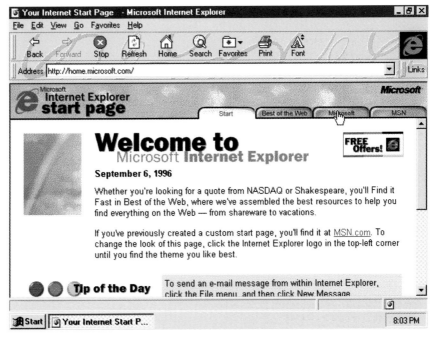

Figure 1.15 Microsoft Internet Explorer's default start page

If you've used Internet Explorer before, you may have noticed that Microsoft has changed the start page that automatically comes up when you start the program. Microsoft has been sorting out their web strategy for the last few years, and in the meantime, a number of different home pages have come and gone. They've now settled into a fairly coherent system:

- The Microsoft home pages relate to the giant software company and its products.
- The MSN home pages are of more general interest. "MSN" refers to Microsoft's online service—the Microsoft Network. MSN started as an America Online–type online service but has retooled itself as a web presence with special content and services for MSN members as well as Internet Explorer users.
- There have been three different major versions of Internet Explorer in the past few years, and each has had a different default home page. If your computer once had an earlier version installed, you may find even your up-to-date Internet Explorer starting at the old page.

If you have created a custom start page, you'll find it at http://www.msn.com, the home page for the Microsoft Network. Previous versions of Internet Explorer used this as the default start page.

Home Page	What It Is
home.microsoft.com	The current default start page for Internet Explorer 3.0. This page displays one of the following four tabbed sections: Start (the default): Profiles new Microsoft products and announcements about the Internet and Internet Explorer. A link near the top takes you to www.msn.com (see below). Best of the Web: Weekly and daily web site recommendations in various categories (Today's Picks, Find it Fast!, News, Business and Finance, Computers & Technology, Sports and Health, Living, Travel & Entertainment, and International). Microsoft: displays the same thing as www.microsoft.com (see below). **MSN** (which leads to a different MSN start page than the ones below).
www.microsoft.com	Microsoft's home page. This page displays information on Microsoft products, announcements, and new releases.
www.msn.com	MSN's default start page. This page can be customized. This is the default start page for Internet Explorer 2.0.
www.home.msn.com	Currently displays the same thing as www.msn.com, but for a while, this page was empty (or displayed the warning, "This page is going away"). This is the default start page for Internet Explorer 1.0.
home.msn.com	Same as www.msn. com and www.home.msn.com.
www.microsoft.com/ie/	The Internet Explorer (product) home page.

Table 1.3 Microsoft, MSN, and Internet Explorer Home Pages

Table 1.3 explains the multitude of Microsoft pages available.

As of version 3.0, Internet Explorer uses a button style that may be unfamiliar to you. Buttons don't look raised in this scheme. Instead, they appear to light up when the mouse pointer passes over them.

Favorite Places

Internet Explorer saves shortcuts to your favorite web pages in a folder called Favorites. Instead of adding a bookmark to your hotlist, as various other web browsers refer to it, you add a page to your Favorites, but the idea is the same.

To add a page (such as the *Wall Street Journal* page) to your Favorites, select Favorites | Add To Favorites (or right-click or click and hold and choose Add To Favorites from the shortcut menu that pops up). A dialog box called Add to Favorites that looks like a standard Save As dialog box appears.

Change the name for the shortcut if you like and then click the Add button. The page will then appear on the Favorites menu as well as in the Favorites folder.

The Favorites folder is a normal folder on your computer's hard disk, but if you select Favorites | Open Favorites, Internet Explorer will display the contents of the folder in its own window (at least for Windows 95). Do you now see why some people think browsing your own computer should be as easy as browsing the web? Click Back to leave the Favorites folder.

Any time you want to return to a favorite page, you can select Favorites and choose the page from the menu.

To get rid of a less-favored shortcut, select Favorites | Open Favorites, select the shortcut, and press DELETE. Then close the Favorites folder.

E-mail with Internet Explorer

Clicking a mailto link (shortcut) in Internet Explorer automatically launches whichever e-mail program you have integrated into your operating system and your local network (if any). See Chapter 5 for more on the differences among various mail programs.

Using a Different Browser

There are many different browsers available. If you have one other than the two I've explained, I think you'll be able to follow along, taking into account that some commands may appear on different menus or with slightly different names, and that some of the latest features may not be supported.

All Circuits Are Busy

Lately, my personal experience has suggested that the current usage patterns may be changing and weekends may be becoming the busiest times on the Net, suggesting that recreation is driving the Net's popularity more than business purposes.

The Internet is still a haphazard collection of networks, and you won't always be able to make the connection you want. Sometimes, especially during peak hours (more or less the normal work week in the U.S.), your browser will fail to connect to the page you want. In general, all traffic on the Internet is highest during these times, and popular servers can slow down or even crash when "hit" by too many clients. Even sites that are available 24 hours a day, seven days a week, still need to shut down occasionally for maintenance or in the event of a crash.

You'll see an error message, perhaps alluding to a "failed DNS server look up" or what have you, but ignore it, as it's usually just a knee-jerk guess as to what went wrong (a symptom of a busy or overworked network). Most of the time, all that happened was that some attempt to connect along the route "timed out"—that is, gave up before connecting successfully.

Sometimes your browser won't acknowledge that it's hung up somewhere. Instead it will just keep churning away as if it's really loading a page, but nothing new will happen, and the thermometer-like readout that shows the progress will stop moving. When your browser gives up, whether it admits it or not, press the Stop button and try again.

Another problem you may run into is not knowing the exact address of or any specific route to the information or site you want to reach. In that case, you'll want to use one of the many search mechanisms available on the Web. See Chapter 3 for more information on searching.

Keeping Up with the Web

There's really no way you can keep up with the web. It's changing and evolving so rapidly I'm not sure it even makes sense to talk about "keeping up" with it. However, there are a few things you can do to stay "in the loop."

One thing I'd recommend is subscribing to *Netsurfer Digest*. To check it out, visit its home page at http://www.netsurf.com/nsd/ (see Figure 1.16). Read the latest issue and see if you'd like to receive it. It comes more or less weekly and is sent as an e-mail message (either in plain text or as an HTML document you can save and then read in your web browser). All sites are linked directly from the newsletter pages.

Figure 1.16 The Netsurfer Digest home page

Another good place to visit is the clnet online home page (http://www.cnet.com). So far, clnet is the leading online source for Internet information (see Figure 1.17).

Figure 1.17 The c|net site is well designed and easy to use and is updated daily

Publishing on the Web

Putting up your own pages on the Web is easier than you might think. See Chapter 10 for how to build your own web site and Chapter 11 for how to set up shop on the Internet.

Finding Information

For the web browser to become a truly useful front door to the Internet, it has to enable you to reach out and find specific information quickly and accurately. Browsing the Web from site to site, following whims and distractions, is a new mode of entertainment and it has its place, but there's more to the Web than just channel surfing. If you want learn how to zero in on specific information, resources, or people, go on to Chapter 3.

The Future of the Web

For now, almost everything on the Web can be thought of as a document, using something similar to the model of a piece of paper (hence the page metaphor used all over the Web). This document model may be changing, however, as new technologies such as Java (a robust programming language designed to allow people to run interactive programs on the Web) and VRML (Virtual Reality Modeling Language, a method of describing three-dimensional spaces that people can navigate with special browsers, not unlike the way people now play Quake and other 3D shoot-em-up games) continue to mature.

Meanwhile, the upcoming revisions of major computer operating systems (namely, Windows and Macintosh) will incorporate web browsing more fully in day-to-day operations on the computer, blurring the distinction between files on your desktop, on the network server down the hall, and "out there" on the Internet.

For the immediate future, though, the document model with hyperlinks should continue to dominate the field. In some ways, the less you know about all this, the better. The advances that succeed will make the Web even easier to navigate and more transparent to the user, with a fully integrated graphical user interface.

CHECK POINT

Now you know the basics of getting onto the Internet and finding sites, information, programs, and people to talk to out there. But there's more to this book than coverage of the World Wide Web. That's because, contrary to all the hype you may have heard recently, there's a lot more to the Internet than just the Web. In fact, the area of the Internet with the highest volume of usage (discounting huge binary files, such as graphics) is still (and probably always will be) electronic mail. Chapter 2 shows you the ropes for using specific web browsers, and Chapter 3 introduces you to the fastest shortcut on the Net—searching for keywords directly—but after that, you'll plunge into the world of e-mail, mailing lists, discussion groups, and so on.

You don't have to read this book straight through. Pick the chapters that interest you. The whole book is thoroughly cross-referenced, so you won't miss anything (unless you want to). Whenever possible, I will include useful or informative web addresses where you can get hands-on experience or find information on any given topic.

Don't let me hold you back! The best service I can render in this book is to offer you a grounding in what's going on on the Internet and to show you how to work the controls of your browser and other software. After that, you have an entire globe full of information and ideas to explore. I'll point you down some likely pathways, but mainly I'm going to get out of your way and let your natural interests draw you toward your own destinations. Welcome to the Internet.

Stuff to Do Once to Make Your Life Easier

INCLUDES

- Choosing a strategy for the Net and the Web
- Setting up Netscape
- Setting up Internet Explorer
- Customizing your browser
- Choosing a different startup page
- Customizing your startup page
- Installing PointCast
- Buying stuff online

FAST FORWARD

Install Netscape ➤ pp. 51-57

Download Netscape Now!

1. Visit the Netscape Now! page:
   (http://home.netscape.com/comprod/mirror/
   client_download.html).
2. Scroll down to the numbered steps and specify the product
   version you want.
3. Specify the platform of your computer, your language, and
   your location.
4. Click the button at the bottom of the screen to display a list of
   download sites.
5. Scroll down to the list of download sites Netscape appends to the
   current page and click one of the links. If it fails to connect (it
   happens), try clicking the Reload button.
6. Choose a directory for the file from the Save As dialog box.
   Your browser will download the file (it will take a while).
7. Double-click the file you downloaded, which starts the
   installation program, approve the suggested folder for installing
   Netscape (or specify another folder), and then let the setup
   program do the rest.

Install Internet Explorer ➤ pp. 57-60

1. Visit the Internet Explorer page (http://www.microsoft.com/ie/).
2. Click Download Software or any other download link.
3. Specify the version of Internet Explorer you want (the platform)
   and click Next.
4. Choose a language and Full, Minimum, or Typical installation.
   Then click Next.
5. Click one of the download links that appears. If it fails to connect
   (it happens), try clicking the Reload button.
6. Choose a directory for the file from the Save As dialog box.
7. Double-click the file you downloaded, which starts the
   installation program, approve the suggested folder for installing
   Internet Explorer (or specify another folder), and then let the
   setup program do the rest.

Customize Your Browser ➤ pp. 61-63

Use Netscape's Options | General Preferences or Internet Explorer's
View | Options command to change the look and feel of your browser.
Changes I recommend include

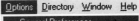

- Minimizing the buttons and doo-dads on the screen
- Turning off link underlining
- Changing your startup page

Choose a Different Startup Page ➤ pp. 63-64, 66-68

In Netscape, follow these steps:

1. Select (or have handy) the exact wording of the web address
   (you can go to the page and copy it from the Location box).
2. Select Options | General Preferences.
3. Click the Appearance tab.
4. Type or paste the address into the Browser Starts With Home Page
   Location box.
5. Click OK.

In Internet Explorer, follow these steps:

1. Go to the page you want to use as your starting page.
2. Select View | Options.
3. Click the Start and Search Page tab.
4. Click the Use Current button.
5. Click OK.

Install PointCast ➤ *pp. 80-83*

1. Go to http://www.pointcast.com/download/.
2. Choose your version and click any of the Download Sites links.
3. Choose a folder in which to save the installation file—and remember what you chose. Your browser will download the installation file—note the name of the file.
4. When the file is downloaded (it may take a while), open the folder in which you saved the file, find the file, and double-click it to install PointCast.
5. Click Launch PointCast or Personalize PointCast (you can always personalize the program later).
6. Click "Use Netscape Navigator to access the web" (or choose one of the direct or modem connection options) and click OK.

One common complaint people have about the Internet is the do-it-yourself, erector-set mentality of much of the software. To get a reasonable Internet setup on your computer you may have to install several different programs and fiddle with them to get them to work together. Then you'll want to upgrade some of your programs from time to time, when improvements come out or annoying headaches are solved by later versions.

The only way to enjoy smooth Internet access is to decide on an approach to take ahead of time. Determine how much poking around you're willing to do, how easy you want things to be, and how much pizzazz you want to extract from your Internet connection.

Your Web and Net Strategy

By fully released, I mean completely tested and officially released, in contrast to beta versions of most programs, which are often widely available and widely in use on the Net, but not fully tested or ready for prime-time release.

To keep yourself sane when you start dipping into the Internet, take a minute or two now to envision how you're going to use the Net and how much of your time you want it to consume. I'll describe three different approaches to Internet use—you determine which fits you best.

The Easiest Way

The easiest approach to web and net access is to use as few programs as possible and to use only the fully released, stable versions of each program. This strategy is similar to my hardware strategy, which is to buy not the latest thing but the next-most-latest thing, which is usually much cheaper. With Internet tools, it's not so much cost that you save (this approach may even be a little more expensive than others), but hassle. Stable, fully released software will break down less often, and the various programs will tend to be compatible (if not capable of all the latest tricks). This is definitely the approach you want to take if you're equipping an entire office or project. Within a single company, you're better off if everyone is using the same tools (within reason).

To minimize the number of different programs you have to install and set up, you can rely primarily on your web browsers and tools that plug into it. This is one type of "easy," since it reduces the amount of configuration and setup you have to do. On the other hand, Netscape Mail and Internet News (the newsreader designed to work with Microsoft Internet Explorer) both leave a lot to be desired compared with competing, third-party programs—so you may want to opt for maintaining separate mail or news programs. Regardless of what approach you take, I will tell you how to install and configure your extra (non-web) Internet tools.

EXPERT ADVICE

If you're completely new to the Net and the Web, consider signing up for a free month with an online service (such as AOL) to get yourself oriented with the least number of new programs to learn. If you like what you find, you'll probably want to switch to a flat-rate Internet service provider (or ISP; see Appendix A for more on shopping for access).

The final aspect of the easy approach is to leave most or all of your programs' preferences set to their original out-of-the-box settings. This saves you work and helps maintain a consistent look-and-feel across all your tools (and workstations, if you deal with more than one).

Beta Tester

If you're always looking to eke out a little extra performance from your computer and you're interested in the improvements available in upcoming software releases, then you might want to take the "permanent beta tester" approach and use software as soon as it's released for testing, upgrading whenever new (even interim) versions come out.

This approach has two real drawbacks:

- You have to download and upgrade software frequently.
- Beta software is not always dependable and can crash on you or freeze your machine.

DEFINITION

Download: *To transfer a file from a remote site to your own computer. Similarly,* **upload** *means to transfer a file from your own computer to a remote site.*

The counterarguments to these objections, by the way, are (1) you have to download and upgrade software frequently no matter what, and (2) all software crashes computers.

One additional benefit of being a beta tester (beyond that of experiencing the latest advances in technology) is that you don't have to pay for beta software, since it's not in actual release yet. You are doing the company that makes and publishes the software a favor by testing it for them.

Multimedia Monster

The third approach—using all the multimedia features the Internet presents—requires some investment in hardware as well. To explore the most advanced (and exciting) tools that the Internet has to offer, you need to make sure first of all that your computer is equipped to play sounds; store (enormous) video files in memory and play them back at a reasonable speed; display high-resolution graphics and redraw the screen quickly; record with a microphone, camera, video-camera, and scanner; and so on.

On the software end, you need to download new web-browser plug-in software (more on this later) and set it up to work with your browser and your Internet connection, so you can see other people; interact with online programs and environments; play games; and edit and post sounds, video, or other multimedia contents to the World Wide Web or to a more local intranet.

Navigator Versus Internet Explorer

For most people on the Net (aside from the diehard Unix-loving, character-only Lynx-using few), the question of which web browser to use has narrowed to just two: Netscape Navigator and Microsoft Internet Explorer. In terms of sheer percentages as well as number of different computer platforms covered, Netscape has for the past year or two looked like the "browser of destiny," still commanding around two-thirds of all desktops by most estimates.

If Internet Explorer were the product of any other company than juggernaut Microsoft, it would not be considered an equal contender for web domination, despite the fact that (at least on the Windows and, to some extent, Macintosh platforms) it matches Netscape, more or less, feature for feature. While Netscape has a natural constituency among those who prefer Internet culture to Microsoft monoculture, there's no denying that Microsoft can buy its way into any market if it really wants to (and it does).

For now, the race is too close to call. Rest assured that you won't go wrong with either browser, and that most web sites will look and feel just about the same in either one. Keep an eye on developments when the newer versions start coming out. If you plan on developing content for the Web, keep one copy of each installed (ideally on more than one type of computer), so you can make sure that your pages look fine on both.

Personally, I still prefer Netscape.

Netscape is revising its flagship Internet program as an all-in-one program called Netscape Communicator, which will include a Netscape Navigator 4.0 browser along with an updated mail and news program called Netscape Messenger, new tools for creating web documents, and additional software modules for online collaboration and intranets. Netscape is taking this step in order to go toe to toe with Microsoft's next expected move: incorporating many of the functions of web browsers directly into the Windows operating system. In the long run, Netscape's success may depend on its convincing you to use its Communicator platform as your primary interface for both the Internet and your local computer and network.

Downloading, Installing, and Setting Up Netscape Navigator

The process for getting a copy of Netscape is not as streamlined as I'd like it to be, but you get used to it. The first question, which may sound silly, is "Do you have access to the Web yet?" You may, if you have an online service (such as AOL) or access through work or school and some other web browser (or an earlier version of Netscape itself).

If you have Netscape installed already, skip on ahead (unless, that is, you want to upgrade to a newer—or beta—version).

If you don't, then you have two choices. You can walk into (or call) a computer software store, buy a shrink-wrapped copy of Navigator, and then install it from the disk in the box. Alternatively, you can sign up with a service provider or accept some other offer that includes a copy of Netscape on a disk (and, as before, install the software from the disk).

Let me start by explaining how to download Navigator (using any browser), assuming that you already have access to the Web. If you have Navigator on a disk (or plan to get it that way), just skip ahead to the section "Installing Netscape Navigator." If you belong to an online service, you may already have Netscape on a disk or installed with the main program, or you can usually download Netscape directly from the service's archives (search for, or go to, Netscape). You may not get the most recent version this way; if not, read the section "UpgradingNetscape," coming up.

Downloading Netscape Navigator

Here's how you download Netscape:

1. Point your browser at http://home.netscape.com/comprod/mirror/ client_download.html (or click any Netscape Now! button, such as the one on Netscape's home page).

EXPERT ADVICE

You can get to Netscape's home page from within Netscape by clicking the spacey N in the upper-right corner of the window.

2. Scroll down to the numbered steps.

3. Specify the product version you want:

   - Specify Standard to minimize the download time.
   - Specify Standard plus components to get extras for 3D browsing and phone-like live chat tools.
   - Specify Gold (with or without components) to get Netscape Editor, a web-publishing tool.

4. Specify the platform of your computer (Macintosh or a version of Windows or Unix), your language (probably U.S. English), and your location (the continent).

5. Click the button at the bottom of the screen to display a list of download sites (see Figure 2.1).

6. Scroll down to the list of download sites Netscape appends to the current page and click one of the links. If it fails to connect

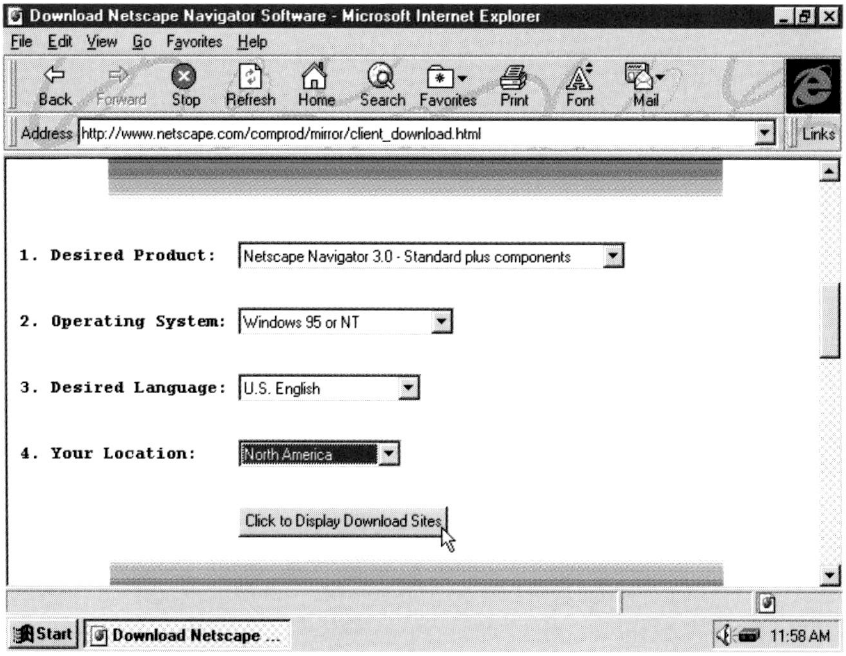

Figure 2.1 Getting ready to download Netscape

(it happens), try clicking the Reload button. If the link still fails after one or two attempts, try another link.

7. Repeat step 6 until you connect. If you fail to connect for ten minutes, take a half-hour break before trying again. If you repeatedly fail to connect, try early in the morning or late at night. When you do connect, your browser will start downloading a file.

8. Choose a directory for the file from the Save As dialog box. (By the way, even if you've never heard of FTP before, you're using it now. See Chapter 8 for more information on transferring files with FTP.) Your browser will download the file (it will take a while).

EXPERT ADVICE

If you feel comfortable hunting through directories, you can point your browser directly at one of Netscape's FTP sites (see Chapter 8 for more on FTP), such as ftp2.netscape.com (through ftp18.netscape.com last time we checked). Once you connect (it may take a while), choose the pub folder, and then navigator, and then the version you want. Specify the platform you use (such as Macintosh, Unix, or Windows), and then download one of the n* files. For Windows users, choose one ending in 32 for Windows 95 or 16 for Windows 3.x.

Installing Netscape Navigator

Installing Navigator is about the same whether you're installing it for the first time or installing an upgraded version over an existing installation. You double-click the file you downloaded, which starts the installation program, approve the suggested folder for installing Netscape (or specify another folder), and then let the setup program do the rest. Once everything's unpacked and set up, you can answer No to the last few questions Netscape asks you (unless you *want* to read the latest release notes or visit the Netscape web site to pay for the software immediately).

EXPERT ADVICE

The setup program may ask you if you want to install CoolChat (a chat program designed to work with Navigator—see Chapter 7 for more on chat programs). If you do, it will also ask if you want to enable something called the CoolTalk watchdog. Click No unless you have a full-time network connection to the Internet.

Upgrading Netscape

If you're installing an upgrade version of Navigator, you should do so in the same folder as the older version *unless* you're installing a beta version or a version you're not sure you want, in which case you should install it in a different folder and leave your older installation of Navigator untouched.

If you've customized Netscape and you want to keep all of your settings without specifying them all over again, be sure to install the new version over the old one (without first uninstalling the old one).

Setting Up Personal, Mail, and News Information

Some providers fill in this information for you.

The first time you run Netscape, you'll be asked to read and accept a license agreement (see Figure 2.2). Then the program will start and attempt to connect to the Netscape home page.

The first thing you should do is tell Netscape who you are and what your e-mail address is (along with some other basic mail and news information). Select Options | Mail and News Preferences. Then click the Identity tab on the Preferences dialog box that appears.

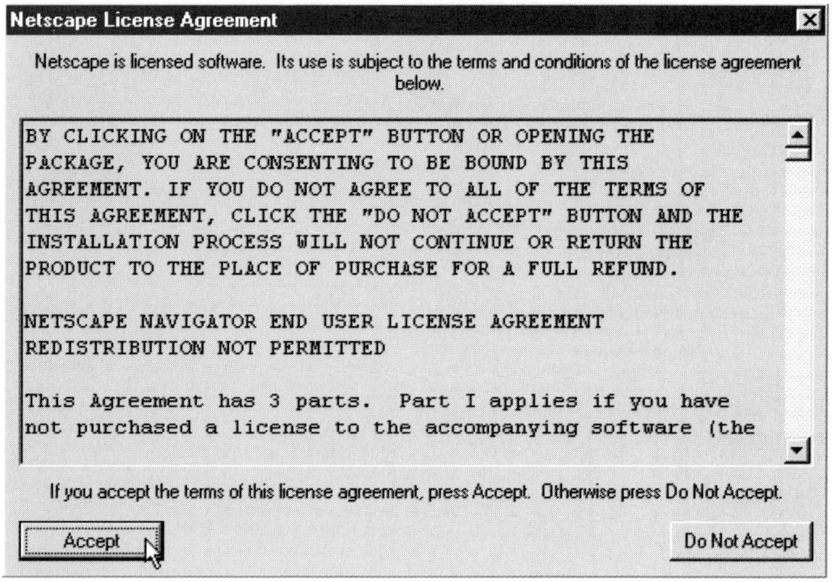

Netscape License Agreement

Netscape is licensed software. Its use is subject to the terms and conditions of the license agreement below.

```
BY CLICKING ON THE "ACCEPT" BUTTON OR OPENING THE
PACKAGE, YOU ARE CONSENTING TO BE BOUND BY THIS
AGREEMENT. IF YOU DO NOT AGREE TO ALL OF THE TERMS OF
THIS AGREEMENT, CLICK THE "DO NOT ACCEPT" BUTTON AND THE
INSTALLATION PROCESS WILL NOT CONTINUE OR RETURN THE
PRODUCT TO THE PLACE OF PURCHASE FOR A FULL REFUND.

NETSCAPE NAVIGATOR END USER LICENSE AGREEMENT
REDISTRIBUTION NOT PERMITTED

This Agreement has 3 parts.  Part I applies if you have
not purchased a license to the accompanying software (the
```

If you accept the terms of this license agreement, press Accept. Otherwise press Do Not Accept.

Accept   Do Not Accept

Figure 2.2 You have no choice but to accept this agreement

Fill in the information on the Identity tab (see Figure 2.3):

1. Type your name as you want it to appear on your outgoing e-mail and then press TAB.
2. Type your e-mail address (if you know it) and press TAB twice.
3. Optionally fill in the organization box.

At this point, you may want to give Netscape your mail and news information. No matter what programs you end up using for mail and news reading, you'll have to enter information like that discussed here. The only reason to set up Netscape for mail and news now is for its two built-in modules, Netscape Mail and Netscape News.

DEFINITION

Server: *A network machine that handles heavy-duty jobs such as sorting and routing mail, maintaining archive sites, and serving web pages to multiple clients.*

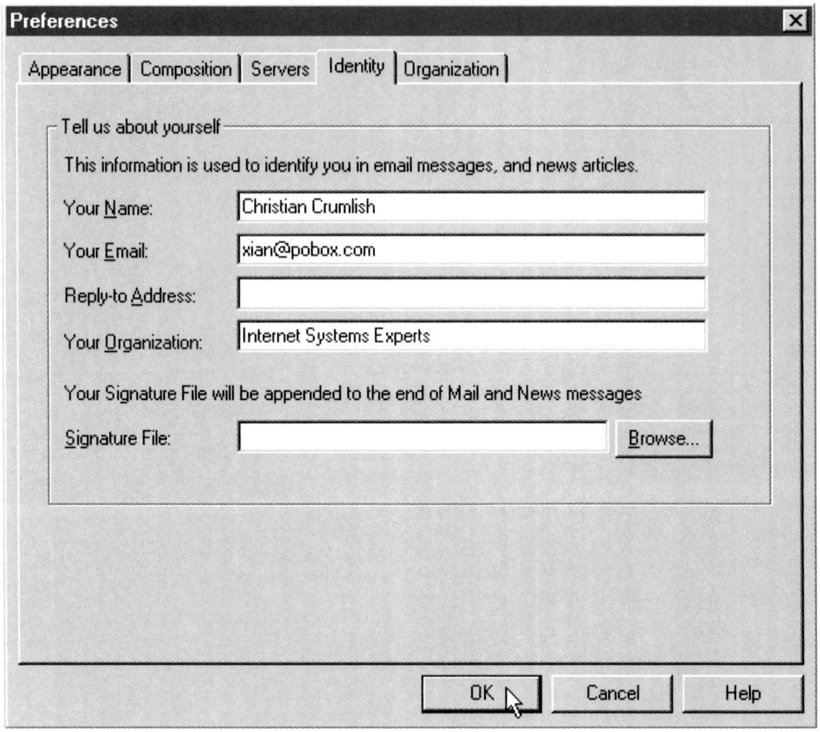

Figure 2.3 My name, e-mail address, and organization on the Identity tab

Chapter 4 explains more about e-mail, and Chapter 6 covers Usenet news and other types of newsgroups.

If the content of the Outgoing Mail (SMTP) Server box at the top of the dialog box is just the word "mail," or if that box or the News (NNTP) Server box is empty, then you'll have to get the addresses of your mail and Usenet news servers from your service provider's technical help staff or from your network's system administrator (and then you'll have to type the server names in these boxes exactly).

That's all you have to deal with. Click OK to accept your preferences. From now on, you can just run the program and forget about the setup (unless you choose to customize Netscape—see "Customizing Your Web Browser" later in this chapter).

STEP BY STEP Set Up Netscape Mail and News Information

1 Click the Servers tab.

2 If it's not already entered, type the Internet address of your outgoing-mail server (your provider or system administrator should tell you this) and press TAB.

Preferences	✕

Appearance | Composition | Servers | Identity | Organization |

Mail

Outgoing Mail (SMTP) Server: `mail.emf.net`

Incoming Mail (POP3) Server: `mail.emf.net`

POP3 User Name: `xian`

Mail Directory: `C:\Program Files\Netscape\Navigator\Mail`

Maximum Message Size: ⦿ None   ○ Size: [   ] KB

Messages are copied from the server to the local disk, then:
⦿ Removed from the server   ○ Left on the server

Check for Mail: ⦿ Every: `10`   minutes   ○ Never

News

News (NNTP) Server: `news.emf.net`

News RC Directory: `C:\Program Files\Netscape\Navigator\News`

Get: `100`   Messages at a Time (Max 3500)

[OK]   [Cancel]   [Help]

3 If it's not there already, type the address of your incoming-mail server and press TAB.

4 Type your username (your e-mail address, up to but not including the @).

5 If it's not entered already, click the News (NNTP) Server box and type the address of your news server.

Downloading, Installing, and Setting Up Internet Explorer

As with downloading Netscape, the first question, silly as it may sound, is "Do you have access to the Web yet?" You may, if you have an online service (such as AOL) or access through work or school and some other web browser (or an earlier version of Internet Explorer itself).

If you have Internet Explorer installed already, skip on ahead (unless, that is, you want to upgrade to a newer—or beta—version).

If you don't, then you have two choices. You can walk into (or call) a computer software store, buy a shrink-wrapped copy of Microsoft Internet Explorer, and then install it from the disk in the box. Alternatively, you can sign up with a service provider or accept some other offer that includes a copy of Internet Explorer on a disk (and, as before, install the software from the disk).

Let me start by explaining how to download Internet Explorer (using any browser), assuming that you already have access to the Web. If you have Internet Explorer on a disk (or plan to get it that way), just skip ahead to the section "Installing Internet Explorer." If you belong to an online service, you may already have Internet Explorer on a disk or installed with the main program, or you can usually download Internet Explorer directly from the service's archives (search for, or go to, Internet Explorer). You may not get the most recent version this way; if you don't, read the section "Upgrading Internet Explorer," coming up.

Downloading Microsoft Internet Explorer

1. Point your browser at http://www.microsoft.com/ie/ (or click any FREE Microsoft Internet Explorer button, such as that on the Microsoft home page at http://www.microsoft.com).
2. Click Download Software or any other download link.
3. Specify the version of Internet Explorer you want (the platform).
4. Click the Next button (see Figure 2.4).
5. Choose a language and Full, Minimum, or Typical installation.
6. Click Next.

7. Click one of the download links that appears. If it fails to connect (it happens), try clicking the Reload button. If the link still fails after one or two attempts, try another link.

8. Repeat step 7 until you connect. If you fail to connect for ten minutes, take a half-hour break before trying again. If you repeatedly fail to connect, try early in the morning or late at night. When you do connect, your browser will start downloading a file.

9. Choose a directory for the file from the Save As dialog box. Your browser will download the file (it will take a while).

EXPERT ADVICE

Some browsers will tell you they don't recognize the type of file you're downloading. If this happens to you, tell your browser to save the file (In Netscape, click Save File).

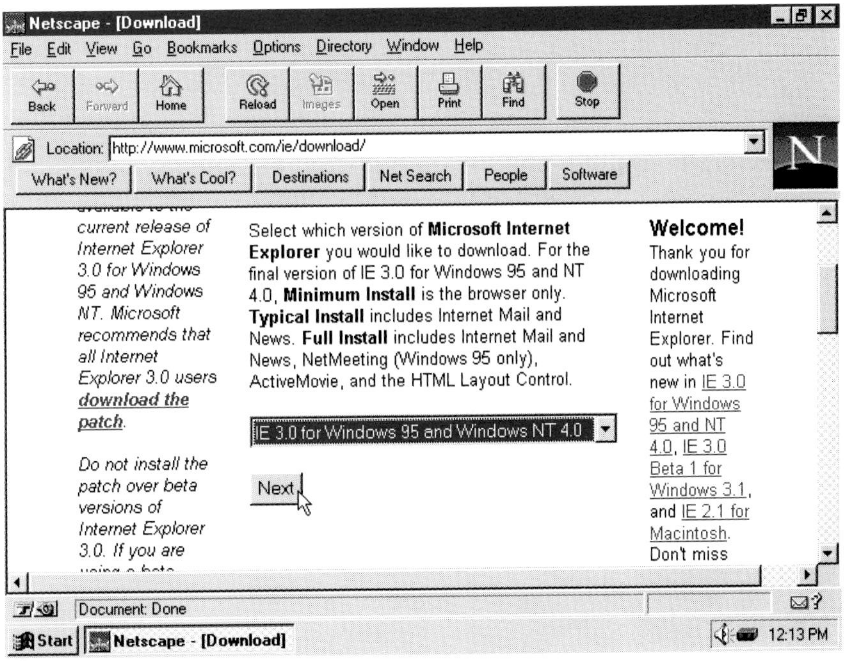

Figure 2.4 Getting ready to download Internet Explorer

Installing Internet Explorer

To install Internet Explorer, double-click the file you downloaded, which starts the installation program, approve the suggested folder for installing Internet Explorer (or specify another folder), and then let the setup program do the rest.

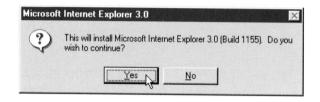

Upgrading Internet Explorer

As with Netscape, if you're installing an upgraded version of Internet Explorer, you should do so in the same folder as the older version *unless* you're installing a beta version or a version you're not sure you want, in which case you should install it in a different folder and leave your older installation of Internet Explorer untouched.

If you've customized Internet Explorer and you want to keep all of your preferences without setting them again one by one, be sure to install the new version over the old one.

Setting Up Personal, Mail, and News Information

Internet Explorer's Full download includes mail and news programs (Internet Mail and Internet News), at least on the Windows platform. These programs will store your name, e-mail address, and other information. Although they are designed specifically to work well with Internet Explorer, Internet Mail and Internet News are conventional news and mail readers that stand alone and can work with any other Internet tools (unlike Netscape Mail and Netscape News, which are part of the Navigator program). See Chapters 4 and 6 for more on mail and news.

Customizing Your Web browser

Most web browsers allow you to change some of their basic settings, affecting mainly appearance. (There are also advanced preferences you can set, but let's not get into that level of detail.) For the two major browsers I'll tell you how to change the look of the screen (you don't have to—you can leave it just the way it is; most people do) and how to change the startup page. I'll tell you what my personal preferences are, but this is really a matter of taste and comfort, and in fact, your preferences will most likely change if you use your browser for a long time.

Customizing Netscape

You've no doubt seen the familiar Netscape window in newspapers and magazines, in books, and on TV shows. Usually it's the Macintosh version of the screen, since most publishers use Macs, but it's always the just-out-of-the-box setup, with all buttons showing words *and* pictures, the most amount of detail possible. As with all programs, very few people change the basic settings of Navigator, but it's worth at least knowing how to. Most of the Netscape illustrations in this book show *my* preferred setup, as I think the screen looks best, but you'll be able to follow along perfectly well no matter what preferences you choose.

Hide the Directory Buttons

I have nothing against the Directory buttons per se, but they take up too much of your precious window. Each of the buttons corresponds to an option on the Directory menu, which has additional options to boot, so just use that menu.

To remove the Directory buttons from the screen, select Options | Show Directory Buttons. The Directory buttons will disappear. Repeat this process to bring them back if you want.

Turn Off Link Underlining

I'm going out on a limb here, but I feel strongly about this: web pages look much better without underlined words all over the screen. Links are already a different color from the rest of the text (usually blue versus black), but the default underlining draws unnecessary emphasis to link words and destroys the typographical design of a web page.

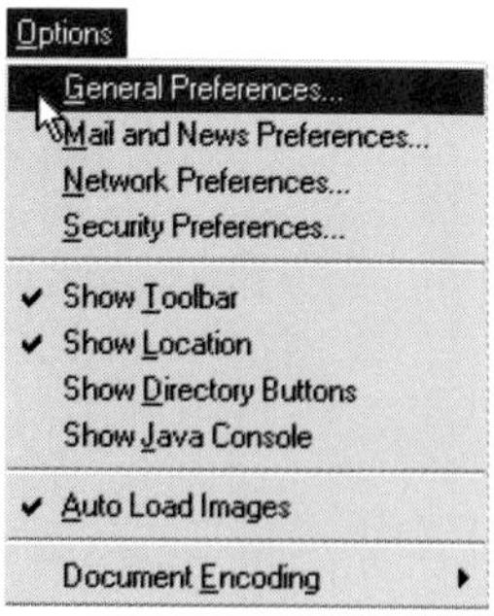

To turn off link underlining select Options | General Preferences. This brings up the Preferences dialog box. Click the Appearance tab if it's not already in front (see Figure 2.5). Click the "Links are" check box in the Link Styles area to uncheck Underlined. While you're at it, decide if you want your toolbar buttons to appear as just pictures, as just text (my preference—they take up less space, and you can read what each button does), or as both pictures and text. When you're done, click OK.

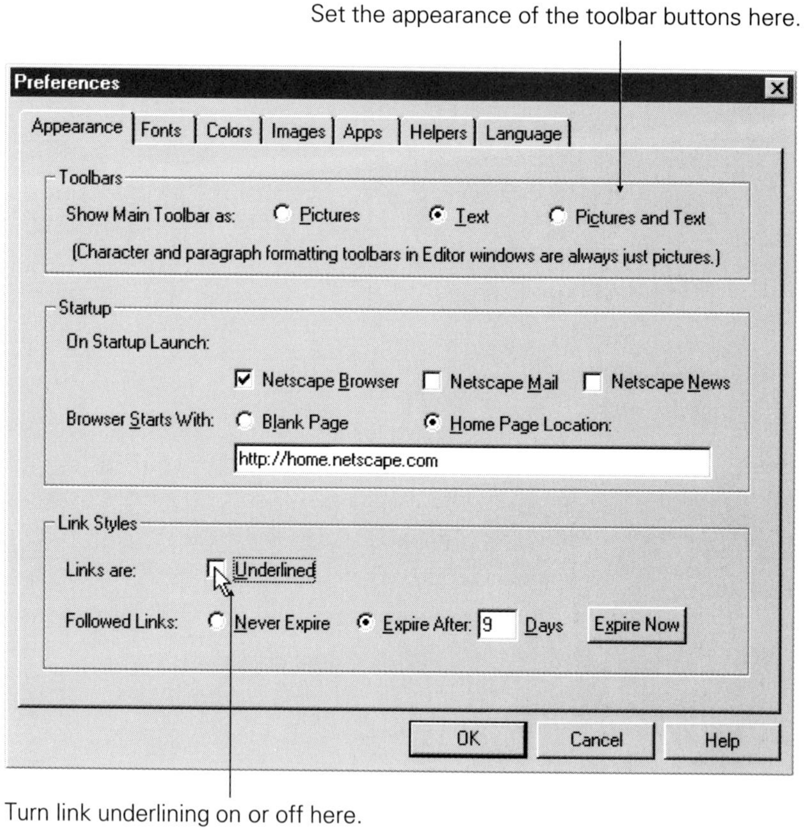

Set the appearance of the toolbar buttons here.

Turn link underlining on or off here.

Figure 2.5 You'll be glad you turned off underlining, believe me

Some of the items in this dialog box are not worth getting into, but you may want to check out the Fonts and Color tabs:

- You can change the size (and typeface) of regular and "typewriter" text on the Fonts tab, but I don't recommend it. It can make some pages look better, but it will mess up most pages.
- You can change the color of various screen elements (the background; regular text; and links before, during, and after they're clicked) on the Colors tab, but it's not worth it, since most web pages look better with their designers' colors.

Choose a Different Page as Your Startup Page

You don't have to start at the Netscape home page every time you run Navigator. (You can always get there in one hop by clicking the N.) If you come across a page you like enough to use as a jumping-off point (such as CNN, Yahoo!, any of the Search pages discussed in Chapter 3), you can make it your default home page or startup page (the one that appears whenever you start Netscape).

1. Go to the chosen page (such as http://www.yahoo.com/).
2. Click the Location box and select the web address of the page you're on.
3. Press CTRL-C (COMMAND-C on the Macintosh) to copy the address.
4. Select Options | General Preferences and click the Appearances tab.
5. Select Home Page Location in the Startup area.
6. Click the Browser Starts With box and press CTRL-V (COMMAND-V on the Macintosh) to paste the address into the box (see Figure 2.6).
7. Click OK.

To create a custom startup page, see "Customizing a Startup Page" later in this chapter.

Click here to set the
home page location.

Click this box and
then paste the home
page address.

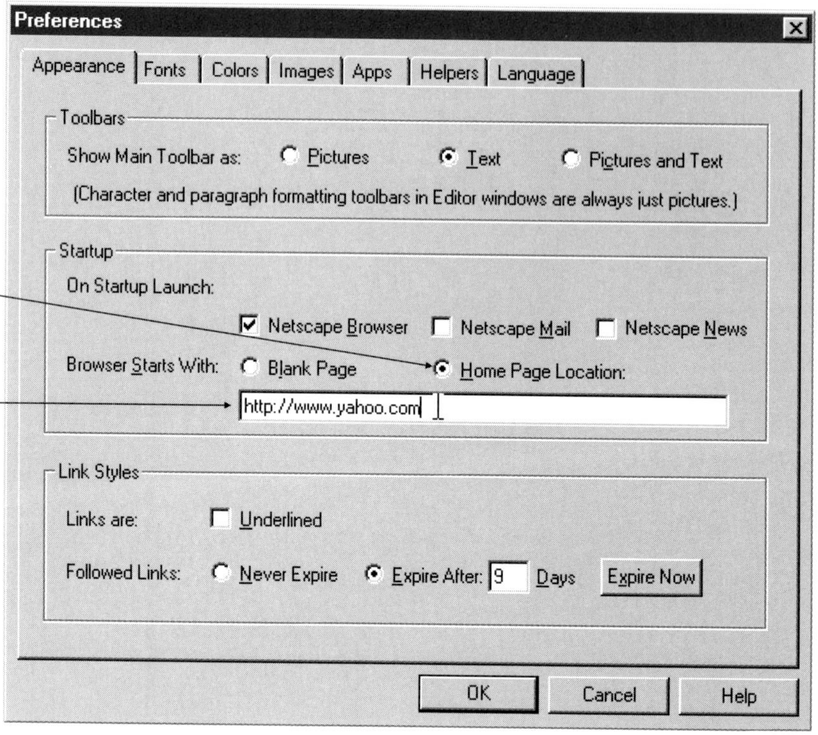

Figure 2.6 Make a different page your home page using the Appearances tab of the
Preferences dialog box

Customizing Internet Explorer

Because I use Internet Explorer as an alternative or back-up browser, I often
leave it set up the way it installed itself. When I find myself using it a lot, though,
I eventually do customize it to more or less duplicate my Netscape preferences.

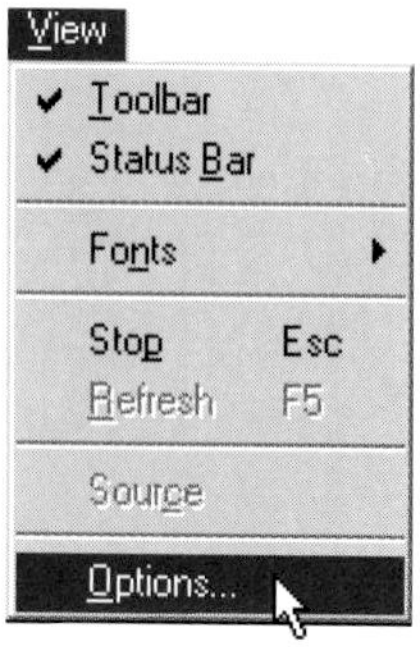

Turn Off Link Underlining

As I mentioned in the Netscape section, I personally think underlined links
ruin the look of most pages (although I admit this is a matter of taste), so I tend
to turn off link underlining as soon as I remember to.

To turn off link underlining select View | Options. This brings up the
Options dialog box. Click the General tab if it's not already in front (see Figure
2.7). Uncheck the Underline links option in the Links area of the dialog box. Then
click OK.

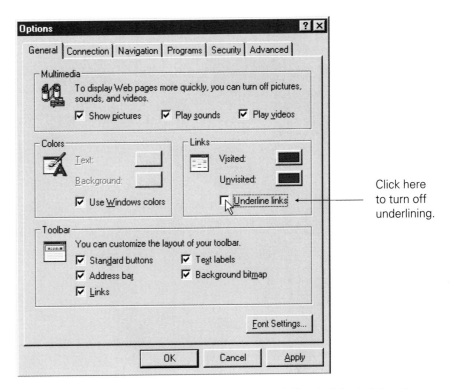

Figure 2.7 As with Netscape, you'll be glad you turned off underlining in Internet Explorer

Change the Buttons and Toolbars

Internet Explorer usually hides its Links buttons (direct links to useful starting places) at the right end of the Address Bar. Click the raised double-groove to the left of the word "Links" to expand the Links buttons and hide the Address bar. Click again to change it back. Both of these strips, along with the quite useful toolbar above them, can be removed from the Options dialog box. I recommend leaving things as they are. Nevertheless, to see the options, select View I Options and the General tab again (as shown in Figure 2.7).

- Uncheck Standard Buttons, Address Bar, or Links to remove any of these items (don't bother).
- Uncheck Text labels to reduce the standard buttons simply to icons (worth doing once you can tell the buttons apart by picture).

See Table 1.3 in Chapter 1 for a complete explanation of the various Microsoft home pages, including the various startup pages used by different version of Internet Explorer.

If you have created a custom start page, you'll find it at http://www.msn.com, the home page for the Microsoft Network. Previous versions of Internet Explorer used this as the default start page.

- Uncheck Background bitmap to remove the abstract swirls on the buttons (again, why bother).

Then click OK.

Choose a Different Page as Your Startup Page

When you run Internet Explorer, it will connect you to its default home page, http://home.microsoft.com.

If you decide you'd like to have Internet Explorer start you off somewhere else automatically, first go to that page. Then select View | Options and following the instructions in the Step by Step box.

If you ever want to return to the Microsoft start page, enter **http://home. microsoft.com** in the Address box and press ENTER. To revert to the original start page, click the Use Default button in the Start Page section of the Navigation tab of the Options dialog box. To create a custom startup page, see "Customizing a Startup Page," next.

STEP BY STEP Change Your Internet Explorer Startup Page

Options ? ✕

General | Connection | Navigation | Programs | Security | Advanced

Customize

You can change which pages to use for your start page, search page, and the Links toolbar.

Page: | Start Page ▼

Name: | Start Page

Address: | http://www.yahoo.com/

[Use Current] [Use Default]

History

The History folder contains links to pages you've visited.

Number of days to keep pages in history: | 14 ▲▼

[View History...] [Clear History]

[OK] [Cancel] [Apply]

❶ Click the Navigation tab in the Options dialog box.

❷ Make sure the Page section displays "Start Page."

❸ Click the Use Current button.

❹ Click OK.

Customizing a Startup Page

Both Netscape and Microsoft offer custom startup pages that you can actually use with any browser (though each is optimized for the company's own browser, of course). In Chapter 3, you'll see that you can create a custom search page in a similar way.

Creating a Netscape PowerStart Page

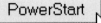

Netscape offers to put together a custom start page for you. If you're interested in trying this, click the N icon at the upper-right edge of the window to go to the Netscape home page. Then scroll down and click the PowerStart button.

This takes you to the PowerStart setup page, which is split into three frames (see Figure 2.8). Often, clicking one of these frames will change the contents of a different frame.

This frame will display a preview of the start page you're building.

This frame will display instructions.

This frame will display choices.

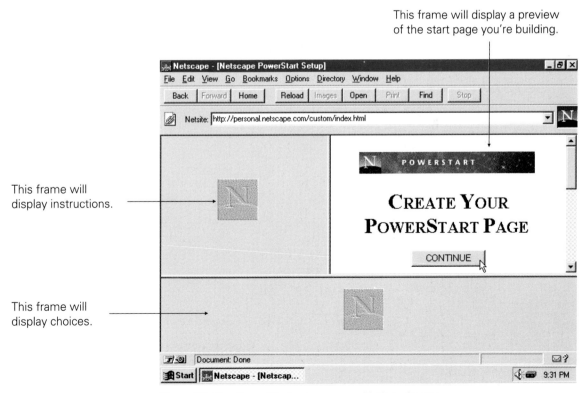

Figure 2.8 The PowerStart setup page, with three frames

1. Scroll through the upper-right frame and read the explanatory text. Then click the Continue button.
2. Read the Instructions paragraph in the upper-left frame. Then scroll down the frame to Choose Your Content, read the instructions, and click the Collection link (see Figure 2.9).

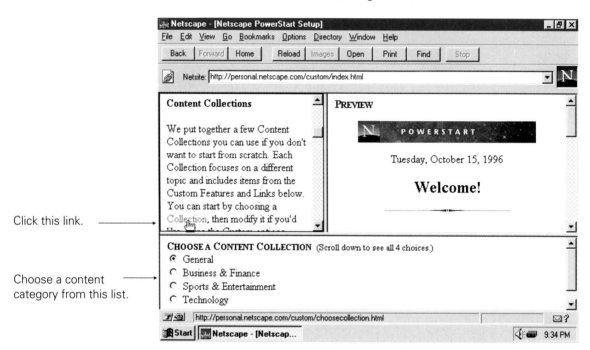

Click this link. ⟶

Choose a content
category from this list. ⟶

Figure 2.9 Choosing a link

3. Choose one of the content categories from the choices that appear in the bottom frame. The upper-right frame adjusts itself (if necessary) to reflect your choice.
4. In the upper-left frame, scroll down to Custom Features, select one of the choices, and click Yes in the lower frame.
5. If you are asked about your choice, answer any relevant questions.
6. Repeat steps 4 and 5 for any other Custom Features choices you want.

7. Scroll further down to Custom Links and choose any of the preassembled link categories listed. Then choose the subcategories of links you want on your start page.

8. To add your own links, click Personal Links in the upper-left frame. In the lower frame, type the name of a page, press TAB, type or paste the URL of the page, and click the Enter button. (See Figure 2.10.) Repeat this step as often as you like.

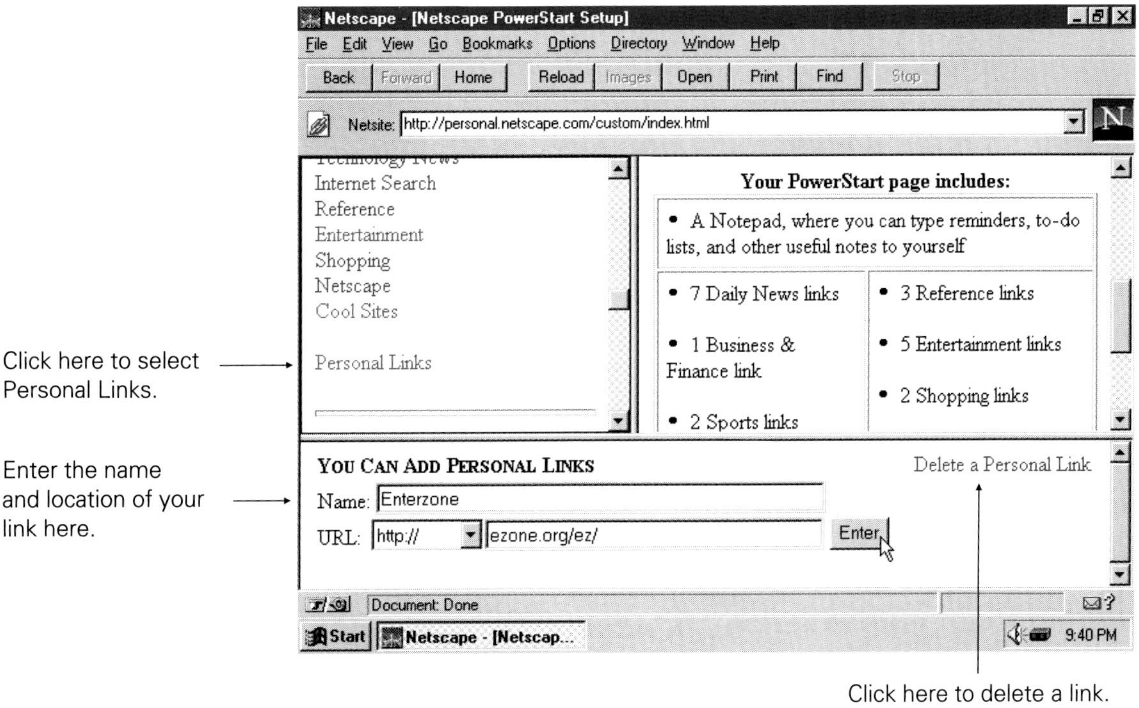

Click here to select Personal Links.

Enter the name and location of your link here.

Click here to delete a link.

Figure 2.10 Adding your own links

9. Repeat step 8 as often as you like. To throw away any mistaken or unwanted links, click Delete a Personal Link.

10. In the upper-left frame, scroll down to Choose Your Page Style, click Style Sheets, and choose a basic style in the bottom frame.

11. To customize the layout further, click any of the Custom Design Elements links in the upper-left frame and make a selection in the bottom frame. Repeat this step as often as necessary.

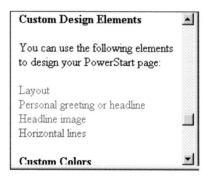

12. To select colors, scroll down further in the upper-left frame to Custom Colors, choose a color category (background, text, links, or visited links), and select colors in the bottom frame. Repeat this step for any of the other color categories you want to change.

13. Scroll down still further and click the Build button.

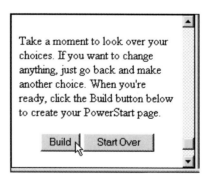

14. Click OK in the congratulatory dialog box that appears.

CAUTION

If you click the Start Over button, all your choices will be lost! Most forms on the web feature two buttons at the end, side by side. The names may change, but the functions are usually the same: submit, and start over. Be careful where you click!

15. Bookmark the page (select Bookmarks I Add Bookmark) or make it your startup page by selecting the URL in the address box and then following the instructions in the section "Choose a Different Page as Your Startup Page" earlier in this chapter.

Creating an MSN Custom Start Page

To create a custom start page, first go to the MSN (Microsoft Network) home page and select the Custom Start Page link (or jump directly to http://www.msn.com/csp/choices/first.asp). Read the Custom Start Options page that appears and then click the first Click here button, just below "Let's get customized!"

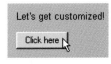

CAUTION

It is likely that this procedure will change a little or a lot in the long run, so don't be too concerned if what you see does not match the following steps exactly. Try to go with the flow.

You'll be taken to step 1, Personal Preferences. Fill out the questionnaire with your name and address (or a fake one—see what junk mail comes!) and then click "setup this page."

EXPERT ADVICE

You may see a security alert whenever you click buttons during this routine. If and when this happens, click OK.

That takes you to step 2, Services. You can choose among options for stock tickers, sports scores, movie listings, and music information, and you can mix and match the options. Then click "setup this page."

For step 3, News & Entertainment, you can choose among categories for an MSNBC newsfeed, request TV listings, select a few comic strips, and choose

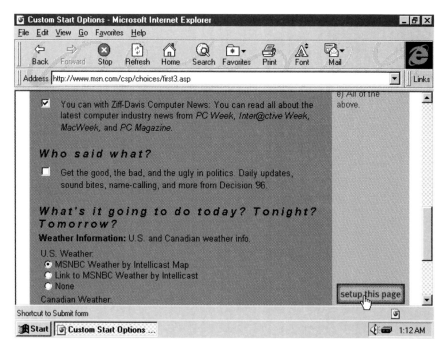

Figure 2.11 MSN's Custom Start Page News & Entertainment step

among a few other custom features in categories such as technology, politics, and weather (see Figure 2.11). Then click "setup this page."

Step 4 lets you select Internet search tools (more on these in Chapter 3). I'd recommend selecting Alta Vista, Excite, and Yahoo, at least. If you want to see whatever new pages MSN feels like touting, select "Bring me a new Web site every day!" or some of the specific categories for sites. Lower down on this page, you can enter the addresses of any pages you'd like to link to automatically. The screen suggests, modestly, that you link to the Microsoft home page, but you can replace the first suggestion with anything you like, as shown in Figure 2.12.

When you've entered as many links as you want, click "setup this page." Your page is created, and you're taken to it. (Microsoft sticks in links to its own corporate pages anyway.) Scroll down through the document to see all your choices or links that lead to them (see Figure 2.13).

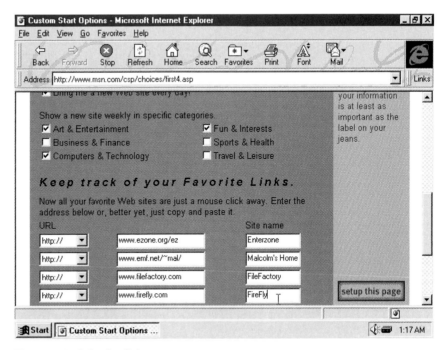

Figure 2.12 Selecting links

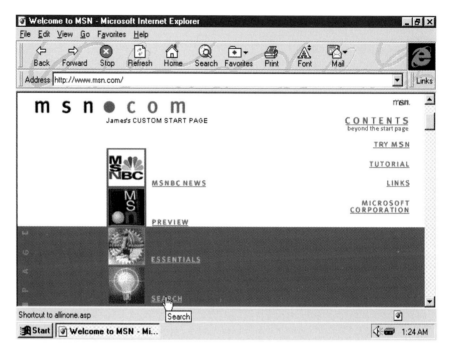

Figure 2.13 An MSN custom start page

Now add this page to your Favorites (select Favorites | Add to Favorites) or make it your default start page, as explained earlier in this section.

Downloading Plug-Ins and Specialty Tools (such as PointCast)

Any web site that requires a plug-in for proper viewing will (if it's worth its salt) include a link directly to the download site for the plug-in needed.

You can download and install a number of third-party programs to extend the capabilities of your web browser. In the early days of web browsers (a year or so ago), the only way to enhance a browser's features was by informing it of stand-alone "helper applications" the browser could start up externally (to display an image, for example). While helper apps (as they're often called) still exist, more and more programs designed specifically to plug directly into a web browser and increase its own ability to display or handle additional file formats are coming out all the time.

There are too many of these plug-ins for me to list them all here, and most of them will be useful to you only if you visit specific web sites that require them to function fully. Some of these plug-ins can produce astounding results and display fascinating effects, but many of them are bulky and take up a lot of disk space and memory when they're running. Your web browser by itself is a bit of a resource hog. Think back to your Internet strategy. If you want to explore the limits of multimedia available online, be ready to install many plug-ins. If you'd rather keep things simple, you may want few or none.

Choosing Plug-Ins

If you have the disk space and the interest in getting additional programs, here are three "must-have" plug-ins:

- Macromedia's Shockwave
- Progressive Networks' RealAudio
- Adobe Acrobat

Shockwave enables your browser to handle Macromedia Director files, which can include animation, sounds, and interactive elements (things that respond differently depending on where you click, for example). You can download Shockwave from http://www.macromedia.com/shockwave/ (see Figure 2.14).

RealAudio is the most popular format for *streaming audio*, or sound files that can start playing soon after they start downloading. You can download RealAudio from http://www.realaudio.com/ (see Figure 2.15).

Acrobat is a compact portable document format that enables publishers to design sophisticated publications and make them available on the Web without the limitations of HTML, the coding language normally used for web documents. You can download Acrobat from http://www.adobe.com/acrobat/ (see Figure 2.16).

Other popular plug-in formats include many competing flavors of three-dimensional (virtual reality) viewers, such as Live3D; video players, such as VDOLive; and Apple's QuickTime movie format. A good central location to check for available plug-ins is BrowserWatch's Plug-In Plaza at http://www.browserwatch.com/plug-in.html (see Figure 2.17).

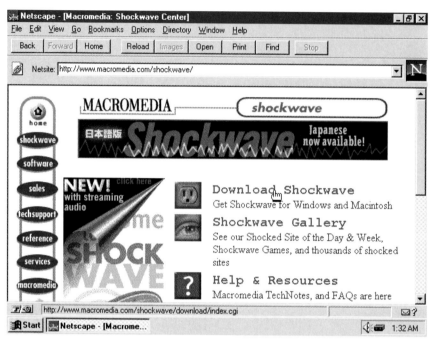

Figure 2.14 Macromedia's Shockwave home page

Figure 2.15 Progressive Networks' RealAudio home page

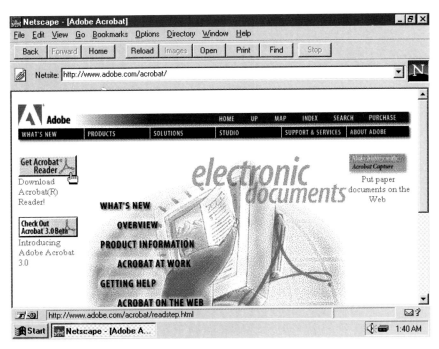

Figure 2.16 Adobe Acrobat home page

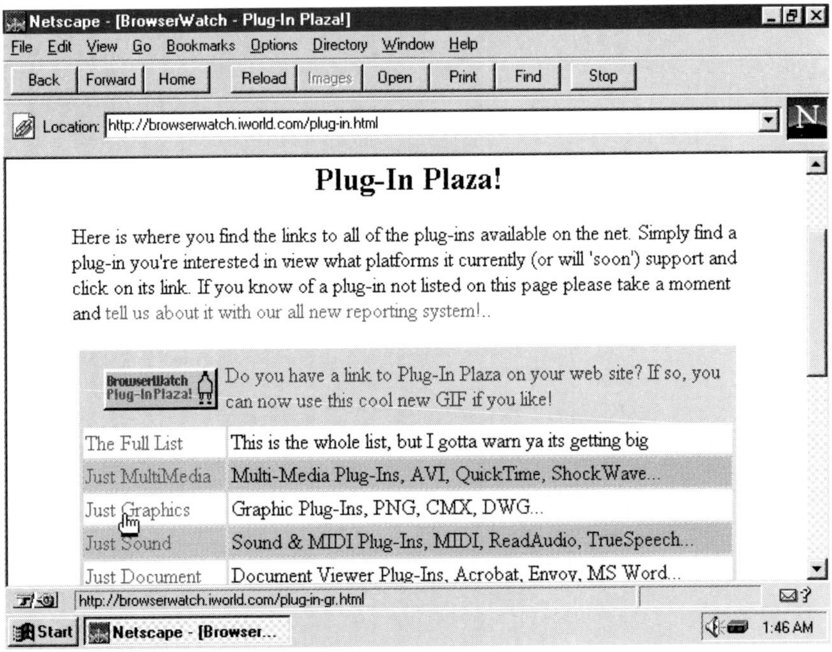

Figure 2.17 Keep up to date with the latest plug-in developments at Plug-In Plaza

PointCast Network

Some programs can run independently on an Internet connection, using the Web but not connected to any web browser. A popular program of this sort is PointCast, which allows you to customize a news and information display. Although you can specify all sorts of preferences, PointCast essentially allows you to be passive: it connects to the Web for you, finding the sorts of news and information items you're interested in, and displays headlines and ticker-tape information in a window (or on your whole screen, functioning as a screen saver).

This software is free, since the program is self-supporting through advertisement. So long as you don't mind seeing ads on your computer screen, you get something for nothing. PointCast, with its direct news feed, may be a new kind of newspaper-of-the-future—or perhaps it is just a maddening never-ending procession of trivial factoids. You can decide for yourself.

Installing PointCast

Install PointCast as follows:

1. Go to http://www.pointcast.com/ and read any of the information at the site, if you still have questions about what the PointCast Network (the product's full name) does.

2. Click any of the "click here to download the PointCast Network" links you see (or go straight to http://www.pointcast.com/download).

3. Choose your version (the current choices are Windows, Macintosh, and Canada).

4. Click any of the Download Sites links.

5. Choose a folder to save the installation file in (my choice is usually c:\temp\install), and remember what you chose. Your browser will download the installation file to the folder you chose (note the name of the file).

6. When the file is downloaded (it may take a while), open the folder in which you saved the file, find the file, and double-click it to install PointCast.

7. Specify a directory for PointCast.

8. Read and agree to the license agreement.

9. Fill out (or erase the contents of) the personal questionnaire and then click Continue.

10. Type your ZIP code and click Continue. PointCast will be installed.

11. Click Launch PointCast or Personalize PointCast (you can always personalize it later).

12. If you use a modem to connect to the Internet, make sure PointCast knows to use the Windows 95 Dialer (and the Dial-Up Networking connection that you use to connect to your provider). If you access the Internet through a network, connect using the "Direct connection (non-modem)" setting.

13. Click "Use Netscape Navigator to access the web" and click OK (see Figure 2.18).

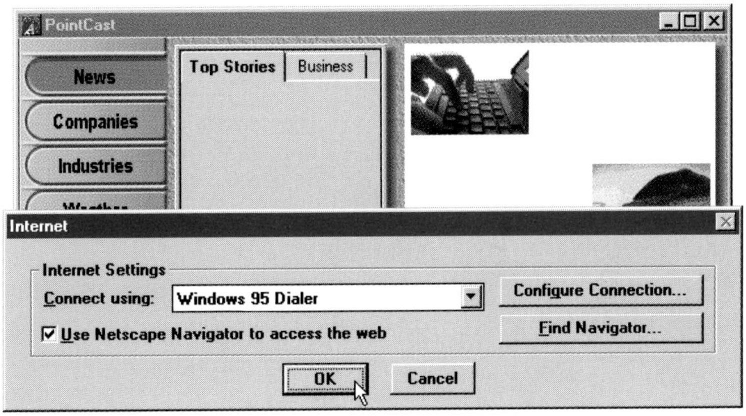

Figure 2.18 PointCast, once you've launched it for the first time

When PointCast offers to get you your first batch of news (while minimized), click Yes. (You can also click the Update button to make this happen.)

When the news is ready, it will appear as headlines in an upper-left pane and as full stories in a lower pane. (The upper-right pane is for advertisements—don't look!)

Updating your PointCast feed can take up to 5 minutes.

By default, PointCast installs itself as a screen saver (in place of your current screen saver if you have one set up). To control whether PointCast functions as a screen saver, click the Options button (or click Stop first and then Options, if PointCast is still downloading news). Make sure the SmartScreen tab of the Options dialog box is showing . Then follow the steps in the Step by Step box. Figure 2.19 shows PointCast in its SmartScreen mode.

STEP BY STEP Control the PointCast Screen Saver Function

① Choose a delay, such as 10 minutes, before the screen saver is activated.

② Choose a corner of the screen as the Activate Now corner. Moving the mouse pointer there will start the SmartScreen version of PointCast.

③ To be able to dispel the SmartScreen by moving the mouse (the way most screen savers work), click "Hold down 'Alt' key and click with mouse" (that's what you'll have to do to display a full story). If you select the alternative option, you choose a story just by clicking it.

④ Click OK.

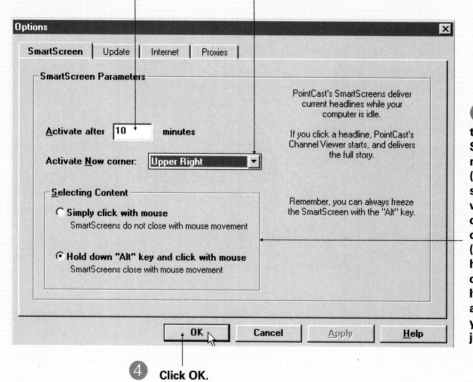

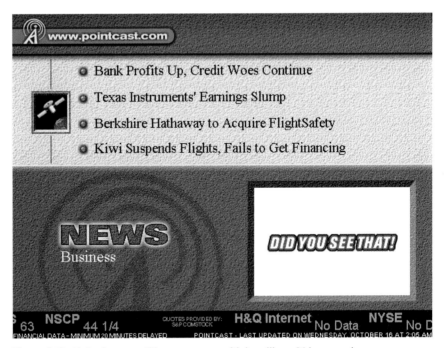

Figure 2.19 PointCast can fill your screen with headlines 24 hours a day

You can choose from a number of different categories and more specific preferences any time you personalize PointCast. To control whether PointCast updates itself manually or automatically, select Options | Updates, choose the option you want, and click OK.

Security, Credit Cards, and Online Purchases

The Internet and the Web are open systems, not designed with security as the paramount consideration, so there's been a lot of concern in the past few years about how to make Net transactions secure and how to reassure potential consumers that they can safely send sensitive information, such as credit card numbers and expiration dates, over the Internet without compromising their security.

(Never mind that most consumers take bigger risks with their credit information in restaurants every day.)

Both Netscape and Internet Explorer use similar solutions. They both have the ability to create secure connections with certain types of web servers out there on the Net (conveniently, for the most part, servers made by the same company as the browser in question) and can notify you that the connection is secure whenever it is. Netscape, for instance, displays a broken key in the lower-right corner of the screen when the connection is *not* secure (most of the time), and it displays a solid key when it is. Netscape also displays a blue border around secure pages; see Netscape's View | Document Info command for a more detailed security report.

Similarly, Internet Explorer displays a lock on the status bar in the lower-right corner of the screen if the current page is secure. You can get more information about a page's security by using the File | Properties command and clicking the Security tab.

Both Netscape and Internet Explorer display a message when you connect to a secure server. Furthermore, when you do attempt to send any type of information to a server, both browsers will warn you if the connection is not a secure one (though they give you the option of turning off the warning screen if you find it intrusive). Here's Netscape's warning message:

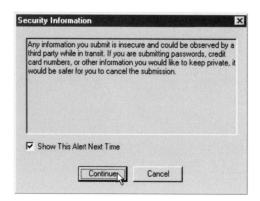

These warning messages can become annoying because they come up so frequently. A very real danger is that you will get in the habit of clicking OK to ignore these warnings, so that they become meaningless. For now, you may want to remind yourself to keep your credit cards private and uncheck the Show This Alert Next Time box.

CHECK POINT

Now you know how to set up your most basic Internet tools, and you can start wandering the Web. If you get tired of poking around aimlessly, Chapter 3 will show you how to search for specific topics and zero in on exactly the resources you want online. After that, you'll see how to use the Internet's most common communication tool, e-mail, and how to participate in ongoing and live discussions. Finally, you'll learn how to connect to remote sites, search the nooks and crannies of the Net, and create and publish web documents.

Easy Searching

INCLUDES

- Searching for topics on the Web

- Guessing domain names

- Performing keyword searches

- Using search engines

- Consulting web directories

- Visiting all-in-one search sites

- Searching for software

- Finding e-mail addresses

- Looking up phone numbers and addresses

FAST FORWARD

Search for Information with Search Engines ➤ *pp. 91-97*

Perform keyword searches at

- http://altavista.digital.com/
- http://www.excite.com/
- http://www.hotbot.com/
- Any of the other sites listed in Table 3.1

Look for Information in Directories ➤ *pp. 97-98*

Look for topics by category at

- http://www.yahoo.com/
- http://www.mckinley.com
- http://www.pointcom.com

Visit All-in-One Search Sites ➤ *pp. 98-102*

Search multiple sites from one web page at

- http://home.netscape.com/home/internet-search.html
- http://home.microsoft.com/access/allinone.asp
- http://www.search.com
- http://www.metacrawler.com

Hunt for E-Mail Addresses ➤ *pp. 106-110*

- Visit http://www.four11.com, type the name, and click the Search button.
- Visit http://www.whowhere.com, type the name, and click the Start My Search button.
- Send a message to mail-server@rtfm.mit.edu with no subject and the words *send* **usenet-addresses/** *name* on a line by themselves.

As you've probably noticed by now, the Internet (not to mention the Web) is a nebulous, amorphous, constantly changing, regularly shifting blob of a network. Fortunately, there are brave souls out there working hard to make it comprehensible, as well as searchable—so when you're looking for information on a rare disease, or you're planning to go scuba diving in South America, or you're looking for a new job, try searching the Net using some of the methods described in this chapter. I'll point you toward some useful search engine, give you some basic search tips, show you how to find software, and run through some of the methods you can use to look for individual e-mail addresses and other information about people.

Searching the Web

The most convenient search tools on the Internet focus on the Web, where most of the action is these days. However, although you can use a web browser to connect to all kinds of parts of the Internet (Gopher menus, FTP file archives, and so on), the search engines generally only *know about* the material that's literally on the Web.

Some topics can be researched more easily using the Usenet (and other) newsgroups, as I'll explain in Chapter 6. For information on how to dig down even deeper into the layers of the Internet, such as searching Gopher or mailing-list archives, see Chapter 9.

Still, most of the time, if you're looking for a web site or a topic, your best bet (and at least the first thing you should try) is the Web, either by guessing the address of the site you want to see or by visiting and trying out one or more of the many web search engines.

Guessing Domain Names

If you're looking for a specific web site (as opposed to a topic), you may be able to guess the address of the site's home page. Many companies, for example, have home pages with an address in the form http://www.*company-name-here*.com. Often you can easily try one or more possible variations of this format to see if you can find the page you want. University sites generally end in .edu, noncommercial sites often end in .org, and government sites usually end in .gov. Another variation to try sometimes is .net, since commercial, educational, and noncommercial sites may have the Net domain name in their address.

EXPERT ADVICE

The fastest way to call up a web site is to type its exact name (such as www.ibm.com). Typing just a single word will result in one or two false hits on your provider's name server before you connect to the site you want.

Netscape tested this same search feature in pre-release versions of Navigator 3.0, but it seems that the search engine companies objected to having to take turns as the target of these casual searches (they're trying to establish brand-name dominance over the field and object to being treated as interchangeable commodities), and the feature was gone by the time 3.0 was released.

The Netscape and Internet Explorer browsers both assume that you want an address starting with http:// if you leave out that part. Netscape also assumes the www. and the .com portions if you type just a single word. This means, for example, that you can type just **ibm,** and Netscape will connect you with http://www.ibm.com.

Go to: ibm

Internet Explorer also has a built-in search feature in its address box. If you type two or more words separated by spaces, IE will send the words as a query to one of the search engines. We'll get to search engines themselves in a moment.

Performing Keyword Searches

The best way to look for a specific topic is to perform a keyword search using one of the many search engines. Each of the competing search sites has different special features that allow you to express sophisticated search requests (called queries), but all of them perform basic searches in about the same way.

DEFINITION

Keyword: (Also key word.*) A word, which when specified with other words in a search, can single out documents or database entries that contain the specified word or words. Good keywords are those that narrow down the number of matching results as much as possible.*

The simplest type of search involves a single keyword. If there's an obvious single word associated with your topic, you can try typing it in a search query form and clicking the button (usually called Submit). You may discover that your search turns up relevant and irrelevant results, especially if your keyword has more than one meaning. In that case, you can try again, entering two words (separated by a space) to see which web pages the engine finds that include both words.

EXPERT ADVICE

You can often get more exact search results by searching for two or more words. In most search engines, you can put two or more words in quotation marks to require that they be found all together in a phrase. Also, try more than one search engine, as their results can differ substantially.

You can perform more advanced search techniques requiring that documents meet additional criteria. For example, you can require that some or all of the search words appear in every document returned, that two or more words be found close together (or in a phrase), or that documents contain one word and exclude some other word.

Suppose you want a copy of the football schedule for the University of California at Berkeley (the California Bears). Just type **Cal Bears football schedule** in the search box of any search engine (more on these later in this chapter). The first set of pages returned in this simple search is largely irrelevant. Since you don't want the Bears' basketball schedule, you can exclude basketball pages by including a minus sign in front of basketball. Add the year to concentrate on the current schedule. A more refined search might put a plus sign in front of "schedule," to indicate the word "schedule" must appear somewhere on the page. Also, you can consider adding "Berkeley" and "California" as well as Cal, so pages that mention the California Bears are returned. A successful search string might be California Cal Berkeley +Bears +football +schedule -basketball.

CAUTION

There are certain small, common words that you can't search for because they show up too often (words such as "is," "and," "the"). These words are sometimes called stop words or buzz words.

Here's a more detailed example. Suppose you're searching for a web page displaying the well-known painting *American Gothic*. If you start by just typing **American Gothic** in the search box, you'll generate a huge number of irrelevant hits on a TV show called *American Gothic*. To avoid this, you can refine your search by requesting information on American Gothic -television -TV (the minus signs means pages that *don't* include that word). The results now are a little better, but many pages still mention the TV show, though without using the words "TV" or "television." To further refine your search, you can add a relevant word: "painting," for example. To make sure that you don't get pages about gothic-style paintings, you can place quotation marks around "American Gothic." This search, "American Gothic" +painting -television -TV, doesn't generate an image of the painting, but one of the sites mentions the artist's name, Grant Wood. The final search, "American Gothic" -television -TV +painting +Grant +Wood, generates a number of copies of the image, plus some modern interpretations of the famous couple with the pitchfork and a page about Anamosa, Iowa–Grant Wood's birthplace.

Search Engines

When I first discovered the Web, I used it mostly by browsing. I wandered randomly through the hyperlinks of the Web, sometimes stumbling over stuff I found really interesting. After a while, I found this approach took up too much of my time. Along the way I had developed the habit of making bookmarks, so from that point on I generally went directly to my favorite, bookmarked sites (although I still did a lot of browsing, especially from my favorite starting points).

Finally, I realized that I was limited to the precincts of the Web I had explored before or that I could get to in a number of jumps from sites I already knew about, and I started guessing addresses and searching for sites. Now most of the time I use the Web like this: I run my browser (usually Netscape), go to the AltaVista search page (http://altavista.digital.com—more on this site in a moment)—at times I've even made the AltaVista page my startup page—enter a keyword or two, and click the Submit button. Then I'm off and surfing.

Actually, there are several different senses in which you can search on the Web. For example, with any web browser, you can search the text of the current page. This can be useful with very long pages. You will also sometimes encounter pages with the notice, "This is a searchable index." Pages with this notice have been designed so that if you type a keyword (or words) in the box provided and press ENTER, you'll receive whatever matching information is available.

In Netscape or Internet Explorer, press CTRL-F to search for a particular word on the current page.

CAUTION

Because the information on the Net ages so quickly, often the pages you find from a search will already have been moved or changed. Try using several search engines to perform as thorough a search as possible.

Finally, you'll encounter pages, such as those outlined in the next few sections, that are really front-ends for search engines. A *search engine* is a program that connects you to a database of web addresses. These databases are generally compiled by computer programs (called webcrawlers, spiders, or robots) that explore the Web, cataloguing pages they find and sending references back to the main database. Search engines therefore can often give you huge numbers of pages in response to a query, though sometimes without much context or filtering. You get what the robots found.

DEFINITION

Search engine: A computer program, especially one accessible via the Web, that can be used to search a database or index of web sites, Internet resources in general, or other reference sources.

These search engines often give you more control over your search than just entering a word or two. These pages usually contain full-fledged forms with most of the features you probably associate with dialog boxes (list boxes, check boxes, and so on). You fill out just as much of the form as is necessary, click a button to submit your form, and then await the results. Some databases have just the titles of documents stored; others have entire documents or abstracts with keywords.

EXPERT ADVICE

If you end up publishing anything yourself on the Web, then you can use search engines for "ego-surfing"—that is, searching for references to yourself or your site on other people's web pages.

Security Warnings

One other thing about search engines (before I show you some): sometimes, when you click a button to submit a form, your browser will display a warning

CAUTION

If you're trying to buy something over the Web and you're about to send your credit card number and expiration date, then you should cancel the transaction if you are the type who tears up your credit card carbons.

dialog box to tell you that your transmission is not secure (as discussed briefly in Chapter 2).

If all you're doing is querying a search index, as in all the preceding examples, then there's nothing to worry about, and you can go ahead and click Continue.

AltaVista

As I mentioned earlier, AltaVista is currently my favorite search engine. I'll discuss it along with a few other search engines, and I'll also show you (later) how to find lists of search engines (you never know when a new one will appear), so you can judge for yourself and choose your own favorite search sites.

AltaVista offers searching tips just below the input box.

The AltaVista search site is run by Digital Equipment Corporation (a computer company based in Massachusetts) and includes both Web and Usenet searching. (See Chapter 6 for more on Usenet.) To use it, go to http://altavista.digital.com, type a word (or words) in the box, and click the Submit button (see Figure 3.1).

AltaVista will return a page with links to the first 10 web sites it found that matched your keyword (and up to 19 additional pages of sites).

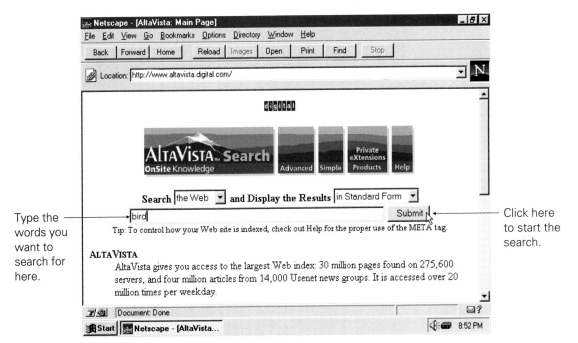

Type the words you want to search for here.

Click here to start the search.

Figure 3.1 AltaVista search screen

Now try AltaVista yourself:

1. Point your web browser at http://altavista.digital.com.
2. Type the words **tornado twister hurricane** into the main box.
3. Click the Submit button.
4. Figure 3.2 shows some of the links AltaVista returns. Click some of these links to see what information you found.

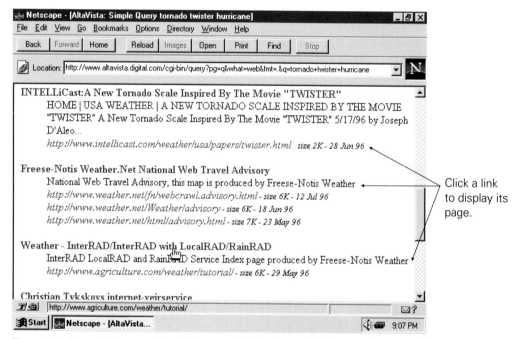

Figure 3.2 Some of the pages found by searching for the words "tornado," "twister," and "hurricane"

To just read the reviews, you can click any of the category listings below the search area.

Excite

Another excellent search site is Excite. Along with Usenet information (see Chapter 6), it includes an option to search reviewed web sites. To use Excite, go to http://www.excite.com and type a word in the box. If you want to read opinionated reviews, click the drop-down list box and choose Excite Web Site Reviews. In either case, then click the Search button (see Figure 3.3).

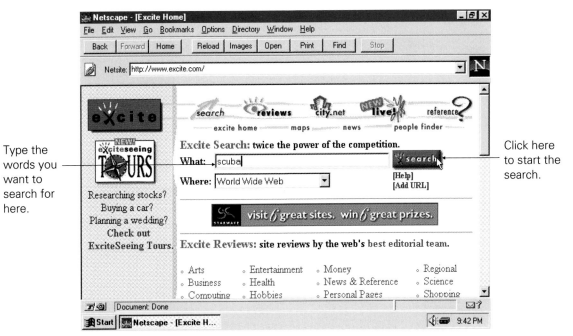

Type the words you want to search for here.

Click here to start the search.

Figure 3.3 Excite search screen

bookmark

You can find the Excite search site at http://www.excite.com.

Excite will return a page with links to the first ten web sites it found that matched your keyword (and a button at the bottom of the page to display ten more).

HotBot

The newest, largest, and possibly fastest searchable index of the Web is called Inktomi, and HotWired, the online publishing network (http://www.hotwired.com), recently attached a new front-end to the Inktomi database, called HotBot. To get there, point your web browser at http://www.hotbot.com. HotBot can also search Usenet, as most of the search engines seem to be able to do these days (see Chapter 6 for more on Usenet).

bookmark

HotBot's at http://www.hotbot.com.

Enter your search word in the main box and then click the Search button. HotBot quickly returns a list of sites, weighted by how closely they match your search words (see Figure 3.4).

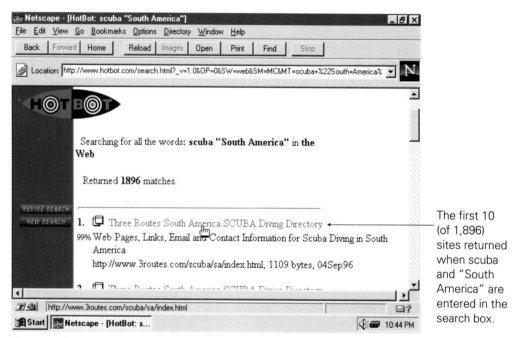

The first 10 (of 1,896) sites returned when scuba and "South America" are entered in the search box.

Figure 3.4 The results of an Inktomi search

And Many More. . .

There are many other worthwhile search engines (and more cropping up all the time), and all of them work more or less the same way. Table 3.1 lists a number of good search engines (including those already mentioned, so you can refer to one place for all the addresses).

EXPERT ADVICE

I'd recommend that you make some bookmarks for these sites, since you'll probably want to visit them more than once. In addition to using AltaVista as my start-up page, I also have a few other search engines at the top of my bookmarks.

Search Engine	Web Address
AltaVista	http://altavista.digital.com
Excite	http://www.excite.com
HotBot	http://www.hotbot.com
InfoSeek	http://www.infoseek.com
Lycos	http://www.lycos.com
WebCrawler	http://www.webcrawler.com
OpenText	http://www.opentext.com

Table 3.1 Good Search Engines

The Difference between a Search Engine and a Directory

You recall that a search engine is a web page that connects you to a database of web addresses. There are also databases that are compiled by people (researchers and editors). These databases are called directories, and they generally don't attempt to include every single web page or resource they can find, but instead they make selective choices about which pages are useful or worthwhile, and then they organize them into categorical hierarchies. The most popular directory site is Yahoo!.

bookmark

Yahoo! is at http://www.yahoo.com.

Despite the technical difference between search engines and directories, on the surface they look very much the same, especially now that most directories are searchable, and many search engines also include subject categories (and even reviews, as you saw with Excite), much like a directory. In the long run, this distinction will probably become blurrier and eventually disappear.

Still, if you're going to hunt for information on the Net, you should know about directories as well. Table 3.2 gives the addresses of a few of my favorite directories.

Directory Name	Web Address
Yahoo!	http://www.yahoo.com
Magellan	http://www.mckinley.com/
Point	http://www.pointcom.com/

Table 3.2 Some of the Best Directory Pages on the Web

Going to Your Browser's Built-in Search Page

Both Netscape and Internet Explorer offer all-in-one search pages where you can access a number of different directories and search engines. If you haven't bookmarked your favorite search sites yet, then using your browser's built-in search page is the easiest way to perform a search.

Netscape's Internet Search Page

One quick doorway to a number of useful search engines is Netscape's Internet Search page. To get there, select Directory | Internet Search (see Figure 3.5)

EXPERT ADVICE

If you're running a different web browser, you can still get to this page by going directly to http://home.netscape.com/home/internet-search.html.

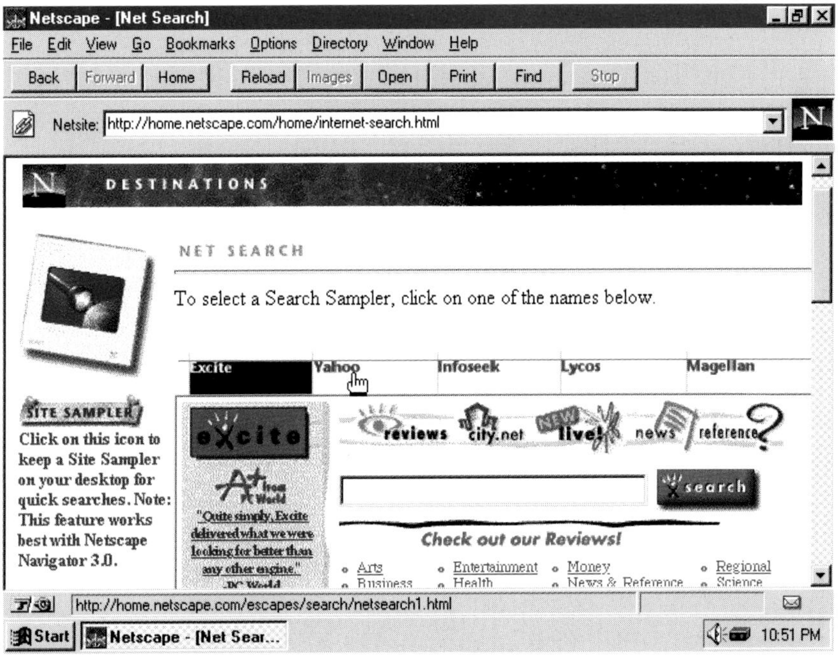

Figure 3.5 Netscape's Net Search page offers easy access to a number of different search options

EXPERT ADVICE

Click the Site Sampler icon to create a floating dialog box for the currently featured search site. You can then perform searches in this separate window.

Net Search currently features five resources in its most prominent position (near the top of the page): Excite, Yahoo!, Infoseek, Lycos, and Magellan (they pay for the exposure). A different one of the five will be selected in the search form, depending on when you visit.

If you scroll down the page, you'll see many links to other useful search and directory resources.

Internet Explorer's Search Page

EXPERT ADVICE

If you're running a different web browser, you can still get to this page by going directly to http://home.microsoft.com/access/allinone.asp or http://www.msn.com/access/allinone.asp, but the page is designed for use with Internet Explorer and may look funky in other browsers.

To go to Internet Explorer's central search page, click the Search button in the toolbar. You can then follow the steps in the Step by Step box to perform a keyword search.

The Internet Explorer start page also features links to a number of specialized search services.

Other Central Search Sites

Besides the central search sites provided by the two major web-browser companies, there are a few others worth visiting as well. The first, clnet's Search.com site, is similar to the two just discussed. The second, MetaCrawler, actually searches multiple sites at once for you, which can save you quite a bit of time and effort.

Search.com

The same people who publish the clnet page, one of the best sources of computer and Internet news, also offer a page called Search.com (found, naturally,

STEP BY STEP Perform a Keyword Search Using Internet Explorer's Find It Fast! Page

① Enter your keyword search criteria.

③ **Click the Search button.**

② **Choose one of the eight engines and directories to search.**

at http://www.search.com), with a number of different search sites built right in (see Figure 3.6). Search.com features a direct front-end for AltaVista, a search form that can be tuned to ten different search or directory sites, and links to many other specialty search pages.

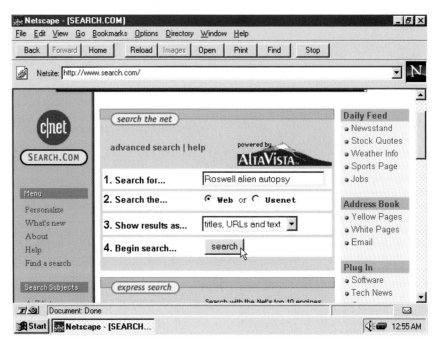

Figure 3.6 Search.com start page

MetaCrawler

A new search site, MetaCrawler, performs *parallel* searches, meaning that it submits your query to multiple search sites at once and then collates the results on one page for you. This can save you the time and trouble of visiting many different sites to make sure you aren't missing a reference out there on the Net. You can try MetaCrawler for yourself at http://www.metacrawler.com (see Figure 3.7).

Good Search Habits

Once you start searching for things on the Net, you'll do it more and more often. You'll begin to rely on searching as a way of navigating this bewildering blob of a network. I recommend bookmarking any search sites you like and possibly even making one your new startup page (as explained in Chapter 2). In general, for important searches you'll want to search more than one site to be sure you haven't missed anything obvious.

Figure 3.7 Enter a key word or two and let MetaCrawler search multiple databases for you

It's possible to do serious research on the Web, but the Net is not as dependable as traditional media, and you can't be sure you'll find what you're looking for even if it is out there. (For research, Usenet is also an invaluable research tool, as discussed in Chapter 6.)

If you perform a search but don't have time to check out all of the returned sites, you can save the search results page as an HTML document on your computer by selecting File | Save As, specifying a folder and file name, and then clicking the Save button. One problem with this approach is that the links on your search results page may age and become out of date, in which case you'll need to perform the search again (the Web changes fast).

Another, similar method of preserving a search is to bookmark the query itself. If you try several searches and come up with a combination of keywords that seems to ferret out the results you want, you can bookmark the results page. What this really does is bookmark the gibberish in the address box that constitutes your search query (as far as the database you consulted is concerned). Later, if you return to this bookmark, the search will actually be performed anew, with up-to-date references.

Finding Software

Besides looking for information and specific web sites, you may also want to hunt for useful software on the Internet. A lot of software on the Net is free, at least during a trial period when you can consider whether or not to buy it. Software you eventually have to pay for is called *shareware*. Software you don't have to pay for is called *freeware*. Sample software that includes only a limited set of working features is called *crippleware*. You can hunt for all the different varieties of programs at clnet's Shareware.com site (see Figure 3.8).

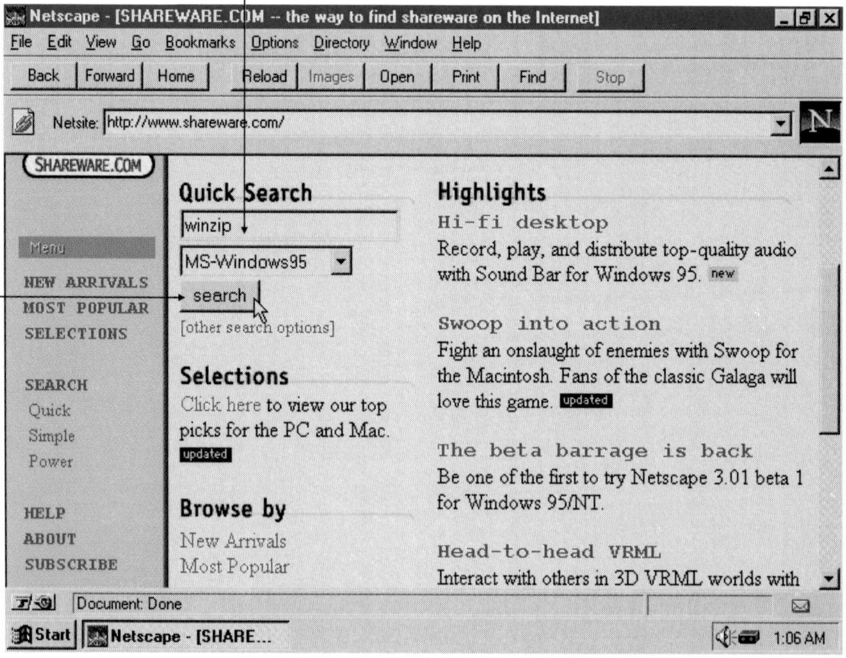

Figure 3.8 Searching for software on the Internet with c|net

bookmark

Shareware.com is at http://www.shareware.com

If you know the name of the program you're looking for, you can search for it directly by name. You can also search for a shorter word or word fragment that you think appears in the name of the program you want. If you have no clue about the program's name, you can still hunt around the site, looking at things such as the latest additions to the listings or the most popular downloads. If you find what you're looking for, Shareware.com won't actually have the file for you to download. Instead, it will give you a list of the FTP archive sites where the file can be found. All you do is click one of the links to get the file you want.

Finding People and Businesses

Aside from looking for information, you might also want to see if someone you know can be reached by e-mail. As with the rest of the Net, e-mail addresses exist pretty much in chaos, so there's no single definitive list of e-mail addresses anywhere, but there are several avenues you can try.

EXPERT ADVICE

If you're looking for the e-mail address of someone affiliated with a university, try the campus Gopher and/or web pages, which may have a list of addresses. This procedure applies to some big corporations as well.

You may also want to find people or companies *off* the Net. I'll show you some Yellow Pages-type listings that give addresses and phone numbers for individuals and companies.

Looking for E-Mail Addresses

There's no guarantee that your friend (or long-lost aunt) will be listed in the online e-mail directories, even if he or she does have an Internet address, but it's worth a try to look. Two sites that specialize in e-mail addresses are Four11 (named for the U.S. telephone system's 411 directory number) and WhoWhere? I'll also show you some of the traditional alternative methods for finding e-mail addresses.

EXPERT ADVICE

Netscape's and Internet Explorer's search pages feature links to Four11 and WhoWhere? and other directory services. You can keep up to date with new sites by visiting those pages from time to time.

Four11

One good place to search for e-mail addresses (and other personal information) is the Four11 site at http://www.four11.com (see Figure 3.9).

Enter as much or as little information about the person whose e-mail address you're seeking.

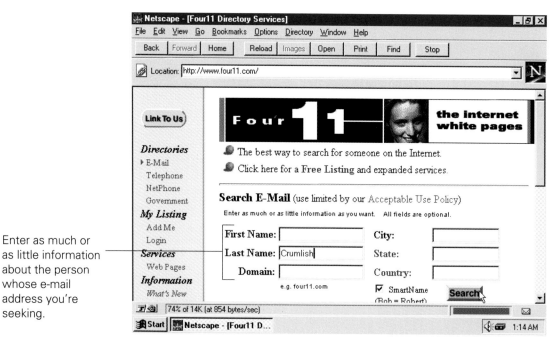

Figure 3.9 The Four11 e-mail search screen

bookmark

Find Four11 at http://www.four11.com.

You can click the linked e-mail address to send mail to the person directly.

Enter as much information as you have available in the boxes of the form and then click the Search button. If Four11 finds more than one listing that matches your submitted name, it will show you them all. For example, I'm listed twice at Four11: once at the Microsoft Network and once at CompuServe.

```
GIVEN NAMES      FAMILY NAME       E-MAIL DOMAIN
--------------   ---------------   ----------------------

Alfred           Crumlish          @postoffice.worldnet.att.net
Alfred P         Crumlish          @well.com
Brian John       Crumlish          @nd.edu
Carol            Crumlish          @AOL.COM
Christian        Crumlish          @msn.com
Christian T      Crumlish          @Compuserve.Com
Danette          Crumlish          @Compuserve.Com
Fred P           Crumlish          @Compuserve.Com
Jennifer         Crumlish          @NIHCU.BITNET
Jennifer         Crumlish          @UBVM.CC.BUFFALO.EDU
Jennifer A       Crumlish          @cu.nih.gov
Kevin            Crumlish          @mail.snip.net
```

To see the e-mail address, click the name that matches most closely:

Christian T Crumlish

Oakland, California,
United States Of America

E-Mail Address:

76770.2325@Compuserve.Com

You may want to search for your own e-mail address, to see if you are listed.

EXPERT ADVICE

*If you don't find your e-mail address and you'd like to be listed, click the
Free Listing link to add your e-mail address to Four11's database.*

STEP BY STEP   Search for Your Own E-Mail Address

① **Go to http://www.four11.com.**

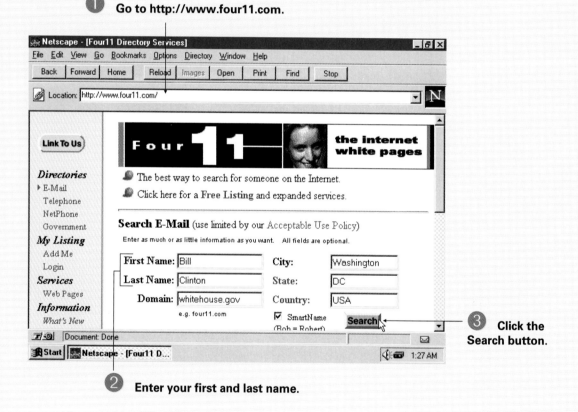

② **Enter your first and last name.**

③ **Click the
Search button.**

WhoWhere?

Another good search site for e-mail addresses is WhoWhere? at http://
www.whowhere.com (see Figure 3.10).

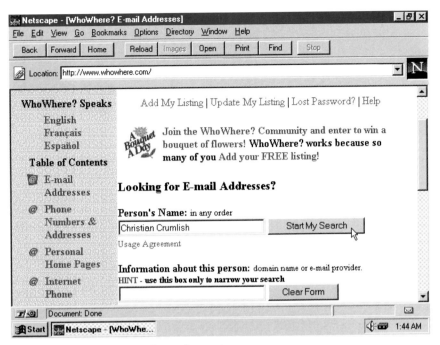

Figure 3.10 The WhoWhere? e-mail search screen

bookmark

The WhoWhere? site is http://www.whowhere.com.

To search for an address, enter the first and last name in the main box. If you know anything else about the person's address, you can enter it in the optional box below. Then click the Start My Search button. WhoWhere? will list any names and e-mail addresses that match even part of the name you entered, with the best matches listed first. As shown here, WhoWhere? found several valid addresses for me—different ones than Four11 found (hmm. . .).

Name: Christian Crumlish   **Info:** [   ]   Search

⊙ all matches ○ only exact matches

◉ **Highly Relevant Responses**

• **Name:** Christian Crumlish
E-mail: xian@netcom21.netcom.com (click to send e-mail)
Service Provider: Netcom Online Communication Services

• **Name:** Christian Crumlish
E-mail: xian@netcom.com (click to send e-mail)
Service Provider: Netcom Online Communication Services
Last Updated: October '96

• **Name:** Christian Crumlish
E-mail: xian@POBOX.COM (click to send e-mail)

*For more on how to send
e-mail, see Chapter 4.*

Usenet Addresses

The kind souls at the RTFM archive site at MIT regularly compile a database of e-mail addresses and associated real names, culled from Usenet postings. If you have patience (it can take a whole day to get a response), send a message to mail-server@rtfm.mit.edu with no subject, and the words

send usenet-addresses/*name*

on a line by themselves (with an actual name entered in place of *name*). The mail-server at the FTP site will search its lists for the name you send and return its results. My e-mail address can be found thanks to my occasional posts to Usenet newsgroups, as shown here. Looks like there's another long-lost cousin out there as well.

Finger

For more about mIRC and chatting on IRC, see Chapter 7.

If you know someone is located at a particular domain (such as whitehouse.gov or mit.edu), you may be able to use the finger command to look up the person or find some information about the person.

The finger command is not available in Netscape directly. You have to download and install a finger program or find a web page that lets you finger (such as http://www.emf.net/cgi-bin/finger). One popular program that you may already have that includes a finger command is mIRC (a chat program for Windows). Choose Tools | Finger and then type a domain (with an @ sign in front) or an e-mail address.

You can finger from the web page at http://www.emf.net/cgi-bin/finger.

Finger is often used to find out more about a person whose e-mail address you already know. If the person has a Unix-style shell account, you can usually find out when the person was last online or received e-mail and whatever information they want to share with you in their "plan." (Fewer and fewer people have shell accounts these days. If the person has a more popular SLIP or PPP account, finger won't tell you anything; this is one reason why fingering someone is not so common an activity anymore.)

A more interesting use of finger, though, is to look up someone when you know his or her domain but not the person's account name. For example, if you know that someone named Stephen Mack has an account at emf.net but you don't remember what his account name is, try fingering Mack@netcom.com. Here is what you get:

```
End of finger session

Trying emf.net
Attempting to finger mack@emf.net

Login name: estephen                In real life: E. Stephen Mack
Directory: /accounts/estephen       Shell: /bin/csh
Last login Thu Oct 17 02:17 on ttyp0 from sjx-ca39-03.ix.n
Mail last read Thu Oct 17 02:17:31 1996
Plan:
        Write.  Write.  Write.

URL:
        http://www.emf.net/~estephen/

Plugs:
        Visit Gray Mansion, a place to explore.  Type:
        lynx http://www.emf.net/~estephen/gray.html

        Read alt.usenet.manifestoes ... Request it by name ...
                                                        --Zeigen

End of finger session
```

Here, even though we fingered "Mack"—a nonexistent account—we found the finger information for the correct account name, estephen. EMF uses the "In real life" information to perform searches for people at emf.net.

Some universities have comprehensive student and staff databases that can be accessed quickly with finger. Fingering @mit.edu, for example, is a good way to find someone at MIT. However, not all domains support finger, and not every domain that supports finger lets you search for people's names.

Traditional Routes

It used to be that if you knew the domain and host portion of someone's e-mail address (if, for example, you knew where a person worked or went to school), you could send e-mail to postmaster@*that-address* and ask politely for the person's e-mail address. Nowadays, there are so many "postmasters" who are so overworked and undertrained that you can't count on this method working for you.

Still, old-fashioned common sense can come in handy. Try calling your friend (or your friend's employer or school) and asking for his or her e-mail address directly.

Phone Numbers and Street Addresses

If you've poked around the Four11 or WhoWhere? sites, you may have noticed that they offer other search features besides just a way to look up people's e-mail addresses. Among other things, they also offer phone numbers and mailing addresses. (A lot of the information that goes into printed Yellow Pages has also been stored in digital form on CD-ROMs, and many such CDs have been uploaded to databases on the Net.)

If you're looking for the phone number or address of a person or company, you can start at one of those two sites:

- At Four11, click the Telephone link.
- At WhoWhere? click the Phone Numbers & Addresses link.

Figure 3.11 shows WhoWhere?'s search form for phone numbers and addresses. Enter as much information as you know and click the Start My Search button.

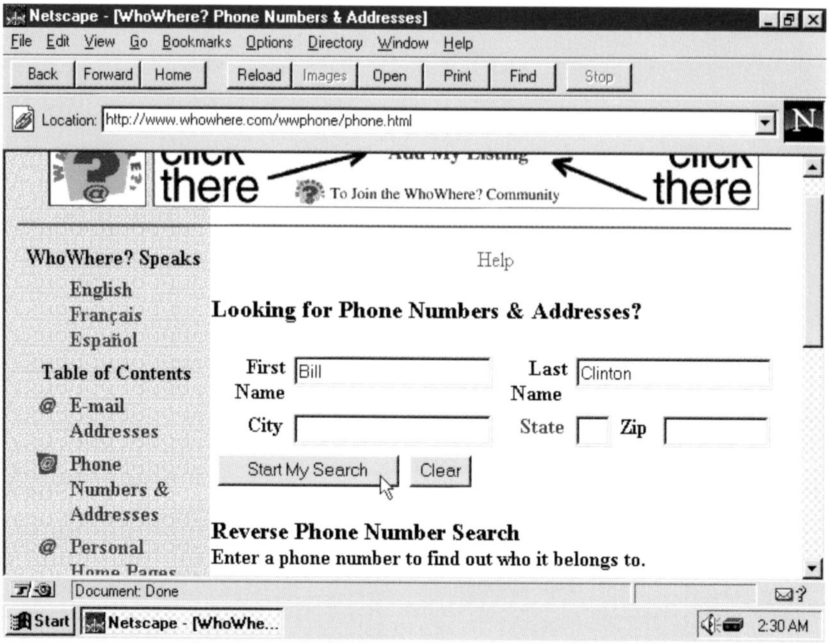

Figure 3.11 Looking for U.S. telephone numbers and addresses at WhoWhere?

Big Book

Big Book is a search site dedicated to phone number and address listings. It can find specific addresses as well as businesses that fit a category you submit.

bookmark

Big Book is located at http://www.bigbook.com.

How Not to Spam

If you found your name in any of these directories, you might be wondering how it got there. Most likely, your Internet service provider added your e-mail address to one of these directories (or to some more generic resource that the

STEP BY STEP **Search Big Book for Phone Numbers and Addresses**

① **Go to http://www.bigbook.com.**

Netscape - [Welcome to BigBook]

File Edit View Go Bookmarks Options Directory Window Help

| Back | Forward | Home | Reload | Images | Open | Print | Find | Stop |

Netsite: http://www.bigbook.com/

BigBook ®

home search your book business center community about help

Welcome to BigBook – A whole new kind of Yellow Pages.

WHO: or	WHAT:	WHERE:	
Diversified	Temporary Help	Oakland	CA
Business (eg, BigBook)	Category (eg, Hotel)	City	State

| Search Now | Categories | More Search Options |

Document: Done

Start Netscape - [Welcome...   2:41 AM

② **Enter the name of a business, a category of business, and the city and state of the business, if you know it.**

③ **Click the Search Now button.**

directory maker may have consulted), or the directory obtained your street address from one of the usual sources.

Most of these sites permit people to remove their own listings to protect their privacy. If this is important to you, you should pursue it. Similarly, the sites also all have strict rules against businesses collecting huge lists of e-mail addresses and then sending them all unsolicited junk mail. Scattershot mailings of that sort are usually referred to online as *spam*, and they violate the spirit of the Internet mail system as well as the letter of the rules of these directory sites.

There's nothing wrong with targeting specific messages to audiences that have expressed some kind of interest in that type of information, but be very careful never to send mailings to large groups of unrelated people. See Chapter 5 for more on mailing lists.

The Importance of Findability

Once you've gotten used to browsing the Net through searching, you'll begin to realize how important it is for businesses and other services that want to gain customers or contacts through the Internet to actually be findable. It helps if they have a sensible domain name that anyone could guess, but it's also important for a site to be listed in the major search engines and directories. In Chapter 11 I'll show you how to list your own web site (once you've built it!) at these search sites.

CHECK POINT

In the first three chapters, you've learned the basics of browsing the Web and connecting to the Internet, mainly as a passive member of a huge global audience. But there's a lot more to the Internet than reading other people's web pages. A big attraction of the Net is the capacity for connecting to and communicating with people all over the place. The next few chapters explain how to use e-mail and mailing lists, how to participate in newsgroups, and how to carry on live conversations in text, sound, video, or even imaginary worlds.

E-Mail: You Have New Mail

INCLUDES

- Understanding Internet e-mail

- Keeping e-mail under control

- Understanding standard e-mail conventions

- Building an address book

- Sending files via e-mail

- Handling e-mail problems

- Using Eudora, Microsoft Internet Mail, and Netscape Mail

FAST FORWARD

Keep E-Mail from Taking Over Your Day ➤ p. 123

Just check your messages a few times a day, instead of staying connected all the time and compulsively checking your messages. (This is one of those "do as I say, not as I do" rules.)

Send Internet E-Mail ➤ pp. 123-125

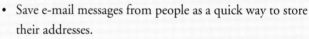

- If you're on a network, make sure it has an Internet e-mail gateway.
- Enter your recipient's e-mail address on the To: line in the standard Internet format: their-username@their.Internet.address.
- Type the topic of your message on the Subject: line.

Prepare for a Vacation ➤ pp. 127-128

I am away from my mail while on vacation.
message when I return on November 20th.

Aloha!

      --xian

- Set up an outgoing vacation message so people will know why you're not responding to your mail.
- Temporarily unsubscribe from high-traffic mailing lists.

Keep Track of Others' E-Mail Addresses ➤ pp. 128-129

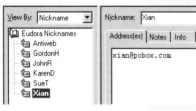

- Save e-mail messages from people as a quick way to store their addresses.
- Create aliases or nicknames for e-mail addresses you use often.
- Set up an address book with names and e-mail addresses.

Attach a File to a Message ➤ pp. 129-130

Attach File

- In Eudora, press CTRL-H, select a file, and click OK.
- In Microsoft Internet Mail, click the Insert File button, choose a file, and click Attach.
- In Netscape Mail, click the Attach File(s) button, click Attach File, choose a file, and click OK twice.
- In some programs, you can drag a file icon onto a mail message to attach it.

Read Your Mail Offline ➤ p. 130

To minimize your connect time, consider running an offline mail program that will let you send and receive your messages all in a batch.

Connection Method:
- ⦿ Winsock (Network, PPP, SLIP)
- ○ Dialup (shell account access)
- □ Offline (no connections)

When on the Net, Do as the Netters Do ➤ pp. 133-136

- When replying to e-mail, quote the salient part of the original message.
- Create a short signature to be attached to each message.
- When not in formal business situations, keep your e-mail tone conversational.
- If you are afraid someone may misinterpret what you say, consider appending a sideways smiley face. :-)

Thanks Karen, I'll definitely be there, unless I get
Forbin project! :-)

--Christian

Set Up Your Mail Program ➤ pp. 138-139

- Put your program on the desktop or in the Start menu for easy access.
- Tell your program your e-mail address and full name.
- Tell your program where to send and pick up your mail.

POP account:
xian@netcom.com

Real name:
Christian Crumlish

When you get past the hype (and truly exciting developments) of the World Wide Web, you'll notice that what really holds the Internet together is e-mail. In a century that has seen the invention and widespread acceptance of the telephone and television, perhaps we've become all too accommodating to each new communication medium. In some ways, though, I'm surprised that the academics, researchers, and military personnel who originally populated the Internet managed to keep such a useful tool a secret for so long.

The biggest advantage of e-mail is convenience. You don't have to print your message, put it an envelope, stamp it, and take it to a post office. In comparison to other forms of telecommunication, e-mail has the advantage that it is not immediate. Sure, e-mail travels much more quickly than traditional paper mail (called "snail mail" by e-mailers), but unlike a phone call, an e-mail message cannot demand immediate response. So e-mail enables you to schedule some of your communication with others and postpone interruptions until you're ready for them.

Unlike voice mail, which is similarly asynchronous, e-mail enables you to keep a written correspondence. Still, you can't yet assume that your e-mail correspondents will necessarily see and respond to your mail in a timely fashion, so for urgent business matters, it's best to employ additional means of communication.

CAUTION

The act of checking your e-mail can easily become addictive and destroy productivity. Be conscious of how you integrate the use of e-mail into your work (or even home) life, so it doesn't eat up more than its share of your time.

DEFINITION

Asynchronous: A geek expression meaning "not happening at the same time."

Compared to other forms of written communication (conventional mail, fax, telex, and so on), e-mail is also relatively cheap. In addition, there's something tangibly more likable about e-mail as compared to other forms of quick communication. Receiving written messages carries some (if not all) of the appeal of finding letters in your "real" mailbox. Also, unlike in phone conversations, you can make sure you've said precisely what you want to say in exactly the right tone before you click the Send button. But I don't need to convince you about e-mail. If you're reading this book, the wave has caught up with you, and you're already on the Net.

In the first part of this chapter, I'll give you an overview of e-mail to help you understand the general procedures and terminology. In the second half, I'll give you the lowdown on three typical e-mail programs: Eudora, Microsoft Internet Mail, and Netscape Mail.

Internet Mail Versus E-Mail in General

The Internet provides a common medium for sharing many different types of e-mail. It doesn't matter if you use Quickmail in your office and the person you want to send mail to uses America Online. With Internet mail addresses, you can send a message to that person just as if you were both on the same network. The only requirement is that the messages must be formatted the same way, with certain standard headers—which your e-mail program will take care of for you. Ideally, your program will hide most of those headers from you as well.

CAUTION

Some online services charge for e-mail received (usually with a certain amount free), and many Internet connectivity services charge for connect time.

The reason you sometimes get e-mail with enormous headers is that the message originated in a different e-mail program.

For now, Internet e-mail is still a plain-text medium, so don't expect your clever use of fonts, boldface, and graphic lines to go over well with your Net correspondents. It may travel across a LAN to an office buddy just fine, but it will not make it through the eye of the needle that is an Internet mail gateway. (Then again, if Netscape has its way, e-mail messages will start looking a lot more like web pages in the near future.) For that matter, the methods for attaching files to e-mail messages are severely limited for mail that has to make it across the Internet before reaching its destination.

DEFINITION

Gateway: *A program or computer that regulates communication between two networks, the Internet and a local network, or any two network media.*

To some people, e-mail is the Internet, and e-mail traffic, after web transactions, still represents the lion's share of Internet activity. Some people distinguish between the larger group of people who can send or receive Internet mail (referring to them as "on the Net") and the smaller but still large group of people who have direct connections to the Internet ("on the Internet").

However you look at it, an Internet e-mail address always appears in this form: username@Internet-address. The Internet-address portion takes the form host.subdomain.domain, with the host name sometimes optional. To send e-mail to someone via the Internet, make sure to enter the address in this form. Generally, e-mail addresses are not case-sensitive (meaning they don't distinguish between uppercase and lowercase letters), though sometimes the username may be. Here are some typical e-mail addresses:

```
President@whitehouse.gov
billg@microsoft.com
jsoames@uclink4.berkeley.edu
estephen@emf.net
kyrie@engr.sgi.com
BIFF99@aol.com
gelezeau@dmi.ens.fr
```

E-Mail for Busy People

When you are really busy, e-mail can be either a blessing or a curse (or both at the same time). Not having to drop what you're doing to reply to a query can help you organize your own time effectively. But don't let e-mail interrupt you! If you're constantly checking your mail and getting involved in more and more casual online conversations, your productivity may suffer, and e-mail may become another black hole that eats up all your free time.

EXPERT ADVICE

Tempting as it may be, don't keep your e-mail program running and connected all day long. Try to limit yourself to checking your mail every hour or so (or even two or three times a day, perhaps at the beginning, middle, and end of your work day, if you have Herculean self-control). Of course, how often you should check your mail depends on how much you need to communicate in this manner.

I don't want to make e-mail sound like a drag, though. Most people really enjoy it as a form of communication—just keep it within reasonable boundaries as part of your work day. The real question is how can you best integrate e-mail into your online existence.

DEFINITION

Queue: *A waiting list of messages to be sent when your e-mail program connects to a mail server to retrieve new mail.*

Later in this chapter, I'll explain the details of three popular (and easy-to-get) e-mail programs and give you enough to go on to use any program to read your mail. Here I'll just outline a generic mail session.

A Typical Mail Session

Here is a summary of a typical mail session:

1. Run your mail program. It will tell you if you have new mail.
2. Select and read mail in your in-box.
3. Reply to (or forward) messages, quoting from the original if necessary.
4. Save messages you'll need to deal with later and delete as much mail as you can.
5. Compose new mail (this is sometimes the first thing you'll do).
6. Send all new messages, if they were queued when written rather than sent immediately.
7. Deal with older saved mail, if the time is ripe.
8. Quit your mail program.

DEFINITIONS

Host: The name of a specific machine in a larger domain or subdomain (such as squinky.microsoft.com), but you don't need to know any of this, really.

Domains and Subdomains: Ways of organizing Internet addresses. Domains are large areas divided by purpose (.com for commercial, .edu for education, and so on), and subdomains are smaller areas within those larger domains (ibm.com, harvard.edu, and so on).

Sending Copies of E-Mail

With e-mail, it's just as easy to send a message to two or more recipients as it is to send it to a single person. To send e-mail to more than one recipient, you can either put the e-mail addresses all in the To: header of the new message, separated by commas (or, in some mail programs, by other characters such as semicolons), or you can enter additional addresses on the Cc: line (Cc originally stood for carbon copy and is now, since the demise of carbon, assumed to mean "courtesy copy"). Addresses on the Cc: line will receive a copy of the mail and will appear in the message headers seen by recipients.

EXPERT ADVICE

It's a good idea to keep copies of your own outgoing mail. Some mail programs do this for you as a matter of course (or let you choose a setting for this purpose). If your program doesn't work this way, you can still send a copy of each message to your own address.

Some e-mail programs also permit the use of a Bcc: line—standing for blind courtesy (or carbon) copy. Addresses in the Bcc: header will receive a copy of the mail but will not appear in the message headers seen by recipients.

Keeping Your In-box Under Control

One of the hazards of e-mail is an overflowing in-box. If you don't keep your e-mail strictly under control, it can easily overwhelm you. To prevent this, you have to develop some good e-mail habits:

- Delete mail as soon as you've read or dealt with it, unless you need it for your records.
- Move messages out of the in-box and into topical mailboxes, either to deal with the messages later or to store them for future reference.
- Read and answer or deal with your mail as expediently as possible.
- Don't store messages in your in-box. It should contain only new mail!

That last item is the most difficult to follow. I myself am guilty of leaving lots of undealt-with mail in my in-box "to remind me." In fact, I have over 50 messages in there right now (and it's only Monday!).

netiquette

If you're too busy to respond to e-mail in a timely fashion, consider sending a brief message saying that you did receive the mail and that you'll respond at length when you have the opportunity.

Filtering and Forwarding Mail Automatically

The future of e-mail is intelligent agents that filter and sort incoming mail, perhaps find information for you out on the Net, and even reply automatically to certain messages. For now, some e-mail programs enable you to set up automatic filtering or forwarding. Filtering means sorting messages (based on keywords) as they come in or go out and either filing them or performing some action on them (such as changing the priority, deleting the message entirely, replying automatically, printing the message, and so on). My Eudora mail program lets me use filters to file my incoming (and outgoing) messages, as shown in Figure 4.1.

Eudora Pro lets you set up filter rules using the Tools | Filters.

New mail is automatically filtered into the proper mailbox.

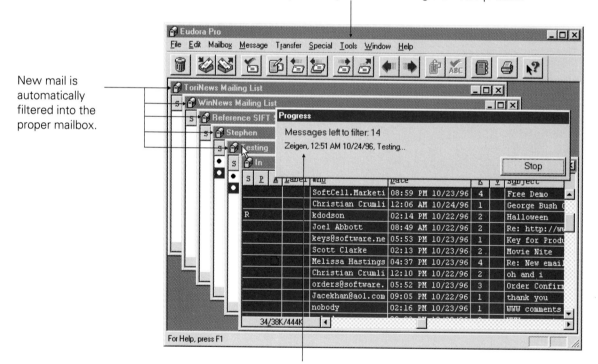

A test mail from Zeigen will be placed in the Testing mailbox automatically.

Figure 4.1 Incoming mail filtered into several mailboxes

EXPERT ADVICE

Filtering is absolutely critical if you subscribe to mailing lists (see Chapter 5). Without it, you have to file by hand every message that comes in from the list!

Forwarding means automatically sending some or all of your mail to another address. (The term "to forward" is also applied to the manual task of sending an individual piece of mail on to another address.) Forwarding can be especially useful if you have more than one e-mail address but you want all your mail shunted to one account so you can check it all in one place. As with a lot of other e-mail developments, though, only Unix systems always provide automatic e-mail forwarding.

Preparing for a Vacation

If you are going to be away from your mail for a while, you may want to set up an automatic vacation message, like the one shown here, to go out to anyone who sends mail to you while you're gone. You do this so no one thinks you're ignoring them.

```
I am away from my mail while on vacation.   I will reply to your
message when I return on November 20th.

Aloha!

        --xian
```

If you subscribe to any very busy mailing lists (mailing lists are explained in Chapter 5), you may want to temporarily unsubscribe to avoid a deluge of mail on your return.

CAUTION

If you go away for a stretch of time and make no special arrangements, your in-box can literally overflow, and you may end up losing mail. Even if you don't max out your in-box, you can end up causing big problems for your mail administrator. Some mailing lists may also unsubscribe you if you start bouncing vacation messages back to the list.

The ability to send out special vacation messages has not yet spread to most Windows and Macintosh e-mail programs. If your e-mail is handled by a Unix machine (and it may be even if you use a PC or a Macintosh—ask your system administrator), though, you can go to a useful page on the Web—Mail Tools— to set up a vacation message and let the web gateway handle the ugly little Unix details for you. To do so, point your web browser at http://charlotte.acns.nwu. edu/mailtools/. Then scroll through the page and follow the directions. They're pretty straightforward. Note that you'll need to have the same kind of information handy that you used to set up your mail program.

CAUTION

The Mail Tools page requires you to send your password over the Web, which is not secure. Consider changing your password after you avail yourself of this service.

EXPERT ADVICE

Open your mail program and look for the menu command and dialog box with a name like Options, Preferences, or possibly Configuration for your mail information.

Some programs, such as Microsoft's Outlook 97, create address books that can be shared by other programs.

Keeping Track of Other People's Addresses

Once you get online, you'll need to start a collection of other people's e-mail addresses. Different e-mail programs have different ways of helping you do this. Most allow you to create an address book or a collection of nicknames or aliases that represent full e-mail addresses.

View By:	Nickname ▼		Nickname:	John Restrick

📖 Eudora Nicknames
- Antiweb
- GordonH
- John Restrick
- KarenD
- SueT
- **Xian**

Address(es) | Notes | Info

jrest@divtech.com

SHORTCUT

The low-tech way to save an e-mail address is to keep a message from that sender (stored in a folder, not cluttering your in-box). Then reply to that message whenever you want to reach the sender.

EXPERT ADVICE

If you need to exchange e-mail addresses with someone who does not remember her address, just ask her to send you mail (give her your address); you'll capture the address in that first message.

More and more often, people are including their e-mail addresses on business cards (some are including web addresses as well).

Sending Files via E-Mail

See Chapter 8 for more (and better) ways to move files around the Net.

Probably the biggest frustration with e-mail these days results from sending files as attachments. Why would you want to do this anyway? Increasingly, when you're working on a file (say a word processing document or a presentation or a spreadsheet), you'll need to send it to someone else. Sure, you can print it (depending on the type of document it is) and send it by mail or courier, but what if you want your recipient to have access to the electronic file itself or even the ability to change or edit the document? Then you have to send the file. Again, you could put the file on a disk, stick it in a cardboard mailer, and entrust it to a delivery service, but it can be much faster (and easier) to simply send the file attached to a piece of e-mail.

DEFINITION

Attachment: *A file that has been encoded as ASCII text and then included as part of an e-mail message. Only if your mail program can't read the encoding will it show you the ASCII gibberish at the tail end of your message.*

You will have no problem if you are working within a given network or within an online service such as AOL or CompuServe, but the methods used to attach files to Internet e-mail are not yet standard for every type of mail gateway. You may have to ask your recipient (or sender) and possibly tech support as well to learn what specifically will or won't work. Even if you can send and receive attachments, you'll still have to agree on file formats that both you and your correspondent can use.

Optional E-Mail Features

Internet e-mail standards are constantly evolving. Here are some useful new features that are not yet widely implemented but are getting there.

See Appendix A for details on connecting to (and disconnecting from) the Internet.

Reading Mail Offline

Because some forms of Internet connectivity charge you the whole time you're connected, you may want to investigate handling your mail offline. This means connecting briefly to download new mail and then disconnecting. You can then read your mail and compose your replies without being connected and then connect again briefly to reply.

Some programs automate the process of off-line mail reading, but with any mail program, you can check your mail, disconnect your Internet connection, and then read and respond to your mail offline. Here's how:

1. Connect to the Internet.
2. Run your mail program (it will check for new mail).
3. Log off from the Internet.
4. Read and respond to your mail at your leisure. (Replies will sit in your out-box until they can be sent.)
5. Log back on to the Internet.
6. Send your mail.
7. Log off from the Internet again.

Composing Mail Outside of Your Mail Program

Some programs, such as Eudora, now automatically correct curly quotation marks.

If you're not completely comfortable in the space provided for composing messages in your e-mail program, you can also write messages in a word processor and then cut and paste them into your mail program (this is different from attaching files).

You have to watch out for the special typesetting characters that modern word processors are forever inserting into your documents (such as curly quotation marks, long dashes, and special symbols such as ™ and ®), because they will generally appear as garbage characters once the mail has passed over the Internet. Here's the best way to do this:

1. Write your message.
2. Save the document as a plain text file.
3. Close the document. Then open it again.
4. Copy the entire document with the Edit | Copy command.
5. Switch to your e-mail program and start a new message.
6. Paste the document into the message with the Edit | Paste command.

Prioritizing Mail

Most mail programs can assign a priority level to messages, from highest, to normal, to lowest, to tell a recipient whether a message is urgent and requires a quick reply. Use this kind of signaling only when necessary or people will start to assume you're always crying wolf. In crises, though, a priority flag can really help a message stand out in a crowded in-box.

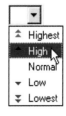

Confirming Receipt of Mail

Some e-mail programs allow you to specify that you be notified when your recipient has received (or even opened) your mail message. This trick isn't supported everywhere on the Net; for now it works only within specific networks.

Maintaining Security and Privacy

E-mail pathways are not secure. As your message flits across the Internet to your recipient, it is copied and stored (at least temporarily) on many computers in between. In some ways, e-mail messages are like postcards. Anyone "carrying" the message can read it, even if most would never do so. The only way to put a message in an "envelope" is to encode it with some form of encryption. Unfortunately, none of the popular e-mail programs yet incorporate an easy way to do this, so don't send anything by e-mail that could damage you or anyone else if read by the wrong person.

Some E-Mail Conventions

After a few replies back and forth, a Subject line may get stale. For example, the original message to you might have the subject "Office Picnic"— but once you reply to the sender and he or she replies to you, you easily may be talking about something else entirely. Using the same Subject line can be confusing. When you get another response a little later, you may put off reading it since the subject still seems to be the by-now-past office picnic. Therefore, it's a good idea to change the Subject line to reflect the current topic.

As a new communication medium, e-mail has developed its own conventions. It's often easy to spot first-time e-mailers, because they tend to borrow from other familiar written styles. An e-mail message is not a postcard, not a letter, not an office memo (but can be similar to all three, naturally).

The headers in an e-mail message (To:, Date:, Subject:, and so on, some of which are filled out for you) make it resemble a memo, but most people write e-mail in a more informal style, reminiscent of conversation.

In the next few sections, I'll describe some of the conventions of e-mail communication, so you can get into the swing of things as quickly as possible.

Providing Meaningful Subject Lines

A good Subject: line describes your message without going into too little or too much detail. You shouldn't need more than a dozen words in the Subject: line. If you're asking a question, it's far better to use a specific subject, such as "Need help locating the new Forbin report," rather than "Important!" or "Need Help" or "Here's a question." On the other hand, an ultra-specific Subject: line such as

"I still need your 53-word response to the 11/15/96 Janan memo because it's been a week already" is too unwieldy and leaves you little to say in the body of the mail. Better to cut the subject down to "Need your response to the Janan memo ASAP!" and leave the details for the body of the message itself.

When writing to someone you don't know or posting to Usenet newsgroups (see Chapter 6), don't try to attract attention by giving your message a provocative but irrelevant subject. Many beginners have tried the old trick of "Subject: Sex!" and then begin the message with, "Now that I have your attention." This kind of bait-and-switch technique generates poor results.

Quoting to Provide Context

It is common to quote some of the message you are responding to in a reply, to provide some context to your message. This is not always necessary, but as soon as you get a message from someone reading "I'm afraid not" or "Yes, let's do it!" and you can't remember what you said in your original message, you'll understand how helpful it is to include some of the original message in a reply.

```
When you wrote:

>If we upsnarch the quince-wimble, I think we'll have the problem
>under control.

I wasn't sure what you meant by "we."

     --xian
```

Most mail programs will automatically include the original message (or offer to do so) when you start to reply. Be sure to trim as much of the quotation as you can so your recipient can save time rereading and to make sure that your reply doesn't get lost in the shuffle. Leave just enough of the original message to provide context. Also, use blank lines (press ENTER) between quoted text and new text so it doesn't all clump together.

CAUTION

When replying to a message, be careful not to excerpt the original message in any way that might change the meaning in its original context. For that matter, you should never edit an original message to alter its meaning.

Some programs allow you to customize the quotation characters or use different characters, such as a vertical bar (|), colon (:), or even the initials of the person being quoted. If you do customize your program, strive for readability.

If you're sending an unrelated message, delete all the quoted text. Change the Subject: line, too, while you're at it.

By the way, the system of quoting using greater than signs (>) or other characters in front of each line comes from Unix mail programs, which until now have dominated Internet e-mail. Some programs change the color, font, and so on to show quotation, but you can't assume that such enhancements will come across correctly on the Internet (as opposed to within your office), where the only common denominator is essentially the standard keyboard characters.

DEFINITION

In-box: *The folder in your mail program that contains incoming mail before it's been deleted or moved to another folder for storage.*

Using a Signature

It is considered boorish in some circles to have a signature longer than four lines.

You may notice that all the mail you get from a correspondent ends with the same tag line, or even several lines. Usually, the person isn't typing that information at the end of each message but instead has something called a signature file that the mail program automatically appends to each outgoing message. The text in a signature file is usually referred to as a signature, but signatures are also called sig blocks, sigs, .signatures, and .sigs (the latter two are Unix terms, pronounced dot-signature and dot-sig, respectively), depending on whom you ask.

So what should you have in your signature, assuming you want one? Well, you'll at least want to include your name and possibly your e-mail address (in case your recipient can't get it from the message automatically), but probably not your phone number. Some people include favorite or inane sayings or elaborate drawings made of keyboard characters (called ASCII art after the name of the standard computer character set—ASCII).

```
--
E. Stephen Mack (Zeigen)                          estephen@emf.net
Winter Weather, Berkeley, CA              http://www.emf.net/~estephen/

        But who are YOU to tell ME to question authority?
```

EXPERT ADVICE

Keep the lines of your message well under 80 characters (the maximum for certain text-only computer systems), so quoted messages will still fit on everyone's screen neatly. I find that 75-character lines work fine.

Assuming you use e-mail for work, keep your signature businesslike. Remember that once you've sent e-mail to anyone, there's a scrap of text with your name attached floating around, and you never know who it might be sent to or where you might end up seeing yourself quoted.

netiquette

It is inappropriate to post others' private e-mail messages to any public discussion group or to forward messages to third parties without the express permission of the original sender.

When you use e-mail for personal correspondence, no one should resend your mail elsewhere without your permission, but it does happen.

Maintaining Informality

Do not be offended if you receive mail that dispenses with the customary (in letters) Dear Sir or Madam type of salutation. Although many people will preface a message with "Hi" or anything from "Dear Ms. Higgenbotham" to "Hey Now!" it is completely acceptable to just plunge directly into a message, in that breathless, late-twentieth-century way.

Some e-mail correspondences resemble long, drawn-out (and thought-out) conversations, and written conversations also provide the potential for wordplay, visual puns, even collaborative poems, and so on. So slip off your shoes and relax before beginning your correspondence.

It's still a good idea to maintain decorum in business correspondence.

Using Smileys :-)

Of course, by now you know about smileys; those sideways faces made from punctuation characters that are also sometimes called emoticons. Because e-mail is said to be a cold medium—conversational, yet lacking the facial, vocal, and body language cues that people use in other forms of communication to smooth out interaction—there is a great danger of misinterpretation, of people taking offense, of arguments.

You may have heard of the practice of "flaming," which essentially means chewing out someone in e-mail or in a discussion group, usually in a vitriolic and sometimes satirically or sarcastically humorous way. Such scurrilous attack messages are referred to as flames. Many flames are provoked through the sort of ambiguity and offense-taking that I just alluded to. Thus the practice arose of appending a smiley, such as the basic one shown here (tilt your head to the left)

```
:-)
```

to the end of anything even mildly controversial. (Certain popular abbreviations, such as IMHO—in my humble opinion—also aim for the same effect.)

There is now an entire vocabulary of smiley faces, many of them silly and rarely used. Semicolons are often substituted for colons to denote winking

```
;-)
```

and the mouth character can be changed to indicate frowning

```
>:-(
```

or other less clear expressions.

There are whole books dedicated to this minor semaphore-like communication form, and I encourage you to pick one up if you are really interested (and not too busy).

Unsolicited Mail and Other Problems

As e-mail becomes a ubiquitous medium, unsolicited e-mail messages, chain letters, and come-ons have started appearing in mailboxes more and more often, just as unsolicited fax messages have started appearing. While this may not cost you money (unless your service provider charges you for mail), it is still a waste of your time as well as rude.

If you receive an unprompted message, reply to the sender asking where the person got your address and telling the person not to send you any more mail (and to take you off any mailing list you may have been put on without your permission). If an unsolicited message continues to be a problem, send a Cc: copy of the message to postmaster@sender's-address (use the same details as after the @ sign in the sender's address), so the person knows you mean business and that the person's mail administrator knows what is going on.

Other Problems with Mail

If you get complaints from friends that their mail to you is bouncing (coming back with "recipient unknown"), or if you experience other problems, contact your own mail administrator. If you are on a small network, you probably know the administrator personally. On a larger network, send mail to postmaster or to postmaster@your-address and ask the administrator to look into your problem.

If you reply to someone's message and your reply comes bouncing back, check the To: header. It's possible that your correspondent's mail program or system is incorrectly configured and that the address is being garbled. Make sure the address on the message that bounced looks like a correct Internet address, with the form *username@something.something.thing* (or maybe just one dot). If it does not, resend the message after editing the To: header manually.

Some bounced messages only tell you that a server along the route is still attempting to send the mail. Not every system on the Internet is up and running 24 hours a day.

Choosing a Mail Program

There are a multitude of e-mail programs out there, and there's no way I could do them all justice in this chapter (hey, I'm a busy person too!). Depending on how you connect to the Internet and what type of computer setup you have, you may end up using one of many different e-mail programs. Fortunately, aside from the inevitable idiosyncrasies in command names, menu placement, and optional features, most mail programs work essentially the same way. In the rest of this chapter, I'll fill you in on the details of three very popular and easy-to-get mail programs: Qualcomm's Eudora, Netscape Mail, and Microsoft Internet Mail.

If you're already set up using a different program, you should still be able to follow most of these instructions, though you may occasionally have to hunt around for the right menu or command. Even if your office still uses, say, cc:Mail for Windows 3.1, you can get any one of these programs and try it out.

Setting up Netscape mail was covered in Chapter 2.

Key Setup Information, No Matter What Mail Program You Use

No matter what mail program you use, you'll have to tell it certain things about your e-mail account. If you work in an office, someone there ought to be able to supply the correct information, but you may be able to figure it out for yourself. Most of what you have to enter is based on your username and Internet address.

DEFINITIONS

POP: Post Office Protocol; a standard method of storing and retrieving e-mail.

SMTP: Simple Mail Transport Protocol; the most common method of distributing e-mail on the Internet.

- If you need to supply a POP account, enter your full e-mail address.

- For your SMTP server (that's the machine that handles your outgoing mail), you can probably enter the part of your address after the @ sign. (If not, your service provider will inform you of this—call your technical support if necessary.)
- For your return address, again enter your full e-mail address.
- If you need to supply a dial-up username (so your mail program can log in to your account to get your mail), include only the username portion of your address (up to, but not including the @ sign).

Figure 4.2 shows a typical e-mail configuration, using Microsoft Internet Mail as a model.

You should only have to set up your mail program once (unless you change service providers).

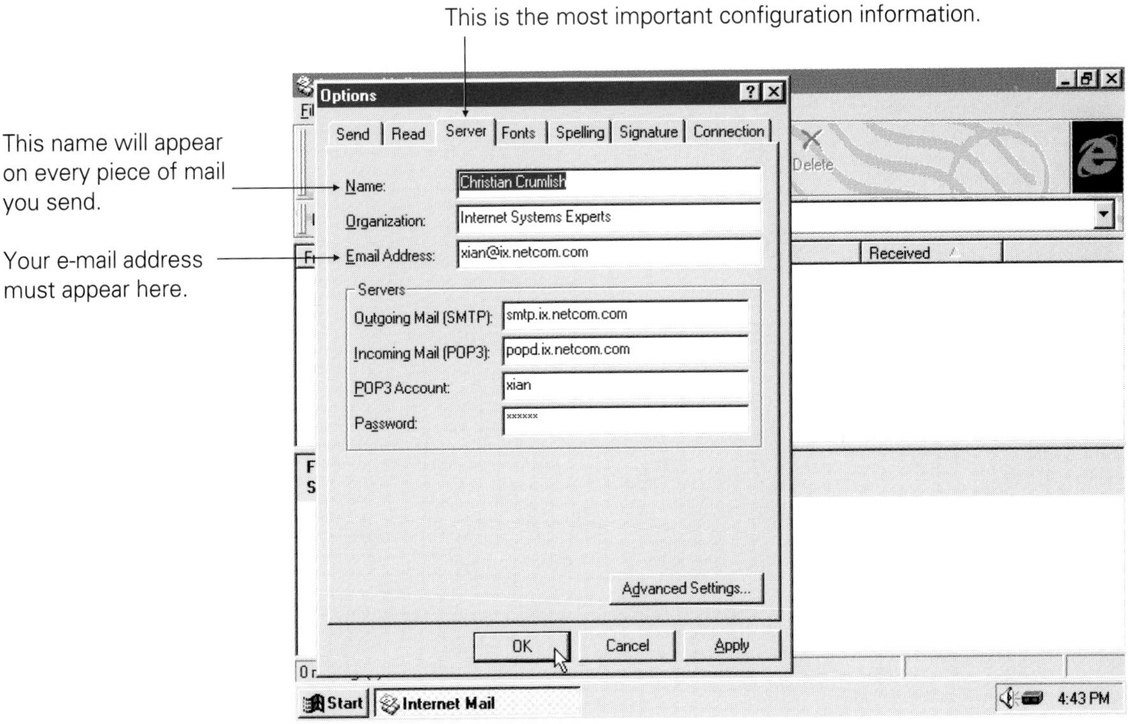

Figure 4.2 A typical e-mail setup

Eudora (Light and Professional)

Eudora was designed specifically for Internet e-mail, and early versions of it were distributed for free on the Internet. More recent versions of it are made by Qualcomm, in two "flavors": Light and Professional. The Light version is free, but lacks some of the advanced features (most notably filters). The Professional version must be purchased.

Pegasus Mail is another pretty good and free e-mail program that you might want to try. You can download it from http://www.pegasus.usa.com/.

Though Eudora was originally written for the Macintosh, new upgrades come out for the Windows platform first nowadays (aimed at the larger installed base of Windows machines), with the changes in the look-and-feel (names of menus, locations of commands, toolbars, layout of windows) eventually trickling down to the Macintosh Pro version and the various Light versions. This section features the most up-to-date Eudora commands and features, so you may find that your version of Eudora differs in small ways. (This mostly means you may have to poke around the Special or Windows menus to find some commands.)

You may as well start with the free version of Eudora, even if it doesn't have the most current look, but if you like it, you'll want to spring for the professional version, for the filters if for no other reason.

Getting and Setting Up Eudora

To get the freeware version of Eudora, point your web browser at http://www.eudora.com/light.html. Fill out the form on that page identifying yourself and then click the Submit button. The Qualcomm web site will then automatically transfer the installation file to your computer (in a folder you specify). When it has fully arrived, double-click the downloaded file and then run the Setup program to install Eudora Light. (The commercial version of Eudora is called Eudora Pro.)

The first time you run Eudora, you'll have to enter some information about your e-mail account. In the Options dialog box (see Figure 4.3), enter your full

DEFINITION

Freeware: Software that's free to download and use, as opposed to shareware, which is free to download, but for which you are expected to pay a licensing fee if you continue to use it after a trial period.

e-mail address and your real name. You may also have to enter your SMTP server name. There are many other categories of options in Eudora (click the scroll bar to see them), but only the Getting Started and Hosts categories are essential.

If you have network access or a PPP or SLIP dial-up account (see Appendix A if you really want to know what all this means), select the Winsock connection

Your POP account is your username and the name of the computer that handles your e-mail.

You can specify a different return address (say, if you have several accounts).

You might have to specify the name of your SMTP server here.

Tell Eudora how often to check for new mail here.

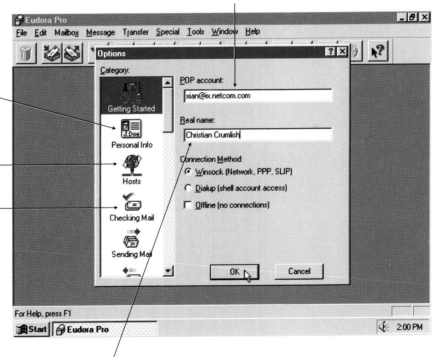

Mail will come From: this name.

Figure 4.3 Eudora's Options dialog box

method. Otherwise, select Dialup. (If you choose Dialup, you'll have to enter the number you want to dial in the Phone number box at the bottom of the Network Configuration area.)

DEFINITIONS

SLIP: Serial Line Internet Protocol; the first popular method of connecting a PC directly to the Internet. Now CSLIP (Compresses SLIP), which compresses headers and makes faster use of a modem, is also available.

PPP: Point-to-Point Protocol; the most common method for connecting a PC to the Internet. It compresses header information, resulting in faster (than SLIP) communication over a modem.

Winsock: A Windows driver that enables network software to perform Internet transactions in the Windows operating system.

To assign a folder for incoming attached files, scroll down to the Attachments category and click the big gray button underneath Attachment Directory. Choose a folder (Eudora still calls them directories) and then click the Use Directory button.

When everything looks good in the Options dialog box, click OK.

Starting Eudora

Eudora

As with any other program, you run your mail program by double-clicking the program icon (or a shortcut to it) or by selecting it from the Start or Apple menu.

When you connect to Eudora, it will immediately check your account for new mail, unless it's set to check for mail every 0 (zero) minutes.

Progress
Connecting to the Mail Server...
Stop

After starting Eudora, you're probably going to read new incoming mail or send new outgoing mail (or maybe do both). I'll explain the procedures for reading mail first, but if you're eager to send a message, feel free to skip ahead.

Reading Mail in Eudora

In most e-mail programs, new mail appears in a window called your in-box. In-boxes generally list just the subject lines of each message. You have to select and open a message to actually read it. Messages are considered new until you've opened (and presumably read) them.

In Eudora, a new message appears with a bullet in the first column. To read a message in Eudora, select the subject line and press ENTER (or double-click it). The message will open in its own window.

Although Eudora automatically checks for new messages when you start up (and at regular intervals), you can check mail manually any time you want. Just press CTRL-M.

Replying in Eudora

To reply to a message (it doesn't have to be open, just selected), select Message | Reply.

Press CTRL-R to reply to a message.

Message	
New Message	Ctrl+N
Reply	Ctrl+R
Reply to All	
Forward	
Redirect	
Send Again	

Eudora will start a new message for you and supply the recipient's name in the To: line. It will also quote the original message for you unless you've told it not to in the Switches dialog box. Erase any part of the message you don't need to repeat and then type your reply (see Figure 4.4). When you are done, click the Queue (or Send) button.

CAUTION

If you're working with Eudora offline and you check Immediate send, then every time you complete a message and click the Send button, Eudora will try (and fail) to connect.

Queue this message (or, if it's marked Send, to send it immediately).

Check the spelling of this message (Eudora Pro only).

Some mail programs add "Re:" to a subject you reply to.

These lines are quoted in my reply.

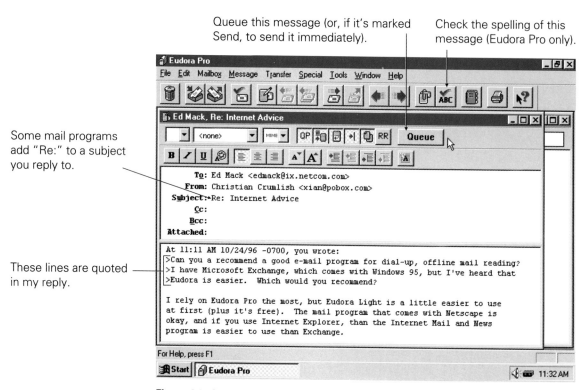

Figure 4.4 A reply message with part of the original message quoted

The difference between Queue and Send is that Queue just adds the message to a list (a queue) of messages and then sends them all at once next time Eudora checks for new mail. Send sends the message immediately. By default, Eudora will send your messages immediately. If you prefer the queue approach, deselect Immediate send in the Sending Mail category of the Options dialog box.

To avoid queuing messages, check Immediate send again. The Options dialog box controls all of Eudora's behavior. Experiment with the other categories of choices to see how they work and how you like them. (Not all the choices in this dialog box exist in Eudora Light, but most do.)

Forwarding in Eudora

Sometimes you'll want to send a reply, not to the original sender but to a third party. To do so, select Message | Forward.

Eudora will quote the original message as in a reply but will leave the To:
line blank for you to enter the new address.

Saving Messages in Eudora

Saving has a slightly different connotation with e-mail than usual. Messages
are automatically saved for you until you delete them, but if you want to keep a
message for informational or other purposes, I recommend moving it to a folder
(or mailbox, depending on the nomenclature of your program). In Eudora, you
can create storage folders on the fly.

To move a message to a mailbox in Eudora, select Transfer | *the folder name*.
At first, there won't be any choices besides the In, Out, and Trash mailboxes. To
create a folder, select Transfer | New. When the dialog box appears, follow the
procedure in the Step by Step box.

STEP BY STEP **Create a Folder for Storing Messages**

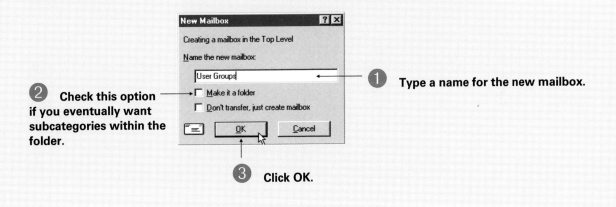

① **Type a name for the new mailbox.**

② **Check this option if you eventually want subcategories within the folder.**

③ **Click OK.**

You can open a mailbox at any point by choosing it from the Mailbox menu.
A new window will appear, showing the contents of the box you selected.

CAUTION

Be careful not to click the Transfer menu when you simply want to open a mailbox, or else you'll move whichever message is currently selected into the box you intended to open. If you do this, just open the box and transfer the incorrect message back to the box it belongs in.

Just press the DELETE key to move selected messages to the Trash mailbox.

Deleting Messages in Eudora

As with saving, deleting means something slightly different when speaking of e-mail messages, as opposed to files. Generally, deleting an e-mail message means moving it to a deleted messages area, not unlike the Recycling Bin or Trashcan on most desktops. These messages are then deleted either when you quit the mail program or when you manually delete them from the holding area.

EXPERT ADVICE

To have the Trash folder emptied whenever you quit Eudora, select Tools | Options, scroll down to select the Miscellaneous category, check the "Empty Trash when exiting" option, and click OK.

To delete a message in Eudora, select it and click the Trash icon on the toolbar. The message will be moved to the Trash mailbox. (You can also select several messages and delete them all at once.)

To empty the trash in Eudora, select Special | Empty Trash.

You can also just press CTRL-N *to start a new message.*

Sending a New Message in Eudora

To send a message in Eudora, select Message | New Message. Eudora will start a message for you in a new window.

STEP BY STEP **Send a Message with Eudora**

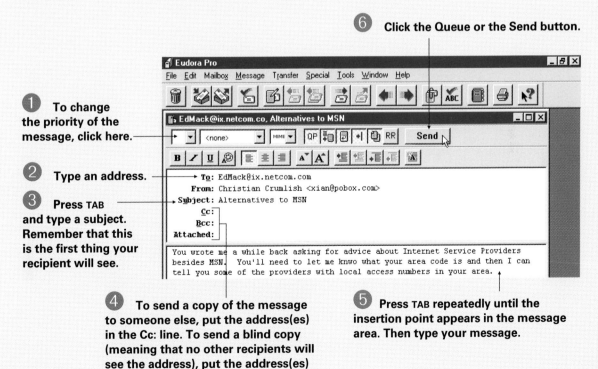

⑥ **Click the Queue or the Send button.**

① **To change the priority of the message, click here.**

② **Type an address.**

③ **Press TAB and type a subject. Remember that this is the first thing your recipient will see.**

④ **To send a copy of the message to someone else, put the address(es) in the Cc: line. To send a blind copy (meaning that no other recipients will see the address), put the address(es) in the Bcc: line.**

⑤ **Press TAB repeatedly until the insertion point appears in the message area. Then type your message.**

If you're using Eudora Light, the command to create a nickname is Special | Make Nickname, not Special | Make Address Book Entry. However, you call them— nicknames, aliases, or address book entries— they're all the same thing.

Saving Addresses in Eudora

Eudora allows you to keep track of e-mail addresses by creating address book entries. The easiest way to do this is to start with an existing piece of mail (you can create a nickname from scratch as well, if you have the address handy). Highlight the message and then select Special | Make Address Book Entry.

In the Make Address Book Entry dialog box, type a short, memorable name. If you want to put this person on your "short list" of addresses available from the menus, click "Put it on the recipient list." Then click OK.

To send (or forward) a message to someone on your recipient list, select Message | New Message To | *nickname* (or Message | Forward To | *nickname*).

SHORTCUT

You can also press CTRL-K to create an address book entry. You can also open the address book by pressing CTRL-L.

To edit nicknames manually, select Tools | Address Book. This brings up the Address Book window, which contains your nicknames. Double-clicking a nickname adds it to the To: list of the current message (or starts a new message if you aren't editing one currently). To create a new nickname, click the New button and then type the address in the Address(es): list box. Close the window by clicking the Close button in the upper-right corner of your screen (or click the To: button to send a message to the selected address). Make sure to save your changes to the address book when Eudora asks you.

Creating a Signature in Eudora

Eudora enables you to set up a signature file to be appended to the end of each message you send. To create a signature, select Tools | Signature in Eudora Light or Tools | Signatures | Standard in Eudora Pro. A small text window will appear. Type whatever you want to appear at the end of each message, press CTRL-S, and then close the window.

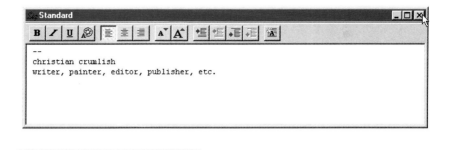

netiquette

It's traditional in Internet e-mail to begin a signature block with two hyphens and a space on a line by themselves. Some mail software looks for those characters as the beginning of the signature.

When sending a message, click the Signature drop-down list box to choose to include the signature or to omit it. (Eudora Pro allows an unlimited number of alternative signatures that you can name whatever you like.)

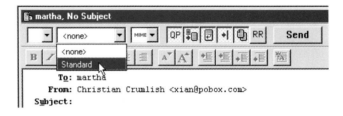

Attaching a File in Eudora

To attach a file to Eudora, select Message | Attach File. This brings up an Attach File dialog box, much like any program's Open dialog box. Choose the file you want to attach, browsing through folders, drivers, and computers as necessary. Then click OK. One nice design feature of Eudora is that it will remember where you last looked next time you attach a file.

CAUTION

Not every recipient will be able to decode an attached document. If your attachments fail to come through clearly, ask your correspondent what encoding methods his or her mailer can handle and see if your copy of Eudora can also use any of those methods.

You can also press CTRL-H to attach a file.

In the third drop-down list box in the top panel of the New Message window, you can choose an encoding method for your attached file. The options are MIME (Multipurpose Internet Mail Extensions, the standard Internet format) or BinHex (the standard Macintosh format, best used when transferring files to or from a Mac—Eudora was first written for the Macintosh, which shows in some of its design features). The commercial version of Eudora can also perform UUencoding (another common Internet format). You can choose a default format in the Options dialog box by selecting Tools | Options and then Attachments, as shown in Figure 4.5.

If you're sending a file to a Macintosh
user, try BinHex; otherwise, use MIME.

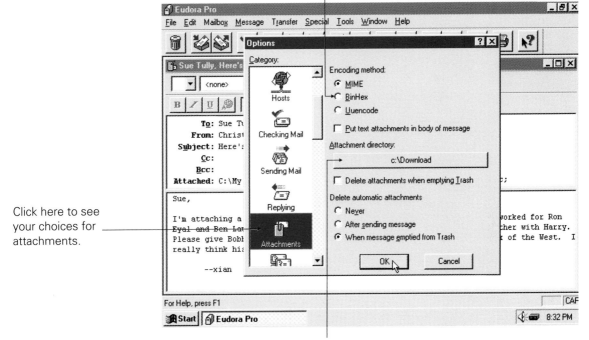

Click here to see
your choices for
attachments.

Place your attachment directory in the folder
where you want downloaded files to appear.

Figure 4.5 Eudora's Attachments

EXPERT ADVICE

*You can attach more than one document to a message (just repeat the
process), but some recipients will see only the first attachment. Consider
creating a compressed file with a program such as WinZip to send all your
files in one attachment.*

Eudora will list the attached file on the Attachments: line of the mail message.

```
          To: martha
        From: Christian Crumlish <xian@pobox.com>
     Subject: Sample Banner Art
          Cc:
         Bcc:
    Attached: C:\Temp\Banners.zip;
```

Attached please find the banner art we discussed earlier, in a .zip file.

    --xian

You can select and delete an attachment if you change your mind about including it.

The free version of Eudora doesn't have filters.

Filtering and Forwarding Mail

The commercial version of Eudora enables you to filter your mail automatically. To do so, select Tools | Filters. Choose a header line for Eudora to base the filtering on and then describe what should or should not be in the header. Usually, you'll filter mail based on the From: line, the To: line (in the case of mailing list messages), or the Subject: line. You can enter a second criterion if you like by changing the "ignore" setting to "and" or "or." If you choose "and," both criteria will have to be met for the mail to be filtered. If you choose "or," either one of the criteria will suffice.

EXPERT ADVICE

There are many possible actions that Eudora can take in filtering mail, including changing the mail's priority or playing a special sound. You can even send back an automatic reply.

To transfer the mail in a different mailbox, choose the first Action field and change it from None to Transfer To. Then click the Transfer To box and choose one of your mailboxes from the menu that pops up. All messages that meet the criteria you chose will automatically be sent to that box (see Figure 4.6). Repeat this procedure for as many filters as you want to set up. When you're done, press CTRL-S and then close the window.

The filter lowest
down on the list has
the highest priority.

Check here to apply this
filter to incoming mail.

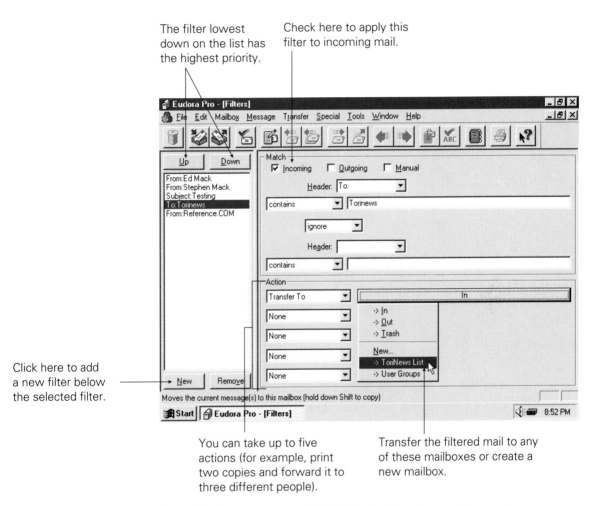

Click here to add
a new filter below
the selected filter.

You can take up to five
actions (for example, print
two copies and forward it to
three different people).

Transfer the filtered mail to any
of these mailboxes or create a
new mailbox.

Figure 4.6 Set up an automatic filter in Eudora to sort some of your mail

Microsoft Internet Mail

Microsoft has offered a number of different e-mail programs over the years.
Some (such as Mail and its successor Exchange) are geared toward local-area
networks. Since releasing Internet Explorer, though, Microsoft has now come out
with a mail program designed for Internet e-mail, named, in Microsoft's inimitable
style, Microsoft Internet Mail. You can download it for free from the Microsoft
web site.

EXPERT ADVICE

Microsoft Internet Mail and Microsoft Internet News come in one package (called, appropriately enough, Microsoft Internet Mail and News), even though they are two separate programs that perform two different functions. The use of Microsoft Internet News is covered along with other Usenet newsreaders in Chapter 6.

Downloading and Installing Internet Mail

Some versions of Internet Explorer come with Internet Mail already installed. If you don't have an icon for Internet Mail, then you'll need to download it.

EXPERT ADVICE

If you use Word 97 (or Word 95), you can make Word your e-mail editor (as part of the installation process). Then Internet Mail will automatically invoke Word whenever you create a new message.

You may be back here to download other Microsoft Internet software later, so consider bookmarking this page.

To get the (currently free) Microsoft Internet Mail and News package (they download together), point your web browser at http://www.microsoft.com/ie/download. Click the "features and components" link or scroll down the drop-down list until Additional Features & Add-ons is selected. Then click the gray Next button.

From the IE Additional Components drop-down list, select Internet Mail and News for Windows 95 or for Macintosh, as appropriate. Click the gray Next button to move to the next step. Since your desired language is most likely US English, when the select language prompt appears, click Next to move on. Now we're getting to the file itself. There are several places from which you can download the mailnews file; scroll down and pick the region closest to you. Then click the blue filename. Internet Explorer will ask you whether you want to open the file or save it to disk. Choose to save it so you can install it. Pick a directory and click the Save button.

When the file has fully arrived, open the folder where you downloaded it and double-click it. A license agreement will appear; click Yes to run the Setup program that installs Internet Mail and News on your system. Enter and confirm your name and organization and then choose whether you want Mail, News, or both. Accept the default folder and then click Finish. You'll probably then have to restart your computer.

The first time you run Internet Mail (from the Programs menu of the Start button), you'll have to configure it. After clicking Next to move past the introductory screen, you'll have to enter your name and full e-mail address.

Now click Next again. You'll need to enter the names of your incoming mail (POP3) server and your outgoing mail (SMTP) server. Hopefully a network administrator or helpful person from your Internet service provider will have already given you these machine names (often the POP3 name and SMTP name are identical).

Now we're getting down to the details. Clicking Next leads Internet Mail Configuration to ask you for your e-mail account and password. The e-mail account name is the part before the @ in your e-mail address. If you enter a password here, then you won't have to enter it each time you get your mail; however, this will make your mail less secure since anyone using your computer will have access to your private mail. Consider leaving the password blank, so you will be prompted for it each time you get mail. Click Next when you've filled in these fields.

Last, you need to indicate what type of connection you use. If you're part of a corporate network, you should choose the first option, "I use a LAN connection." If you want to work offline or have several different ways you can connect, choose "I connect manually." If you use a modem to dial in to your account, choose the third option, "I use a modem to access my email" and then select your dial-up networking connection from the drop-down list (see Appendix A if you haven't set up dial-up networking yet).

Internet Mail Configuration

When connecting to your POP3 and SMTP servers, you can connect in several different ways. Please specify the type of connection that you will use.

○ I use a LAN connection

○ I connect manually

● I use a modem to access my email

Use the following Dial-Up Networking connection:

Netcom ▼

Properties   Add...

< Back   Next >   Cancel

That's it! Click Finish to begin using Internet Mail.

Internet Mail

Using Internet Mail

Double-click the Internet Mail icon to start the program.

SHORTCUT

In Windows, you can start Internet Mail by clicking Start | Programs | Internet Mail.

In Internet Mail, new messages appear in boldface. To read a message, select it. The message will open in the lower half of the window.

To reply to a message, click Reply to Author (or Reply to All if you want to reply to an entire list of recipients).

SHORTCUT

You can also press CTRL-R to reply to a message. You can also press ALT-S to send a message.

*Press CTRL-F to forward
a message.*

Internet Mail will start a new message (in its own window), supplying the recipient's name in the To: line and quoting the message to which you're replying. Edit the quoted material if necessary, type your reply message, and then click the Send button on the toolbar.

To send a reply not to the original sender but to a third party instead, click the Forward button. Internet Mail will quote the original message as in a reply but will leave the To: line blank for you to enter the addressee. Type a recipient's address or click the To: button and follow the instructions in the section "Sending a New Message in Internet Mail" later in this chapter.

To store a message in a folder in Internet Mail, you first have to create the folder:

1. Select File | Folder | Create.
2. In the Create New Folder dialog box that appears, type a name for the folder and then click OK.
3. Select Mail | Move to | *folder name.*

To view the contents of a folder, click the Folders drop-down list box and choose the folder you want:

- Any folders you created with the File | Folder | Create command will appear in this list box.
- The Deleted Items folder contains mail you have deleted.
- The Outbox folder contains any outgoing mail you've prepared, which will be sent when you click the Send and Receive button.
- The Sent Items folder stores a copy of mail that has been sent.

To delete a message in Internet Mail, click the Delete button on the toolbar. The message will be moved to the Deleted Items folder.

EXPERT ADVICE

To have the Deleted Items folder emptied whenever your quit Internet Mail, select Tools | Options, click the Read tab, check the "Empty messages from the 'Deleted Items' folder on exit" box, and click OK.

Just press DELETE to delete a message or a number of selected messages.

To permanently get rid of messages, just delete them from the Deleted Items folder. Internet Mail will warn you that these will be permanently deleted.

To send a new message in Internet Mail, click the New Message button on the toolbar. A New Message window will appear. Type an address in the To: box or click the little phone-file card icon to bring up the Select Recipients dialog box, which allows you to select names from your address book.

In the Select Recipients dialog box, choose a name from the list in the left window and click the To: button to add it to the recipient list, or click the New Contact button to create a new entry in the address book. This brings up the Properties dialog box.

If you consider your message to be very important, click the stamp (in the upper right of the window) and choose High Priority from the menu.

Enter the new name, e-mail address, and any other information you want to add and then click OK. (*Then* click the To: button to add it to the recipient list.) Repeat this process if you want to add other recipients. Then click OK again to add the recipient(s) to the message.

Tab down to or click the Subject: box and type a subject line. Then press TAB again or click the message area and type your message. When you're done, click the Send button.

To attach a file in Internet Mail, click the Insert File button on the toolbar.

In the Insert Attachment dialog box that appears, select the file you want to include and then click Attach. You can look in any drive or folder for the file you want to attach.

SHORTCUT

If you don't want to send the actual file, you can send a shortcut to it instead, if the file is accessible via the Internet or your intranet. To do this, click the Make Shortcut to this file check box.

The file will appear as an icon in a pane at the bottom of your message window.

Oh, by the way, I've attached a little artwork that shows my high spirits!

Celebration!.gif
(11K)

You can also just press CTRL-M to deliver your messages.

Delivering Your Messages

When you "send" a message in Internet Mail, it's placed in your Outbox folder. Messages in the folder are not actually sent until you deliver them. To do so, click the Send and Receive button.

Netscape Mail

The next release of Netscape will be a suite called Netscape Communicator and will include a complete mail program called Netscape Messenger.

Another mail program you might consider using is Netscape Mail, which is actually a module of Netscape Navigator. It's still limited in some ways compared to full-fledged mail programs, but if you have Netscape, you have this module already, and you might consider using it. (Some offices have standardized on Netscape Mail, so you may not have a choice.)

Starting Netscape Mail

You can start Netscape Mail by selecting Window | Mail in Netscape Navigator or by clicking the envelope icon in the lower-right corner of the Navigator window.

Reading Mail in Netscape Mail

Folders appear in the upper-left pane of the Netscape Mail window, and message subjects appear in the upper-right pane. To read a message, select it. The message will open in the lower pane (see Figure 4.7).

Replying in Netscape Mail

To reply to a message, click the Reply button (or click Reply to All if you want to reply to an entire list of recipients).

Press CTRL-R to reply to a message.

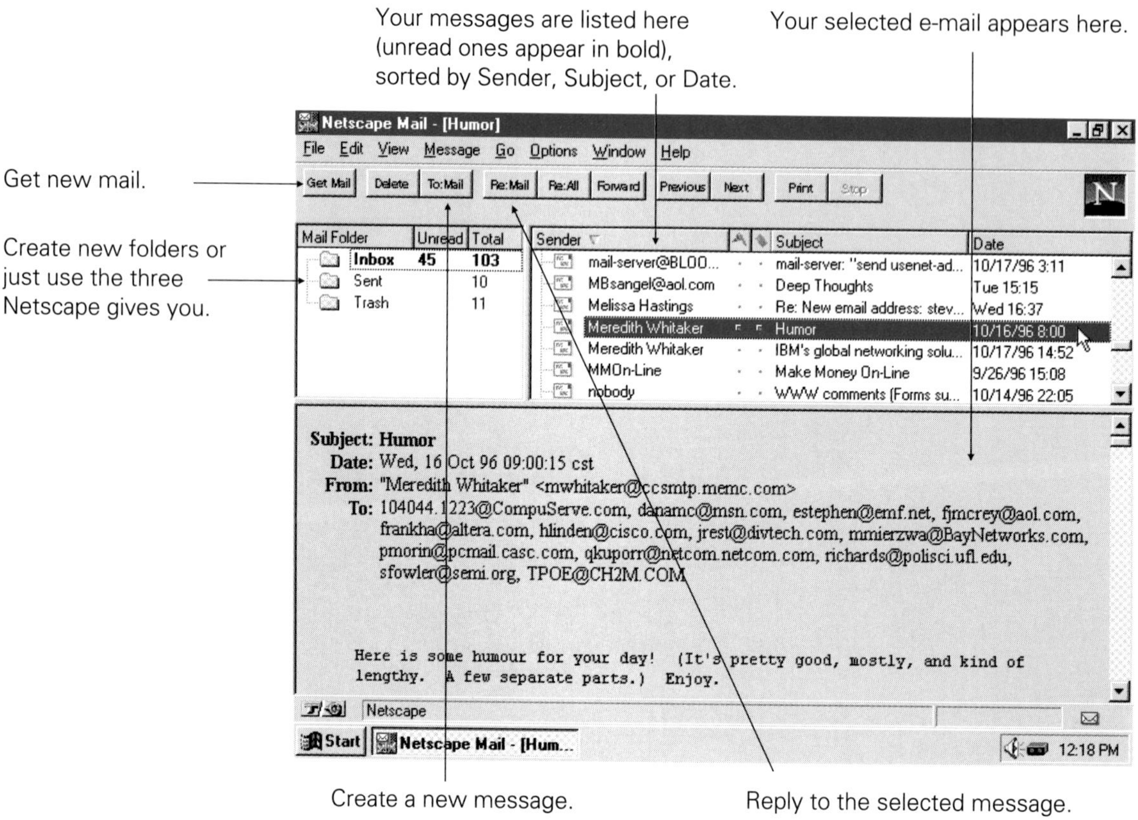

Your messages are listed here
(unread ones appear in bold),
sorted by Sender, Subject, or Date.

Your selected e-mail appears here.

Get new mail.

Create new folders or
just use the three
Netscape gives you.

Create a new message.

Reply to the selected message.

Figure 4.7 Reading mail in Netscape Mail

Netscape Mail will start a new message (in its own window), supplying the recipient's name in the To: box, and quoting the message to which you're replying. Edit the quoted material if necessary, type your reply message, and then click the Send button on the toolbar.

You can use the Options | Deferred Delivery command to work offline, queuing your message to send them later. You can use the Options | Preferences command to set your servers and options for mailing.

Press CTRL-F to forward a message.

Forwarding in Netscape Mail

To send a reply not to the original sender but to a third party instead, click the Forward button.

Netscape Mail will quote the original message as in a reply but will leave the To: line blank for you to enter the addressee. Type a recipient's address or click the To: button and follow the instructions in the section "Sending a New Message in Netscape Mail" later in this chapter.

Saving Messages in Netscape Mail

To store a message in a folder in Netscape Mail, you first have to create the folder:

1. Select File | New Folder.

2. In the dialog box that appears, type a name for the folder. Then click OK.

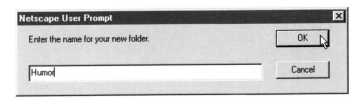

3. Select Message | Move | *folder name.*

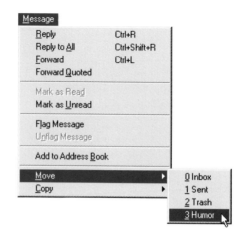

To view the contents of a folder, just click the folder you want in the upper-left pane.

Deleting Messages in Netscape Mail

To delete a message in Netscape Mail, click the Delete button on the toolbar.

SHORTCUT

Just press DELETE to delete a message or a number of selected messages.

Sending a New Message in Netscape Mail

To send a new message in Netscape Mail, select File | New Mail Message or click the To: Mail button on the toolbar, shown here:

Press CTRL-M to start a new message.

A New Message window will appear (see Figure 4.8). Type an address in the To: box. Tab down to or click the Subject: box and type a subject line. Then press

TAB again or click the message area and type your message. When you're done, click the Send button.

Netscape - [Message Composition]

File Edit View Options Window

| Send | Quote | Attach | Address | Stop |

Mail To: send@mmonline.com, postmaster@mmonline.com

Cc: psb@lbl.gov

Subject: Complaint about unsolicited e-mail

Attachment:

```
To whom it may concern,

I am writing to complain in the highest possible terms about some unsolicited
commercial junk mail I received the other day from one of your users.  This kind
of spam is a genuine waste of resources, and I hope you remind your users that
unsolicited e-mail could even be illegal under U.S. law.

Please make sure that your user is aware of the Terms of Service of your
up-stream internet backbone; mass-mailing of unsolicited junk mail is
definitely a violation of the terms of service.

Above all:  REMOVE ME FROM YOUR LIST!

Sincerely,

Christian Crumlish
```

Netscape

Start | Netscape Mail - [Make Mo... | Netscape - [Message...   1:04 PM

Figure 4.8 Click the Mail To: button to add a recipient from your address book

Attaching a File

To attach a file in Netscape Mail, click the Attach File(s) button on the toolbar.

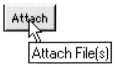

In the Attachments dialog box that appears, click Attach File. In the "Enter file to attach" dialog box that then pops up, select the file you want to include and click Open. Then click OK.

Trying Out E-Mail

Now that you've learned how to handle e-mail, why not pause to try it out for yourself. If you'd like, feel free to send me a message (xian@pobox.com). If you do send e-mail to me, be sure to include the word "Busy" in the subject so my mail filter can put your message in the right place (no, not the trash!).

Start your mail program and create a new message. Then follow the instructions in the Step by Step box.

STEP BY STEP **Send E-Mail**

④ **Click the Send button.**

① **Enter the recipient's address in the To: line.**

② **Tab down to the Subject: line and type a subject**

③ **Tab down to the main area and write your message.**

Eudora Pro

File   Edit   Mailbox   Message   Transfer   Special   Tools   Window   Help

xian@pobox.com, Busy People for Internet Comme

B   I   U | | | A   A | | | | | Send

To: xian@pobox.com
From: Herbert Stencil <hstencil@ppush.mcei.gov>
Subject: Busy People for Internet Comments
Cc:
Bcc:
Attached:

Christian,

I'm just writing to share my opinions of the Internet for Busy People book. I've read through Chapter 4 in great detail, and if nothing else I know that I now know how to send you e-mail with my opinion!
Thanks for all of your help! I'll try to make sure you don't get audited this year. I've got some buddies in the IRS.

--Herbert

For Help, press F1

Start   Eudora Pro   1:20 PM

CHECK POINT

Besides helping you to keep up with all your old college buddies around the globe, e-mail enables you to join mailing lists and participate in online discussion groups. Chapter 5 explains all about lists. Chapter 6 will show you the more public Usenet news groups, which have thousands of additional forums for discussion. Later chapters will introduce the research and file transfer facilities of the Internet.

Joining Mailing Lists

5

INCLUDES

- Using different types of mailing lists
- Using mailing lists in digest form
- Finding mailing lists
- Subscribing to mailing lists
- Unsubscribing from mailing lists
- Contributing to mailing lists

FAST FORWARD

Understand Mailing Lists ➤ *pp. 171-174*

```
    To: Coworkers, KarenD, Martha
  From: Christian Crumlish <xian@pobox.com>
Subject: My vacation
    Cc: GordonH
   Bcc:
Attached:

Hi Everyone,

I'll be on vacation for a few weeks starting September 15.
you all know ahead of time so you can cover for me.

     --xian
```

A mailing list is

- An impromptu list of addressees in an e-mail To: header
- An alias (nickname or address-book entry) associated with a list of e-mail addresses
- An e-mail address that corresponds to a list of subscribers

Find Lists That Interest You ➤ *pp. 175-177*

```
Location: http://www.NeoSoft.com/internet/paml/
```

```
any form, except through normal Usenet distribution chanr
author.

This is a list of mailing lists available primarily through the
is different from a newsgroup because you do not receive
be added to a mailing list, please mail a note to the contact
lists mentioned may be available as limited-distribution new
```

1. Point your Web browser at the subject index of the Publicly Accessible Mailing List site (http://www.neosoft.com/internet/paml/bysubj.html).
2. Choose a topic that interests you.
3. Note the subscription information for one or all of the lists indexed under that subject.

Figure out If a List Is Human- or Robot-Administered ➤ *pp. 178-179*

```
To subscribe, send email to
   majordomo@teleport.com
and in the body of the message, put
   SUBSCRIBE HEATHER-GIGS-L your-email-address

List owner: seafire@teleport.com (Philip R. Obermarck)

Last change: May 96
```

The information about the list should include how to subscribe. If it doesn't, it should at least give the contact address.

- If the contact address starts with listserv@ or majordomo@, and/or if the contact address does not contain the name of the list, then assume that the list is robot-administered.
- If the contact address starts with *listname*-request@, then the list may be administered by a real person, but there's no guarantee.

Subscribe to a Human-Administered List ➤ *pp. 179-180*

```
Please add me to the fabulous Really Deep Thoughts list about
Tori Amos.  Thanks.
     --xian
```

Send a message to *listname*-request@*list-address* (not the mailing list address itself!) asking in plain English to subscribe.

Subscribe to a Robot-Administered List ➤ pp. 181-182

Send a message to the contact address (often listserv@*somewhere*, not the mailing list itself!), typing **subscribe** *listname* on a line by itself, with no signature or subject. Substitute the name of the list for *listname*. For some list servers, you type the command **join**, not subscribe, and you may need to add your real name to the end of the command.

```
To subscribe, send email to
   majordomo@lists.village.virginia.edu
and in the body of the message, put
   subscribe feyerabend
```

Unsubscribe from a Human-Administered List ➤ p. 182

Send a message to *listname*-request@*list-address* (not the mailing list itself!), asking in plain English to unsubscribe.

```
Sorry, due to time constraints I'm not able to keep up with the list,
so please unsubscribe me from Really Deep Thoughts (xian@pobox.com).
   --xian
```

Unsubscribe from a Robot-Administered List ➤ p. 182

Send a message to the contact address (often listserv@*somewhere*, not the mailing list itself!), typing **unsubscribe** *listname* (or **signoff** *listname*) on a line by itself, with no signature or subject.

```
unsubscribe feyerabend
```

Learn about a List Before Posting to It ➤ pp. 182-183

- Lurk for a while to get up to speed with ongoing conversations.
- Ask about and read the Frequently Asked Questions (FAQ) list.

```
1)    WHAT ARE FAQs?
1.1)  What does FAQ stand for?
1.2)  How is FAQ pronounced?
1.3)  What do FAQs contain?
1.4)  What are FAQs used for?
1.5)  Where are FAQs found/kept/hidden?
```

Reply to Posted List Messages ➤ pp. 183-185

1. Decide whether the reply should go to the original poster or to the entire list.
2. Use your e-mail program's Reply command.
3. Make sure the address in the To: header is either the individual or the list address (different lists are set up differently), depending on to whom you wish to reply.
4. Trim as much of the original message as possible.
5. Write your reply and send it.

```
To: precious-things@smoe.org
From: Christian Crumlish <xian@pobox.com>
Subject: Re: Bootleg CD crackdown hits home
Cc:
Bcc:
Attached:

Rusty wrote:
>i went into my favorite local independent record store today to look
>around and possibly buy a few things and i noticed that all of the
>bootleg cd's that normally cover the wall were gone, replaced with UK cd
>singles.

Could it be that they were simply sold out of the bootlegs? Or maybe
they are hidden in a back room.
   --xian
```

Stop Lists When You Go on Vacation ➤ *p. 186*

➤ *p. 186*

`set ALLMUSIC nomail`

Temporarily unsubscribe from any mailing lists you're subscribed to by following the steps for unsubscribing. When you want to read the mailing list again, you'll have to resubscribe.

If your mailing list is a robot-administered list with the name "listserv" in it:

1. Send a message to the listserv address (not the mailing list itself), typing **set** *listname* **nomail** on a line by itself, with no signature or subject, when you start your vacation.
2. Send a message to the listserve address (not the mailing list itself), typing **set** *listname* **mail** on a line by itself, with no signature or subject, when you return from your vacation.

One of the Internet's greatest benefits is that it lets you easily find and converse with like-minded people no matter where they're located physically. There are several types of discussion groups on the Net, but the most basic type is a mailing list.

What's a Mailing List?

A mailing list, often referred to simply as a list, is made up of e-mail addresses, usually with a single e-mail address set up that forwards all messages sent to it to every address on the list. This facilitates a group conversation in which anyone on the list can participate and which can potentially spawn various threads from a single original post.

DEFINITIONS

Post: *A message sent to a public forum of any kind, such as a mailing list or Usenet newsgroup (from the analogy of posting a message to a bulletin board). Also called an article.*

Thread: *An ongoing conversation on a single topic or theme, usually with each message under the same subject.*

Lists do have their downsides as well, especially for a busy person. A high-traffic mailing list will flood your in-box in no time. It's natural to join and quit (subscribe to and unsubscribe from) mailing lists freely, as your interests wax and wane or as the traffic on a list changes. If you're too busy for any kind of conversational lists, you may still be interested in some announcement-only lists, which essentially broadcast information without providing a forum for discussion.

Impromptu Lists

The simplest form of mailing list is a list of addressees, separated by commas, on a To: or Cc: line in a message. Anyone who receives such a message and replies to it with their mail program's Reply All command will be posting that reply to the entire original list of addressees. This can become annoying for anyone on the original impromptu list who does not wish to keep receiving follow-up messages, especially because the list is an unofficial one and has no administrator to appeal to, just a lot of individuals who have the entire list attached to an e-mail message in their mail programs.

Simple Alias Lists

The next most simple type of mailing list is a list of e-mail addresses associated with a single alias (or nickname or address-book entry, depending on your mail program). This type of list is only slightly different from the previous type: in this case, the original sender does maintain an official list, but the recipients will all see the expanded list of e-mail addresses on the To: line, so after the first post, the effect is the same.

If you have a group of friends or associates to whom you occasionally wish to broadcast a message, setting up an alias for all their e-mail addresses is a good way to go (just use whatever method you normally use to create an alias, but enter a list of addresses instead of just a single address). A lot of large-scale, interesting, public mailing lists started off as impromptu lists among friends and then outgrew their original charter.

Figure 5.1 shows a list of addresses associated with an alias (or nickname) in Eudora Pro. The figure uses the nickname "Coworkers" to identify a simple list of a few names.

Although similar in many ways to mailing lists, Usenet newsgroups (explained in Chapter 6) do not send posts directly to your mailbox, but instead keep them in a central location you can visit at your own discretion. Mailing lists are often less "noisy" than newsgroups and more often have archives of past articles.

"Real" Mailing Lists

The most sophisticated type of mailing list is an actual e-mail address associated with a list of addresses. When the mail server of the main address receives incoming mail, it automatically forwards it to every address on the list. Such mailing lists are maintained either by human volunteers or by robotic mailing list programs (controlled by e-mail commands).

Eudora treats a nickname for a list just
as it treats any other nickname.
You can include Eudora nicknames and e-mail
addresses in your list; just type one entry per line.

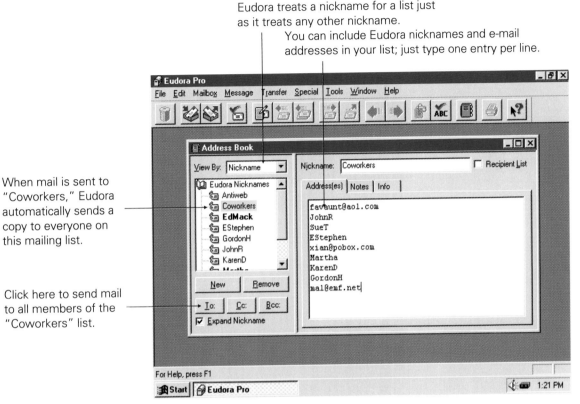

When mail is sent to
"Coworkers," Eudora
automatically sends a
copy to everyone on
this mailing list.

Click here to send mail
to all members of the
"Coworkers" list.

Figure 5.1 A simple list of just a few names

The main thing you need to know before subscribing to a list is whether it
is administered by a human or a robot. With human-administered lists, you send
plain English messages to the administrator when you want to join the list, quit
it, inquire about it, or change your status on the list. With robot-administered
lists, you send carefully worded messages that include commands for the program
that controls the list.

DEFINITION

Robot: *On the Internet, usually refers to an automated process that may or
may not behave like a real person (as opposed to a mobile tin can in a
science fiction movie). Also called bots or agents.*

Digests

Some mailing lists can also be subscribed to in a "digestified" form, meaning that all the messages from that day (or every ten or so messages, or every 20 or 40 kilobytes worth of messages, or all the messages from a single week) are lumped into a single digest and sent out. Digests can help reduce the number of messages appearing in your in-box for a high-traffic list. Digests often have the feel of a newsletter—often a very democratic newsletter in which anyone can participate and there is no editor.

Moderated Lists

Some mailing lists have a moderator, a volunteer who screens messages sent to the list and posts only those that are on-topic (directly related to the topic of the list) and noninflammatory. Moderated lists tend to have fewer posts, which can make them more appealing to busy people.

What Do Mailing Lists Offer You?

There are lists on every imaginable topic—science, academia, business, music, hobbies, social groups, television shows—you name it. You may find useful advice and collegiality in a mailing list related to your work, or you may find relaxation and escape from your work in a list devoted to your favorite rock and roll band, gardening, sports, or what have you.

EXPERT ADVICE

If your mail program can create a Bcc: line in a message, this is the best place to put an alias to a list of addresses, as none of the recipients will have to see the entire list, and the problem of an impromptu list floating around is avoided.

Supportive lists can link together a community of people who've faced a similar problem and give up-to-date options. For example, real lists can help people who've suffered through cancer, diabetes, and miscarriages—and all types of common and rare illnesses—share experiences and trade the names of medicines and therapies that may not be widely known.

Finding Mailing Lists That Interest You

Because mailing lists are being formed (or dying out) every day, it would be a full-time job to keep up with the entire set of lists. Fortunately, the Internet community includes many people who voluntarily maintain references to exactly that kind of information. You just have to know where to look.

Probably the definitive source of mailing lists is a document called, naturally enough, Publicly Accessible Mailing Lists, currently in 20 parts and containing descriptions of over 1,500 mailing lists.

Finding Lists on the Web

Point your Web browser at http://www.NeoSoft.com/internet/paml to go to the Publicly Accessible Mailing Lists (PAML) web site (see Figure 5.2).

Read the main page and then click the Index link. You'll be able to choose an index by name (click Names) or by subject (click Subjects). Clicking Subjects displays the page shown in Figure 5.3.

Note that paml stands for Publicly Accessible Mailing Lists, so that's an "ell" at the end of paml, not the number "one."

This link leads to some more information about the PAML page.

Clicking here takes you to the Index page for the list.

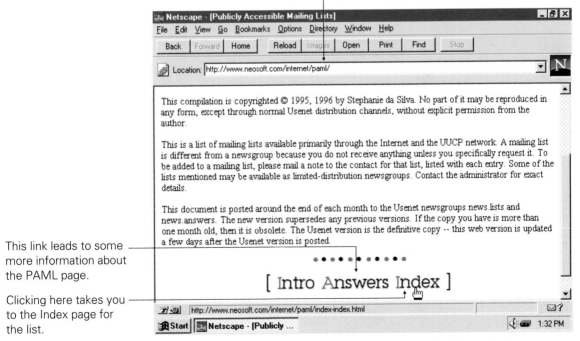

Figure 5.2 The main page of the Publicly Accessible Mailing Lists web site

To go straight to the subject index
in the future, bookmark this page.

These awards show
how popular this page is.

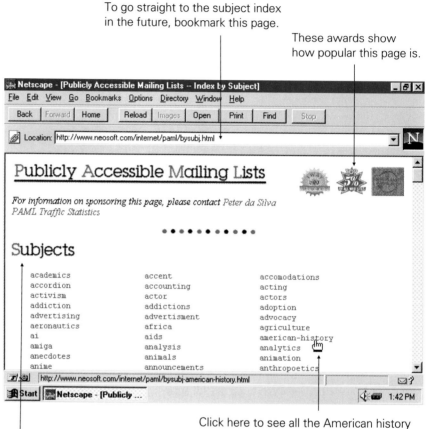

Click here to see all the American history
mailing lists known to PAML.

New subjects are added all the time; this link leads to a mailing list on generative
anthropology. PAML doesn't let you search for words in mailing list descriptions
themselves, so scan carefully for your subject.

Figure 5.3 The Index by subject of the Publicly Accessible Mailing Lists site

If you have any trouble connecting to the PAML site, you can find the same
information (in a less structured form) at http://www.cis.ohio-state.edu/hypertext/
faq/usenet/mail/mailing-lists/top.html. It lists the (currently 20) parts of the PAML
document in the form that it's posted to Usenet newsgroups. Or you can try directly
accessing the archive site where the posted documents are stored at ftp://
rtfm.mit.edu/pub/usenet-by-group/news.answers/mail/mailing-lists/.

CAUTION

The RTFM site is frequently busy and difficult to connect to. Try the wee hours of the morning for an easy connection.

SHORTCUT

To search for mailing lists, you can also just point your browser directly at one of the PAML indexes (at http://www.neosoft.com/internet/paml/byname.html or http://www.neosoft.com/internet/paml/bysubj.html).

If you don't find what you need in PAML and you want to look for other lists of mailing lists, try Yahoo!'s big central listing at http://www.yahoo.com/Computers_and_Internet/Internet/Mailing_Lists/ (see Figure 5.4).

Two mailing lists you might want to check out are Liszt.com (http://www.liszt.com/), which is searchable and lists over 66,000 lists, and Post Office Central (http://ourworld.compuserve.com/homepages/djessop/), though it lists only 300 or so lists.

Finding Lists by E-Mail

If you're looking for mailing lists on a specific subject, you can send mail to listserv@listserv.net with no subject and no signature. Your message should be just one line:

list global / *topic*

but you should replace the word topic with the subject you're interested in. Figure 5.5 shows the e-mail I received when I sent the command "list global / music" to that address. The search yielded several dozen mailing lists, including one promising one, ALLMUSIC. To subscribe to ALLMUSIC, I'd send a message to listserv@listserv.net with the words **Subscribe ALLMUSIC**.

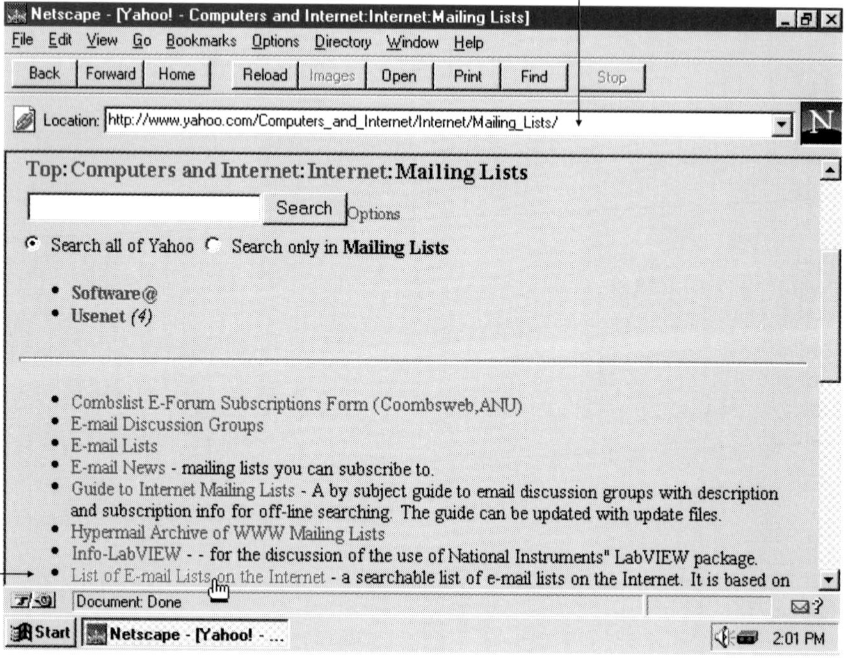

Type this URL or navigate through Yahoo!'s menus (Computers and Internet, then Internet, and then Mailing Lists).

Visit Liszt.com's searchable list.

Figure 5.4 Yahoo!'s list of mailing list lists

How to Subscribe

Subscribing to a list means requesting that your e-mail address be added to the list so that a copy of each post to the list is sent to you. The methods for subscribing vary, depending on whether the list is human-administered or robot-administered.

netiquette

Be very careful not to send a subscription request to the list itself. There is always a separate mailing address for such administrative matters.

Careful! Don't send a message to this address asking to subscribe—this address is for messages to all the subscribers of ALLMUSIC only.

```
Eudora Pro                                                    _ 🗗 ✕
File  Edit  Mailbox  Message  Transfer  Special  Tools  Window  Help

[toolbar icons]

L-Soft list server , 11:22 AM 10/26/96, File: "LISTSERV LISTS"    _ □ ✕

  [icons]  ▼  | Subject: | File: "LISTSERV LISTS"

       Excerpt from the LISTSERV lists known to LISTSERV@LISTSERV.NET
       ---------------------------------------------------------------
                          26 Oct 1996 11:22
                         (search string: MUSIC)

  Network-wide ID   Full address and list description
  ---------------   ---------------------------------
  ACTMUS-L          ACTMUS-L@UBVM.CC.BUFFALO.EDU
                    Asian Contemporary Music Discussion Group

  AFRIMUSE          AFRIMUSE@IUBVM.UCS.INDIANA.EDU
                    Music & Performing Arts of Sub-Saharan Africa

  ALLMUSIC          ALLMUSIC@AMERICAN.EDU
                    Discussions on all forms of Music

  ATTENTION-SCREAM  ATTENTION-SCREAM@LISTSERV.AOL.COM
                    MusicSpace monthly newsletter from America Online

For Help, press F1

🏁 Start  | 🐸 Eudora Pro                                    📢🔊  2:27 PM
```

There are a fair number of lists with the word "Music" in their descriptions or titles—only some of the A's are shown here. Scroll down to see the rest.

Figure 5.5 My results from my search for mailing lists on the subject of music

Subscribing to Human-Administered Lists

For human-administered lists, the administrative address is a variant on the list address, usually the word "-request" appended to the part of the address before the @ sign. So to subscribe to a (fictional) mailing list called busy@syx.com, you'd send a message to busy-request@syx.com, saying "Please subscribe me to the list."

CAUTION

Robot-administered lists often have a listname-*request address as well, so the presence of such an address is no guarantee that you're dealing with a real person.*

If you try to subscribe to what you think is a human-administered list and instead get back a reply from a robot, then follow the instructions in the next section. Figure 5.6 shows such a response. The lines with >>>> in front are what I sent to the robot; the lines with **** in front are what the robot sent in return. As you can see, although robots don't understand plain English, they're very patient about telling you they don't know what you're talking about.

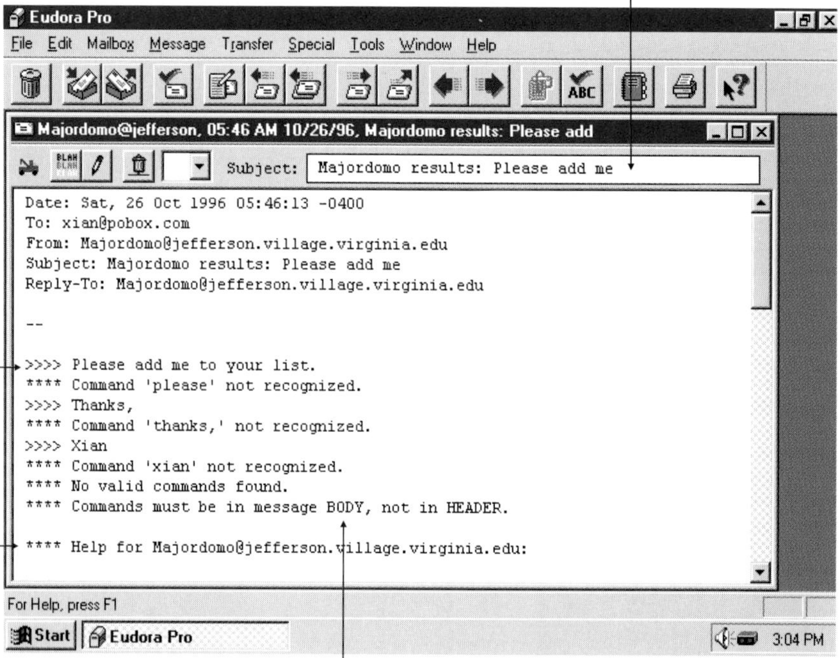

The two most popular mailing-list programs are majordomo and listserv.

These instructions would be clear to a human administrator, but to a robot, they don't make any sense.

At least the robot sent me back a list of the commands it *does* recognize.

```
Date: Sat, 26 Oct 1996 05:46:13 -0400
To: xian@pobox.com
From: Majordomo@jefferson.village.virginia.edu
Subject: Majordomo results: Please add me
Reply-To: Majordomo@jefferson.village.virginia.edu

--

>>>> Please add me to your list.
**** Command 'please' not recognized.
>>>> Thanks,
**** Command 'thanks,' not recognized.
>>>> Xian
**** Command 'xian' not recognized.
**** No valid commands found.
**** Commands must be in message BODY, not in HEADER.

**** Help for Majordomo@jefferson.village.virginia.edu:
```

Majordomo tells me not to use the Subject: line when subscribing to a robot-administered list (commands must appear in the body of the message).

Figure 5.6 A robot's reply to a subscription message sent to a list mistakenly assumed to be human-administered

Subscribing to Robot-Administered Lists

For robot-administered lists (often called list servers or listservs, after the listserv program that maintains the lists), the subscription address is usually completely different from the mailing list (because it's a central administrative address for a number of lists). The subscription address is often majordomo@*such-and-such* or listserv@*so-and-so*, and your subscription request must be of the form

subscribe *listname*

for majordomo lists, or

subscribe *listname your name*

for listservs.

EXPERT ADVICE

To get an e-mail message outlining the commands understood by a list-serving robot program, send a message to the address with just the word **help** *on a line by itself.*

To subscribe to the (real) Allergy mailing list, send e-mail to listserv@tamvm1.tamu.edu and in the body of the message type this:

subscribe Allergy *your name*

You may get back an automated reply telling you that you must confirm your subscription by sending a confirmation message to a certain address. If so, just follow the instructions in the mail you receive.

If you get back a confusing result or an error message, send a message to the majordomo or listserv address with just the word **help** in it, and you should be sent a complete list of correct commands.

When sending mail to a robot, leave out your signature. It will only confuse the poor thing. (Or you can type the word **end** on a line by itself at the end of your message. Everything after it will be ignored.) Also, leave the subject line blank (it's ignored anyway).

CAUTION

Don't send any of your administrative requests to the mailing list itself. This will annoy all of the subscribers!

Saving the Subscription Information

When you join a list, you're usually sent a welcome message, a set of instructions for unsubscribing, and other useful information. Save this message. Create a special folder for it in your mail program and add the similar messages you get from other lists when you join them. Eventually, they'll come in handy.

Chapter 4 explains how to save a message in a special mailbox or folder in your mail program.

Unsubscribing

If and when the time comes to quit a list, send your request to the same address you originally sent to when you joined. For human-administered lists, send a message to listname-request@address asking in plain English to be unsubscribed. For robot-administered lists, send a message to the majordomo address, typing **unsubscribe** *listname* (or, if that fails, or if it's a listserv list, try **signoff** *listname*) and nothing else.

Start off by Lurking

Mailing lists (and newsgroups) usually have many more readers than participants. It is considered totally normal (and is actually recommended) that you read a list for a while before you post for the first time. This is called lurking. Despite the sinister sound of the term, lurking is good netiquette and restrains new people from jumping into the middle of old conversations without understanding the background and ideas that have led up to the current point. Once you get the hang of the topic threads and have a feel for who's who, you can contribute more intelligently and with less likelihood of stepping on toes.

Frequently Asked Questions

Quite a few Usenet newsgroups (as explained in Chapter 6) are devoted to FAQs, such as news.answers and alt.answers.

For every list, there are certain questions that are frequently asked, especially by new contributors (also called newbies). The questions themselves may be perfectly reasonable, but after you've been on a list for a while, it gets tedious to keep seeing (or answering) the same questions. Because of this, a tradition had arisen on the Net for lists and other discussion groups to assemble Frequently Asked Question lists, usually referred to as FAQs (pronounced "facks"). FAQs often evolve as a collective effort, though usually one person must take responsibility for maintaining the document.

CAUTION

RTF: Also called RTFAQ; it stands for "read the FAQ" and is a generic answer to frequently asked questions in a mailing list or Usenet newsgroup. (This is roughly the equivalent of responding, when asked the spelling of a word, "look it up in the dictionary.") Not to be confused with RTFM, which stands for "read the (ahem) manual."

When you join a list, wait or ask for the FAQ to be posted so you can get answers to the most common questions before piping up with your own. Some FAQs are posted regularly to Usenet and archived at sites accessible from the Web. People on the list will tell you where to look (they'll appreciate your finding the answers to those questions yourself rather than bothering them).

Contributing to a List

To contribute to a mailing list, all you have to do is send mail to a list address. If you're responding to a previous post, you can usually just reply in your mailer (but make sure that the To: address is the mailing list and not the individual who posted—how you can reply depends on how the list is set up). As with any mail, trim off as much of the quoted material as you can, but retain enough to make the context of your reply clear.

Keep your posts to a mailing list on-topic. It's natural for threads to occasionally drift from the main purpose of the list, but take your conversations to private e-mail as soon as they're obviously out of the scope of the list.

Responding Privately

As a general rule, err on the side of replying to individuals instead of to the list as a whole. There's nothing wrong with posting to the list, but some conversations naturally spawn side chats that really have nothing to do with the list. Before you post to a list, ask yourself if you're really just talking to the previous poster. If so, send the mail directly to her or him.

EXPERT ADVICE

Any time you're replying to a list post, check the To: line of your e-mail message to make sure you're sending the mail where you think you are.

Some lists are set up so that your mail programs' Reply command automatically posts back to the list. Others are set up so that your reply goes automatically to the individual poster. Here's how to make sure you respond to the right recipient:

1. Select the e-mail address of the sender and copy it (CTRL-C).
2. Press CTRL-R (or use your mail program's Reply command).
3. Check the address in the To: line.
   - If the address is that of the original poster, leave it alone.
   - If the address is to that of the list, delete it and replace it with the address of the original poster as shown in Figure 5.7.

Delete this list address
by pressing the DELETE
key and then paste
(or type) the original
poster's personal
e-mail address.

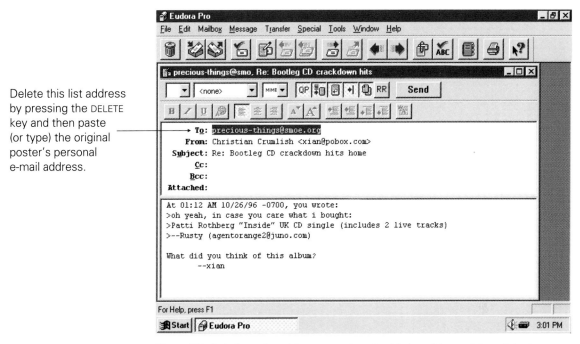

Figure 5.7 Deleting a list address to replace it with the address of the original poster

Avoiding Flame Wars

Probably because the communication is not face to face, e-mail makes it easy for people to lose their tempers and send insulting mail to each other. Such messages are called flames, and when they're sent to a mailing list they can engender a long series of flames and counterflames, known collectively as a flame war. It may be tempting to get in there and mix it up with everyone, especially the first time you see this happening, but it's really a waste of everyone's time. Often the original offense was simply a poorly worded message that a reader construed as an insult. Stay out of flame wars and don't fan the fire.

Some people like flaming so much that they post deliberately inflammatory messages, called flamebait. If you read something that fills you with the urge to immediately reply in terms as scathing as possible, pause for a moment and think about whether that is precisely how the writer hoped you would respond. Don't give the writer the satisfaction.

If someone misinterprets something you wrote and takes offense, just apologize. No harm will be done, and you may make a new friend. Many a flame war has been headed off by a timely apology. Later, think about what you wrote and be more careful in the future about how you put things.

Chapter 4 explains how to let your e-mail correspondents know you'll be away for a while.

Going on Vacation

If you'll be away from your e-mail for a while, you may want to temporarily unsubscribe from your mailing lists. For most mailing lists, you'll have to send an unsubscribe message as described earlier: mail to the list-request address (not the list itself!) with an empty subject, and the word unsubscribe followed by the name of the list.

Listserv mailing lists have an option that keeps you on the list but halts the sending of mail. To invoke this, send mail to the listserv (or listproc) address, typing **set** *listname* **nomail** on a line by itself. When you return, send the message **set** *listname* **mail** to start the messages coming again. (Don't type the word "*listname*"—substitute the actual name of the list, just as you did when you first subscribed.) You won't be sent the messages you missed, but if your mailing list has an archive of old articles, you can hunt for them there (if you have the time).

Trying Out a List

Are you ready to subscribe to a mailing list? How about Win Treese's popular and sporadic (thankfully) list of Internet trivia, called the Internet Index (modeled somewhat on the famous Harper's Index). This is a one-way list, by the way, not a discussion list.

STEP BY STEP Subscribe to a List of Internet Trivia

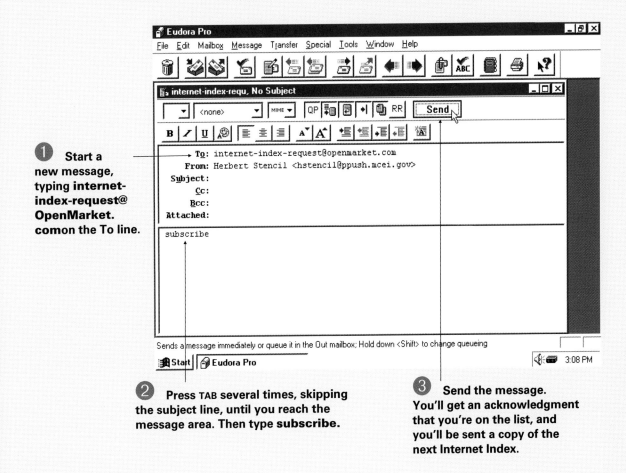

1 Start a new message, typing **internet-index-request@ OpenMarket. com** on the To line.

2 Press TAB several times, skipping the subject line, until you reach the message area. Then type **subscribe**.

3 Send the message. You'll get an acknowledgment that you're on the list, and you'll be sent a copy of the next Internet Index.

Where to Now?

Once you've tried out some mailing lists, you'll probably want to explore the largest set of discussion groups on the planet: Usenet. Chapter 6 explains Usenet, and Chapter 7 tells you how to have live, real-time conversations. Later chapters cover information and software resources on the Net.

Once you've dipped your toes into the world of mailing lists, your e-mail experience starts to expand from a private world of you, your friends, family, and

coworkers, to a much larger public world. In this worldwide e-mail network, you'll meet people from all walks of life, many of whom you may never have met in person, regardless of your shared interests. Communicating with others in ongoing mailing-list conversations is one of the popular pleasures of the Internet. It can also crowd your in-box and your time. Another way to discuss matters with others on the Internet is through the Usenet newsgroup system, explained in Chapter 6.

Reading Usenet Newsgroups

INCLUDES

- Understanding newsgroups
- Using Usenet as a public forum
- Using newsgroups as information sources
- Using moderated newsgroups
- Avoiding flames
- Understanding the basics of newsreading
- Choosing a newsreader
- Searching the Usenet feed

FAST FORWARD

Understand Usenet ➤ pp. 192-193

Subscribed Groups

	49	alt.folklore.urban
	1	alt.food.coffee
	5	alt.irc
	10	alt.religion.kibology
		ba.forsale
	26	ba.jobs.contract
	106	ba.jobs.offered
		news.announce.important

Usenet is

- A set of worldwide special-interest electronic bulletin boards
- A network of networks sharing public messages
- A huge system of discussion groups
- Organized hierarchically
- More or less a synonym for "newsgroups"

Usenet is *not*

- The Internet (though it mostly lives there)
- Part of some online service
- Private
- Accessible only in the U.S.

Read about Usenet Online ➤ pp. 193-197

Welcome to Usenet! This periodic posting describes the the major Usenet announcement newsgroups. There are the four moderated newsgroups in the news.announce.hierarchy -- news.announce.important, news.announce.newgroups, news.announce.newusers and news.announce.conferences. The moderated groups news.admin.technical, news.answers and news.lists are also described, since they are closely related to the announcement newsgroups.

- Check out the Usenet Info Center FAQ.
- Read the articles in the news.answers newsgroup.
- Spend some time lurking in newsgroups before posting questions.

Set Up a Newsreader ➤ p. 200

User	**System**	Online
News Server:		
Email Server:		

To set up a newsreader, you generally have to supply

- The Internet address of your news server
- The location of your Newsrc file (if you have one)

Read Newsgroups (General Procedure) ➤ pp. 200-202

1. Run a newsreader (or connect from an online service).
2. Subscribe to newsgroups.
3. Select a newsgroup.
4. Choose an article or thread.
5. Read and possibly respond to an article.

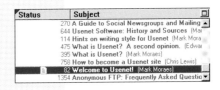

You can then move from article to article and from thread to thread and post new articles.

Read Newsgroups with Netscape News ➤ p. 204

1. Enter a newsgroup name in the Location box (in the form news:*newsgroup.name*).
2. Click an article to read it.
   - To respond by e-mail, click the Reply (Re: Mail) button.
   - To post a follow-up to the newsgroup, click the Post Reply (Re: News) button.
   - To post a new article to a newsgroup, click the Post New (To: News) button.

Go to: news:misc.answers

Read Newsgroups with Agent or Free Agent ➤ pp. 212-213

1. Select a newsgroup by double-clicking its name in the Subscribed Groups pane.
2. Read an article by selecting it in the Newsgroup pane.
   - To respond by e-mail, press R.
   - To post a follow-up, press F.
   - To post a new article, press P.

You've probably heard the words "Usenet," "Netnews," and "newsgroups" by now, but you may not be sure what they really refer to. All three terms are more or less synonyms. *Usenet* stands for User's Network and is often spelled in all capital letters. It is an international network of networks, distributed largely via the Internet but not exactly equivalent to the Internet. There are people not on the Internet with access to Usenet and vice versa. For the most part, though, if you have Internet access, you have access to the Usenet newsgroups.

Netnews is a synonym for Usenet, referring to the news system in general. Articles posted to Usenet discussion groups are often referred to as news or Usenet news, although the analogy to newspapers is not a perfect one. The discussion groups are called *newsgroups*. The contents of newsgroups are contributed by the readers, who post articles and respond to articles previously posted in the group or by e-mail.

CAUTION

If you're really busy, resist Usenet; it's highly addictive and can eat up all your time, even if you find just a newsgroup or two to read every day. It's not surprising that a lot of the traffic is college students, who often have time on their hands.

Before the Web's popularity soared, Usenet was the biggest attraction on the Internet. Because of its interactive nature, Usenet still constitutes the public space of the Net, where ideas are hashed out and personal relationships are formed. If there is an Internet culture, it derives largely from the communication in Usenet newsgroups (along with e-mail and live chatting).

A large number of newsgroups are technically not part of the Usenet system. From your point of view, the only real difference will be that non-Usenet newsgroups are not carried as widely or as consistently by some Internet service providers. I'll go into more detail about distinguishing Usenet from non-Usenet groups later in this chapter.

There are many different ways to get access to newsgroups, but don't let this confuse you—although the way newsreaders look and operate varies, the basic functionality stays the same. All newsreaders provide a way to display news articles and respond to them in a number of ways. In this chapter I'll first show you, in general, how to operate a newsreader and read Usenet newsgroups, so that no matter what method you use, you'll have some idea of what you're doing. Then I'll demonstrate several different ways to read news—via an online service such as Microsoft Network, through a web browser such as Netscape, and by using several different popular Windows newsreader programs.

For more background on Usenet, check out a highly informative document called the Usenet Info Center FAQ, available on the Web at http://sunsite. unc.edu/usenet-i/info-center-faq.html.

On the other hand, if you just need to look busy, Usenet is perfect, because you'll seem to be hard at work when you're really comparing memories of when you first saw Star Wars, or whatever.

DEFINITION

FAQ: *A list of frequently asked questions (FAQs), usually created collaboratively by the members of a discussion group (such as a mailing list or newsgroup) and maintained by volunteers. Pronounced "fack."*

The Mechanics of Usenet

One advantage newsgroups have over mailing lists is that the messages (articles) posted to them do not appear in your mailbox, but are instead stored in a central location. All your computer or software has to keep track of is which messages you've already seen. You can read or ignore any article or even entire threads—ongoing conversations, with responses linked to preceding comments.

Most news servers eventually "expire" old messages, clearing them away to make disk space available for current news, but I doubt that anything ever posted to Usenet is completely erased, considering how many machines all over the planet even briefly carry the news articles, and considering that many networks regularly back up their disks.

In fact, in the same way that many mailing lists maintain archives of past articles, Usenet articles (from the recent past to today or possibly yesterday) are now being stored and indexed at search sites, available to anyone who cares to look. (Eventually, back articles may be added to the databases as well.) We'll get to those search sites later.

To continue with the news metaphor, deciding to read a group regularly is called subscribing to it, even if all that means is that the name of the group appears in your regular list whenever you run your newsreading program. (That is, you won't see the articles in the newsgroup unless you explicitly check for them.)

Because news posts propagate outward from the author's news server to the rest of the news servers on the globe, you can't always be sure that you're seeing articles in the same order in which they were written (you also can't be positive that you're seeing *every* article, for that matter). This can lead to threads that go in circles as old comments are reiterated.

One expert estimates that, taken together, there are now over 20,000 Usenet and alternative newsgroups (and more are created every day).

DEFINITION

Thread: In a newsgroup, an ongoing conversation consisting of an article and a series of related follow-ups.

Categories of Usenet Newsgroups

Newsgroups are organized hierarchically, into categories and subcategories. Ideally, this organization helps you find the newsgroup you want, but it's not always clear where to look. The official Usenet hierarchy includes seven main categories, as shown in Table 6.1. These categories are divided into newsgroup names by dots, Unix-style—so the newsgroup for discussing the Microsoft Windows operating system, for example, is called comp.sys.os.mswindows.

Newsgroup Hierarchy	Meaning
comp	Computers
misc	Miscellaneous (could be anything)
news	News (Usenet news, that is—information on the Usenet system itself)
rec	Recreation (music, sports, games)
soc	Social (social groups, discussions of society)
sci	Science
talk	Talk (mostly debate)

Table 6.1 The "Big Seven" Usenet Categories

There's talk of it now being the "Big Eight" with the addition of a humanities hierarchy (to help balance the heavy math/science orientation), but so far there are not many newsgroups in this eighth hierarchy.

There are assorted other top-level categories beyond the Big Seven Usenet newsgroups. The most popular is *alt* (which stands for "alternative"), where many of the more provocative newsgroups can be found. Newsgroups in these other categories work about the same way as the Big Seven newsgroups do, but they can be formed much more easily (creating a newsgroup in one of the Big Seven categories requires a formal discussion and voting process), though they are not as well distributed.

CAUTION

Users with female (or female-sounding) names or usernames may experience unwanted solicitations from male adolescent types just for posting publicly. It's best to develop a thick skin about this kind of thing or affect a gender-neutral username. This problem is worse in the more controversial, sex-related newsgroups.

Usenet as a Public Space

Usenet is essentially a public space. You should never post anything to a newsgroup that you wouldn't feel comfortable reading in the newspaper. Even e-mail is not as private as it seems, because so many people can look at unencoded e-mail as it happens to pass through their system, but Usenet posts are intended for a public audience and are not suitable for private or sensitive information.

CAUTION

Remember never to post someone's private e-mail messages to public discussion groups, Usenet or otherwise. Also bear in mind that unscrupulous business people feel no compunction about scooping up e-mail addresses from newsgroups and adding them to junk mailing lists.

In general, posting publicly can result in e-mail responses. This is fine when you are looking for information or contacts, but it can be a nuisance if you are trying to keep your e-mail under control. If you receive unwanted mail, be polite but firm about not wanting to receive it and then delete anything else that comes from that same source.

Using Usenet to Find Information

See Chapter 3 for more on searching the Net for specific information.

Usenet is not really an information medium, although information abounds in the groups—in other words, it is not a reference library. Because the contents are always shifting and no one is obliged to answer your questions for you, it's difficult to go to newsgroups with a specific question and be sure of getting an answer. Then again, it doesn't hurt to ask.

netiquette

When checking into a new group, ask if there is a FAQ available that might answer your question without burdening the entire newsgroup with a question the group sees all the time.

Remember that the people who contribute to newsgroups do so voluntarily, so if you want to ask a question, try lurking on the group for a while first to see if your question is answered and to get a feel for the preferred mode of discourse there (every group is different).

There is a joke on Usenet that the best way to get information is to post wrong information and wait for people to correct you. Naturally, people won't appreciate it if you knowingly post incorrect information, but this gives you a sense of at least one dynamic at work on the Net: one-upmanship.

DEFINITION

Trolling: Deliberately posting incorrect information for the purpose of eliciting know-it-all responses. Trollers get a big kick out of watching people leap to correct others: "Telly Savalas was not the Captain of the Love Boat!" and so on.

There is a set of newsgroups whose names end in the word "answers" (such as news.answers, misc.answers, alt.answers, and so on) that regularly post FAQs and other informational documents. Try looking in these groups when you need an answer. (You can't post questions to these groups—however, there are some newsgroups whose names end in the word "questions" where you can.) Figure 6.1 shows the news.answers newsgroup.

Usenet Culture

Some people will barge into a newsgroup, start asking questions, demand answers, and then complain about not being served. The response to this type of behavior will range from "hey, we're not the reference room staff; we live here" to "don't let the door hit your behind on the way out." Newsgroup regulars tend to think of their group as a location, a place where they can expect to see their friends and where people interact in some agreed-upon way. Some newsgroups (such as alt.callahans, for example) have elaborate ongoing metaphors that establish an imaginary space (in the case of alt.callahans, a bar that is featured in a series of science fiction stories) and a lot of play-acting. Most groups don't take the concept that far, but many have cliques, running jokes, and traditions.

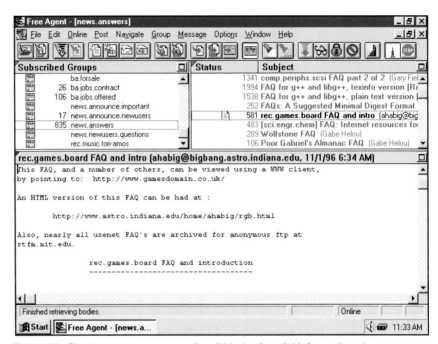

Figure 6.1 Check out news.answers for all kinds of useful information about Usenet itself

Moderated Newsgroups

Some newsgroups, such as the *.answers groups, are moderated, meaning (just as with moderated mailing lists) that a volunteer screens all potential posts to the group and passes on only those that are on-topic. Most newsgroups are not moderated (which will become readily apparent to you once you start poking around). To post a message to a moderated group, just do what you'd normally do. Instead of immediately posting your article, the news software will mail your submission to the moderator. The moderator may or may not send you an automated response to indicate that he or she has received your post. You may also get a note telling you whether your article was accepted or rejected, as shown here. If it was accepted, it will appear in the newsgroup.

Dear Contributor,

Thank you for your recent submission to alt.usenet.manifestoes.
Your submission has been approved. (All articles are accepted that
are on topic, non-commercial and not cross-posted.) Look for your
submission to appear shortly. If your submission does not appear
within three days, please let me know.

To submit another manifesto, please send it to manifesto@emf.net.

To view the archive, browse http://www.emf.net/~estephen/manifesto.html

Thanks again. Thanks to you, alt.usenet.manifestoes is a success.
This has been a recording. To receive a personal reply, please
send e-mail to manifesto-request@emf.net.

E. Stephen Mack
Moderator, alt.usenet.manifestoes

Flames and Flame Wars

As with mailing lists—but even more so—in newsgroups there is always the danger that an insensitive phrasing, a raw nerve, or a deliberate baiting will result in flames: either serious or hilariously exaggerated attacks on another poster. Flames often bring counterflames and sometimes erupt into full-fledged flame wars.

Along with the trollers out there having fun at the expense of earnest newbies, there are also flame baiters who deliberately post articles that skewer the sacred cow of a particular group. When you are presented with a post that obviously, after a moment's thought, is designed to enrage you, the best reaction is to delete the thing and forget it. The key here is the moment of thought you take before responding. Don't give flamebaiters what they want.

EXPERT ADVICE

The best newsreader programs allow you to create killfiles, essentially lists of undesirable authors or topics to screen out preemptively.

The Basic Newsreading Drill

More important than learning the specific menu commands and keyboard shortcuts of a particular program is to first get a feel for what is entailed in reading newsgroups. Then the specific commands and techniques will have a context (plus you can always refer to this chapter if you forget a specific command).

One-Time Setup

Usually the first time you run a newsreader, you may have to do some setup. You'll need to know the Internet address of your news server (this can be a name, such as news.net-provider.com, or a number, such as 192.0.2.1). You may also have to set up a file called a Newsrc (the name comes from Unix) that keeps track of the groups you've subscribed to and what articles in them you've seen. See Chapter 2 for information about news servers.

Subscribing to Groups

Subscribing to groups is not a one-shot deal. You can add or subtract groups from your subscription list at will.

Most newsreaders will start you off automatically subscribed to a few informational newsgroups, such as news.announce.newusers, but some will try to subscribe you to the entire list of available groups (depending on your newsfeed, there could easily be over 10,000), and others will start you off unsubscribed to any groups.

It's then up to you to browse the list of available groups and choose the ones you'd like to subscribe to, at least to begin with. You can unsubscribe and resubscribe as often as you like.

Reading the News

It's possible to search all newsgroups for key words, but not with a typical newsreader program. See "Searching the Vast Usenet Feed" later in this chapter.

Reading the news itself mainly consists of selecting threads and articles to read or ignore (based on their headers) and then reading what you choose. Some groups have a very low signal-to-noise ratio, meaning that there are a lot of useless articles crowded around the interesting ones. With these groups, you do as much news weeding as newsreading.

Navigating Newsgroups

Not all newsreaders are "threaded," or capable of displaying and providing link relationships among articles, but most are. Technically, a threaded newsreader has to be able to read an "overview" database to track the relationships between articles. Other newsgroups approximate threading by sorting articles by their Subject lines (including those that start with "Re:", for instance). With a threaded newsreader you can read an article and then jump directly to an article that replies to it or to an earlier article in the same thread. Outside of threads, navigating a newsgroup consists of moving from article to article.

Marking Articles

Most newsreaders allow you to select the articles you want to read first and then read only those articles. Some let you mark articles as read without actually reading them, as a way of clearing them out. A few newsreaders let you grab news headers and make your article selections offline and then connect again (briefly) to download only those articles and threads you marked.

Killing Threads and Bozos

Some newsreaders let you "kill" an entire thread, or mark it so your newsreader will ignore the thread and not show you its headers. This capability can make news weeding a lot easier, especially in very noisy newsgroups.

If you explore Usenet long enough you will encounter the online equivalent of "lone gunmen," who see their calling as inhabiting discussion groups and distorting them, inflaming them, or otherwise drowning out the group's signal with their noise. With any good newsreader, you can also kill (list in your killfile) a name or e-mail address whose posts you'd like filtered out of the newsfeed *before* you see it. Poof! Bozo is gone.

Responding to Articles

Usenet is an interactive medium, so if an article inspires you to respond, whether to agree or argue, you can do so either by sending mail to the author of the article or by posting a follow-up in the newsgroup. Which you decide to do depends mainly on the context of your reply and whether your follow-up bears directly on the topic of the newsgroup and is of general interest. If your response is of interest only to the author, send a personal e-mail.

EXPERT ADVICE

When responding to an article, check the headers for a Follow-ups to: line. Watch out for follow-ups leading to nowhere—some people want to have the last word so badly that they make follow-ups to their article appear in a completely irrelevant group.

Posting a New Article

You can also start your own threads in most newsgroups, without having to respond to an existing article. If you're posting for the first time ever, consider posting to one of the test newsgroups, such as alt.test, misc.test, new.test, and so on. You can experiment without bugging anyone, and autoresponding robots will send you replies from various news servers to let you know your test was successful.

CAUTION

Some pranksters set the "Follow-Ups To" header on their posts to test newsgroups to trick unwary responders into accidentally posting there. The result is a mailbox full of test replies.

EXPERT ADVICE

If you do want to post a test, definitely do post to a test group. Posting tests to nontest groups will make people mad at you. If you don't want tons of autoresponders to reply to your message, just stick the word "Ignore" somewhere in the subject line.

When you post an article, it may not appear immediately. In fact, it might take several hours or even days to appear. Don't resubmit your article just because you don't see it immediately, or else you risk having your post appear more than once—a major annoyance to other users.

Some articles are cross-posted to more than one newsgroup, and some have a Follow-Up header directing posted replies to a specific newsgroup. Pay attention to where your follow-ups are going so you don't accidentally post where you didn't mean to.

Appending Signatures

As with e-mail programs, some newsreaders can append a signature file to the end of your replies and newsgroup posts. You may recall from Chapter 4 that a signature is a tag line or block of text attached to the end of some or all of your e-mail messages (or, in this case, newsgroup posts). It's traditional to keep signatures to four lines or fewer on Usenet, and overtly commercial signatures are unwelcome in some newsgroups.

Newsreading Offline

Some newsreaders can function when not connected to the Internet, allowing you to choose threads, read downloaded articles, and compose replies without using any connect time. Then the newsreader can go online briefly to update newsgroups and post your replies.

EXPERT ADVICE

Newsreaders that enable offline newsreading (such as Agent, described later in this chapter) can help prevent a lot of wasted time online for busy people.

Ways to Read the News

As with e-mail, Usenet messages carry headers that enable newsreaders to sort the messages and relate them to other messages. Not all newsreaders, however, take advantage of all the available information, so each newsreader offers a different subset of possible features.

Your Internet service provider will give you access to a newsfeed (via an NNTP address), but it won't necessarily give you a newsreader. You have to choose your method for reading the news. The three most common ways to browse newsgroups are with a newsreader program (or module), from within an online service, or by using a Usenet-search web page.

If you use a newsreader (the traditional approach), then you have to choose a program. Some are built in to or designed to work with web browsers (such as Netscape News and Microsoft Internet News). Of the stand-alone newsreaders out there, most are native to one specific type of computer (such as Windows, Macintosh, or Unix), and some are designed for both mail and newsreading.

With online services, you use the service's basic software to read newsgroups in exactly the same way as you read their members-only bulletin boards or forums. Look for Internet or Newsgroups as keywords.

The web sites that index the Usenet feed have grown from basic search sites into web-based newsreaders from which you can also post articles.

Choosing a Newsreader

The only way to choose a newsreader is to try some out and find one whose commands and layout are comfortable for you. They all give you access to the same news. If you want to download shareware or demo versions of some browsers, visit clnet's Shareware.com and Download.com web sites.

In the rest of this chapter, I'll show you how to use Netscape News, Microsoft Internet News, Agent (and Free Agent) for Windows, and News-Watcher for the Macintosh.

I use a text-only Unix program called Trn to read the news, but I'm a fossil. Even most Unix-heads use Tin instead.

Netscape News

The News module of Netscape Navigator (to be supplanted by Netscape Messenger in the expected Netscape Communicator release), does a fair job of presenting a traditional news interface (a place to choose newsgroups, a place to choose articles, and a message area) while sticking pretty close to its own more comfortable web interface.

Netscape's approach means that images can be embedded in news articles as they are on the Web (as explained in Chapter 10), though this leaves out the non-web-enabled people out there.

I showed you how to set up Netscape News in Chapter 2.

Any URLs mentioned in news posts are automatically treated as hyperlinks. Click one, and the Navigator (browser) window swings back in front of the News window and connects to the linked reference.

One-Time Setup for Netscape News

As with any newsreader, you have to tell Netscape the name or address of the news server from which it should get its feed. To do so (after writing down the correct information), select Options | Mail and News Preferences and click the Servers tab. Click the News (NNTP) Server box and type the address of your news server.

Subscribing to Groups with Netscape News

To start reading the news in Netscape, select Window | Netscape News. Double-click the correct news server if more than one is offered. To add a newsgroup to your subscription list,

1. Select File | Add Newsgroup.
2. Type the newsgroup's name in the dialog box that appears and click OK.
3. Click the subscription check box to add a yellow "subscribed" check mark.

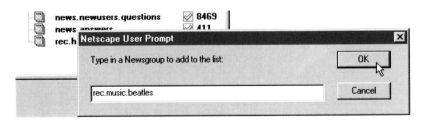

If you want to see what all the choices are (you'll have to be patient—there are hundreds of categories now, most of them bizarre or junk or full of spam), select Options | Show All Newsgroups and then go take a walk around the block.

DEFINITION

Spam: Unsolicited mail, especially mail sent to multiple unrelated recipients, often commercial mail. (From the Vikings in the Monty Python sketch who sang "Spam Spam Spam Spam," eventually crowding out all conversation.)

To add an additional news server to your choices, such as Microsoft's public news server,

1. Select File | Open News Host.
2. Type the server's address (such as msnews.microsoft.com) and then click OK.

Netscape User Prompt	✕
Open News Host	OK
msnews.microsoft.com	Cancel

Reading Netscape News

To start reading a newsgroup, click its name.

SHORTCUT

You can jump directly to a newsgroup from the browser module by typing news: newsgroup.name.here *in the Location box.*

To read an article, simply click its title in the list of articles (see Figure 6.2).

Posting a Follow-Up in Netscape News

To post a follow-up article, click the Post Reply button ("Re:News") on the toolbar.

Forward this post to a friend via e-mail.

Submit
a joke
of your
own to
rec.humor.
funny.

Active
newsgroups
(a check
mark means
you're
subscribed)

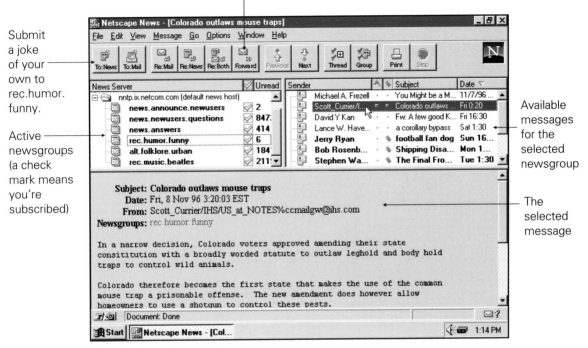

Available
messages
for the
selected
newsgroup

The
selected
message

Figure 6.2 Clicking an article

This brings up the Send Mail / Post News window. Netscape News quotes the article for you automatically. You may want to resize the window so the lines wrap correctly.

Type your reply and trim as much of the quoted article as possible. Then click the Send button (see Figure 6.3).

To reply by e-mail, click the Reply button ("Re:Mail") on the toolbar. This will bring up Netscape's Send Mail / Post News window with the author's name already in place in the Mail To: box. Otherwise, the procedure is the same as for posting a reply to the newsgroup.

Posting a New Article in Netscape News

To post a new article to a newsgroup, click the Post New ("To:News") button on the toolbar.

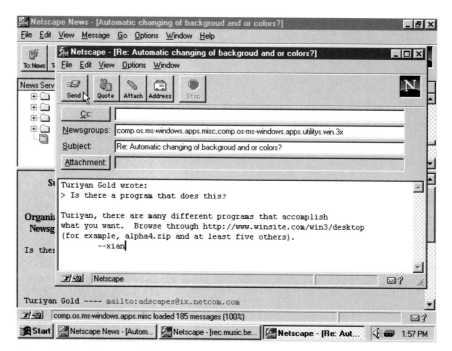

Figure 6.3 Posting an article to a newsgroup

Type in the Send Mail / Post News dialog box that appears. When you're ready (and sure you want to post), click the Send button.

Netscape Newsreading Miscellany

Netscape supports signature files.

1. Select Options | Mail and News Preferences.
2. Click the Identity tab and enter the name of the sig file in the Signature File box.

EXPERT ADVICE

To approximate offline newsreading with Netscape, click on all the articles you want to read, one after another (without stopping to read them). Netscape will store those articles in its cache. You can now disconnect from the Internet and read the selected articles at your leisure.

Netscape does not have the capability to filter out nuisance posts with killfiles (lists of threads to ignore), nor can you read news offline with it (yet).

Microsoft Internet News

Microsoft Internet News looks and feels exactly like Internet Mail (as discussed in Chapter 4). It's a reasonably good news interface, well integrated with Internet Explorer.

You have to tell Internet News the name or address of the news server from which it should get its feed. The first time you run Internet News, it will prompt you for this information using the Internet News Configuration wizard. Click Next to begin entering information.

Microsoft's approach means that images can be embedded in news articles as they are on the Web (as explained in Chapter 10), though this leaves out the non-web-enabled people out there.

1. Enter your name and e-mail address and then click Next.
2. When you are prompted for the name of your news server, enter the machine name (your Internet service provider should have told you what it is).
3. Most likely you won't need to log on, so leave the Logon settings fields blank.
4. Click Next and indicate whether you use a network, manual, or modem connection. Then click Next, and you're done.
5. Click Finish, and you can use Internet News and begin subscribing to newsgroups.

If you ever need to change any of this setup information (for example, after changing Internet service providers), use the News | Options command and click the Server tab.

After you've finished setting up Internet News, you'll automatically be prompted to subscribe to new groups. You don't have to subscribe to all of them now; any time you want to add a new newsgroup to your subscribed list, you can click the Newsgroups button on the toolbar.

To add a newsgroup to your subscription list, select it from the list of Newsgroups that is displayed. You'll have to be patient the first time, since there are bezillions of newsgroups, and the list takes some time to download. Since it's inefficient to scroll through such a long list, you can type a keyword in the "Display newsgroups which contain" box at the top of the screen. Only those newsgroups containing your keyword will be listed. You can then select the newsgroup you want to subscribe to. If you want, next enter a different keyword to get a new list. Repeat this process until you have subscribed to several groups.

STEP BY STEP Subscribe to a Group

1 **Type a keyword here.**

Newsgroups

Display newsgroups which contain:

humor

Newsgroups

- alt.humor.oracle
- alt.humor.puns
- bln.humor
- chile.humor
- fido7.humor
- han.rec.humor
- mn.humor
- rec.humor
- rec.humor.d
- rec.humor.funny
- rec.humor.oracle
- rec.humor.oracle.d

Subscribe

Unsubscribe

Reset List

3 **Click the Subscribe button.**

All   Subscribed   New

Go to   OK   Cancel

2 **Click a newsgroup you're interested in.**

To start reading a newsgroup, you can click its name in the Newsgroups dialog box and then click the Go to button. Wait for the headers (the list of subjects, authors, dates, and sizes) to appear.

SHORTCUT

You can jump directly to a newsgroup from the Internet Explorer browser module by typing news:newsgroup.name.here in the Location box.

To pick a different newsgroup from your subscribed list, click the drop-down Newsgroups box below the toolbar. To see the full list of newsgroups again, click the Newsgroups button on the toolbar. If you know the name of the newsgroup you want, you can just type it in the Newsgroups box and press ENTER.

To read an article, simply click once on its subject in the list. It will be displayed in the lower half of the screen. If you'd prefer to read the article in its own window, just double-click.

To post a follow-up article,

1. Select the article you want to reply to and then click the Reply to Group button on the toolbar.
2. In the window that appears, type your reply and trim as much of the quoted article as possible.
3. Click the Send button.

To reply by e-mail, click the Reply to Author button on the toolbar. Your default e-mail program will appear (probably Internet Mail), with the author's e-mail address automatically selected in the To: box. As with posting, you'll want to trim down the original article's text and type your reply before clicking the Send button.

To post a new article to a newsgroup, click the New Message button on the toolbar.

The Newsgroups header line will contain the name of the currently selected newsgroup. You can type one or more different newsgroup names here, or use the News | Choose Newsgroups command to help you pick the desired newsgroups. Make sure you have an appropriate subject line (see Chapter 4 for suggestions); press TAB twice and type your subject. Press TAB again to type the body of your message. The Post Message button is the first button on the toolbar.

Internet News will let you add a signature to your messages if you want. Use the News | Options command and then click the Signature tab. You can type the signature in the Text box or indicate the location of a file. If you leave the "Add signature to the end of all outgoing messages" option checked, Internet News will automatically append your signature to every new article and follow-up you post. If you'd rather add the signature manually, uncheck this option and add your signature only when you desire, using the Insert | Signature command.

Internet News cannot create a killfile or bozo filter, nor can it ignore a particular thread. However, it does have excellent offline reading capabilities. Using the Offline menu, you can select messages, threads, and even entire Newsgroups for downloading and later perusal.

Windows-Only: Agent and Free Agent

Agent

There are many other newsreaders. Of those designed specifically for Windows, Agent seems to be the most full-featured, and the Free Agent version of the program is available for, uh, free.

Other Windows newsreaders include WinVN and News Xpress.

netiquette

A long-standing practice of software developers on the Internet is to make available a free reduced-function version of a program (such as Eudora Light versus Pro) and also to beta test new software by allowing users to download and use it for free. If you opt for the more expensive version of a program, you usually get more features and technical support. These approaches are similar to a shareware agreement, by which you can try out a program for free but are morally obliged to pay for it if you continue to use it. You can minimize your chances of encountering bugs by paying for commercially released software.

Agent's pluses and minuses are as follows:

- **Pluses:** Its supports multiple signature files; it offers thread selection and killing; it has a flexible window design; and it allows offline newsreading
- **Minuses:** It offers almost too many options (confusing); its window design takes some getting used to; it can use up lots of disk space with downloaded articles, unless you purge often

The following table summarizes the essentials for Agent and Free Agent.

Where to get it	http://www.forteinc.com/store/ or http://www.forteinc.com/getfa/download.htm
Set it up	Options	General Preferences (it prompts you for setup information the first time you run it).
Subscribe to a group	Group	Show	All Groups. To subscribe to a group, select it and press CTRL-S (which also unsubscribes a subscribed group).
Select a newsgroup	Click its name in the Groups pane to see previously retrieved messages. Double-click the newsgroup name and click Get All Message Headers to download a list of current messages.
Read an article	Select it in the Message List pane and press ENTER or double-click it (go online—press CTRL-O—if nothing happens).
Navigate a newsgroup	Use the Navigate menu (keyboard shortcuts are listed on the menu).
Mark articles and kill threads	Use the Message menu (keyboard shortcuts are listed on the menu) or right-click the message in the Message List pane.
Respond by e-mail	Press R.
Post a follow-up	Press F.
Post a new article	Press P.

Macintosh-Only: NewsWatcher

For the Macintosh, NewsWatcher seems to be the most popular newsreader. The following table summarizes the basic commands for NewsWatcher.

NewsWatcher

Where to get it	ftp://ftp.acns.nwu.edu/pub/newswatcher/ (or try http://www.shareware.com)
Set it up	Edit | Preferences
Subscribe to a group	Special | Subscribe
Select a newsgroup	Double-click it in the Full Group window (or your own window)
Read an article	Double-click it
Navigate a newsgroup	News | Next Article, News | Next Thread
Mark articles and kill threads	News | Mark Read
Respond by e-mail	News | Send Message
Post a follow-up	News | Reply
Post a new article	News | New Message

Using News Search Sites to Keep Up with Usenet

The Web itself is turning into a sort of news interface, not just with programs such as Navigator Internet News, but also at web sites where you can search the newsfeed and post to newsgroups. In some ways, mail, news, and the Web are all converging into a platform that anyone can use to compose messages or multimedia documents or other objects and publish them on the Web, post them to newsgroups, or send them to e-mail recipients.

If you want to filter the articles by newsgroup, date, author, or subject (you can use wildcards), click the Power Search link and choose "Create a query filter." On the page that appears, enter a newsgroup, date range, and author name and/or subject and then click the Create Filter button.

Two of the most popular Usenet search sites are Deja News and AltaVista.

Searching the Vast Usenet Feed

Finding anything on Usenet is difficult. For one thing, articles expire after a while. For another, you can never keep up with all the newsgroups where a given topic might be discussed. The Deja News web site is designed solely for searching the newsfeed. So far, it goes back only a few years, but its archives will keep growing, and new articles appear within a day or so of their posting.

To search Usenet articles for a topic, point your web browser at http://www. dejanews.com.

Location: http://www.dejanews.com/

Type a word (or words) to search for in the "Quick Search for" box. Then click the Find button. The Quick Search looks for recent articles that contain all of the keywords that you have entered.

If you'd like to search the entire database, you'll want to do a Power Search instead. The Power Search lets you change various options. If you want to see articles that match any of the words and not all of them, click Any next to "Keywords matched:". To search the older database, click Old instead of Current next to "Usenet database:".

When you're ready, click the Search button. Deja News will quickly generate a list of articles matching your search criteria (see Figure 6.4). Click the subject of an article to read it or click the author's name to see a profile of that author's Usenet postings.

Deja News found 35 articles containing my search terms; the first 25 are displayed on this page.

Refine your search by editing the keywords and clicking this button.

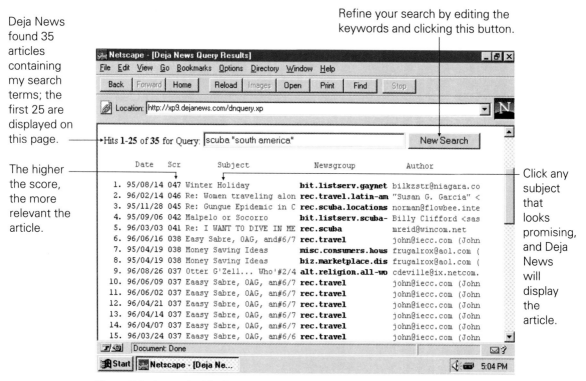

The higher the score, the more relevant the article.

Click any subject that looks promising, and Deja News will display the article.

Figure 6.4 I searched for "scuba" AND "South America" and got these articles

Reading News from a Usenet Search Site

At AltaVista, you can limit your search to a specific newsgroup by including +newsgroups:*news.group.name* as part of your search request. While you are reading articles, references to preceding posts in the thread will appear as numbered hyperlinks, so you can follow discussions as in a newsreader. E-mail addresses are hyperlinks, so you can reply to anyone by mail by clicking the person's address (the mail module or program associated with your browser will handle this). AltaVista does not currently let you post to Usenet, but Deja News does.

To post an article with Deja News,

1. Click an article from a search result. At the bottom and top of the article is a row of buttons, including a Post Article button. Clicking there will take you to a page giving guidelines and rules for posting.

STEP BY STEP Search News with AltaVista

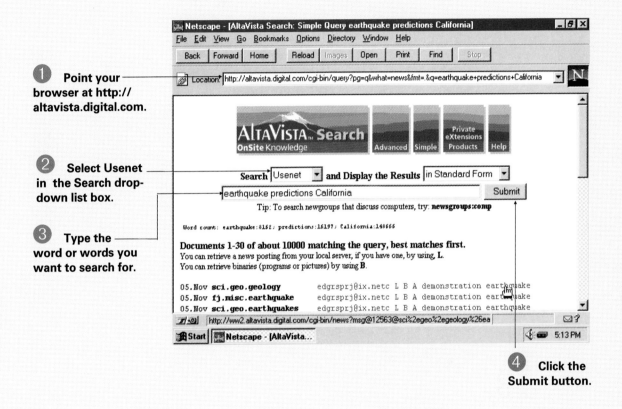

① Point your browser at http://altavista.digital.com.

② Select Usenet in the Search drop-down list box.

③ Type the word or words you want to search for.

④ Click the Submit button.

2. If you're not a Deja News registered user, you'll have to send Deja News a separate e-mail to confirm your post. (It's easy–and currently free–to register.) Fill in the required fields (your e-mail address in the From: field, a subject, and a list of newsgroups to post to, with the latter already filled in for you), type in a body, and then click the "Check your posting:" button.

3. If everything looks okay (including the spelling), click the gray "Looks OKAY, send it to me for confirmation!" button. Deja News' final screen tells you that your article has been spooled for authorization and that a confirmation e-mail was sent to your e-mail address. You'll have to return the e-mail (follow the instructions in that letter) to actually get your article to post.

Figure 6.5 shows a Deja News screen.

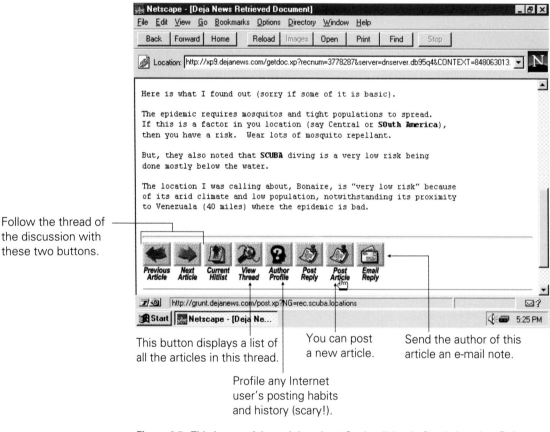

Follow the thread of the discussion with these two buttons.

This button displays a list of all the articles in this thread.

You can post a new article.

Send the author of this article an e-mail note.

Profile any Internet user's posting habits and history (scary!).

Figure 6.5 This is one of the articles about Scuba diving in South America; Deja News gives me several options, including posting (without a separate newsreader)

CHECK POINT

Now you've seen most of the ways that people communicate on the Net. They send e-mail, join mailing lists, and post to Usenet. All of these ways of communicating have a feature in common: they take place over a stretched-out period of time, with everyone participating at their leisure. The Internet can also be used for live conversation. Chapter 7 will tell you how to converse with people in real time, if that's your thing. (You still do it mostly by typing, but new forms of live communication are appearing all the time.)

After that, I'll show you some of the back channels of the Net and how to develop and publish web pages.

Chatting, Conferencing, and Virtual Worlds

FAST FORWARD

Understand Chatting ➤ pp. 224-227

Internet Relay Chat FAQ

What is IRC?

IRC stands for "Internet Relay Chat". It was originally written by Jar 1988. Since starting in Finland, it has been used in over 60 countries as a replacement for the "talk" program but has become much much

- Chatting means communicating live (in real time) with other people over the Internet, often just by typing but sometimes also via voice or video or some other medium.
- Many chat programs use the Internet relay chat (IRC) system, in which users communicate in discussion areas called channels.
- Other programs live on the Web or place the user in an imaginary world.

Participate in a Typical Chat Session ➤ pp. 229-239

```
<rackum> linty hi how r u
* GOLEM looks around the channel then
  wonders why Tex_Cowboy's clothes are
<rackum> lady
<Linty2> fine, how are you?
```

1. Run an IRC client or other chat program.
2. Connect to a server.
3. List channels.
4. Join a channel.
5. Type conversation.
6. Quit.

Talk (for Real) with Internet Phone ➤ p. 240

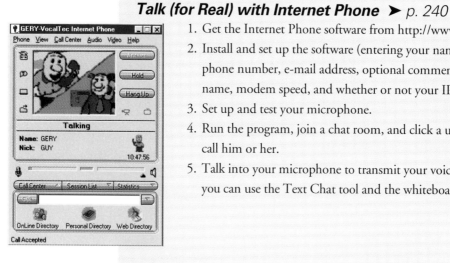

1. Get the Internet Phone software from http://www.vocaltec.com.
2. Install and set up the software (entering your name, nickname, phone number, e-mail address, optional comment, mail server name, modem speed, and whether or not your IP address is fixed).
3. Set up and test your microphone.
4. Run the program, join a chat room, and click a user's name to call him or her.
5. Talk into your microphone to transmit your voice. In addition, you can use the Text Chat tool and the whiteboard.

Run a Meeting over an Intranet (or the Web) ➤ pp. 241-242

1. Download NetMeeting from http://www.microsoft.com/ netmeeting/ (click the Download link and choose the appropriate version and language).

2. Double-click the file to install it. Fill out some personal information for the User Location Service (ULS), decide whether you wanted to be listed as available to take calls from other Internet Users, and then follow the instructions to test and set up your microphone.

3. Browse the list of online NetMeeting users to find someone to talk to (highlight the person's name and click the Call button), or enter the e-mail address of the person you want to speak with by using the Call | Place Call command.

4. Talk to others, share applications and documents, collaborate in shared programs, exchange files, draw on a shared whiteboard, and send typed messages with the Text Chat tool.

5. Click the Hang Up button when you're finished.

Chat in a 3D Virtual World ➤ pp. 242-244

1. Download the Worlds Chat demo from http://www.worlds.net/ (click the download demo link or go straight to http://www.worlds.net/wcg/wcg-download.html).

2. Fill out the registration form and submit it to download and install the Worlds Chat software.

3. Use the arrow keys to move around the gallery. Choose an avatar (online representation of yourself) by clicking the mouse button and then clicking the avatar you want to be. Enter the Worlds Chat space station.

4. Explore with the mouse or arrow keys. Type text and press ENTER to say something.

5. Use the File | Exit command to quit.

Some recent computer games, such as Monopoly, take advantage of the IRC infrastructure (without making a big deal of it) to enable players to compete over the Internet.

Online services such as AOL, CompuServe, and MSN all offer their own private chat facilities (limited to members of the service only). In AOL and MSN, they are called chat rooms, and in Compu-Serve they are called CBs (as in the '70s car-radio fad; remember "10-4, good buddy"?). None of these programs uses IRC, and the names of commands may differ; however, the principles underlying them are the same.

Besides the post office and bulletin board methods of communicating, the Internet also has the capability of supporting real-time interactive conversation. First there was a program called Talk that enabled two users to carry on sentence-by-sentence conversations. Next came chat, which enabled multiple users to communicate in this way. The current live-talk infrastructure on the Internet is called IRC, which stands for Internet relay chat. As with many other Internet facilities, IRC is a client-server system in which individuals run client programs to connect to centralized servers (and thence to other users).

There are also a number of newer technologies that incorporate more than just text in real-time transmissions. Many of these programs, such as Internet Phone, actually take advantage of the IRC protocols. The demands of fast-paced business today sometimes require *virtual* conferences, linking participants all over the globe in real-time meetings and strategy sessions. Besides enabling participants to talk to and possibly see each other, some of the new conferencing programs allow people to collaborate over the Net and even to share software.

Meanwhile, the live chat model has mutated and spread to the Web (where a number of web-based non-IRC chat systems reside) and to imaginary three-dimensional virtual worlds. Oh, to be young and have free time again!

Chat: Not for Busy People

I can't wholeheartedly recommend chatting with any of the various types of real-time communication software to anyone who's really busy, because it can be

I'm not going to go into the multi-user domains, or MUDs, that thrive on the Internet, powered mainly by the energy of college students staying up or procrastinating.

a slow way to talk (with lots of stray conversations passing through), and because it can suck you in so that hours go by without your noticing.

On the other hand, when my Internet dictionary was being translated into Portuguese in Brazil, the translator needed to ask me some questions, and we found e-mail to be slow going (we were sending many messages back and forth each day). We agreed on a convenient time to get together on IRC and had our conversation that way. So used cleverly, chatting can aid you in your busy schedule.

What Is IRC?

The basic unit of conversation in IRC is called a channel. At any given moment thousands of channels are active (and anyone can start a new one at any time). Interested users join the channel and communicate among themselves. You can type messages to everyone on the channel or send private messages to individuals.

In addition, at any given moment hundreds or thousands of channels are active on a particular server. There are hundreds of servers, most of which are networked together (the three major IRC server networks are Efnet, DALnet, and Undernet) and some of which stand alone. Most channels have fewer than a dozen participants, and some have just one or two, but some popular channels can involve hundreds of people at a time.

For more background information on IRC, see the IRC FAQ on the Web at http://www.kei.com/irc.html or the central reference to IRC-related documents (http://ftp.acsu.buffalo.edu/irc/WWW/ircdocs.html).

CAUTION

There are a lot of adolescent types on IRC, and you'll see many channels with bizarre names and lurid descriptions. Remember that the purpose of a system like IRC is to allow people to talk about what they want without getting in anyone else's way, so just ignore any channels with topics that bother you.

As with Usenet, IRC has various pockets containing different subcultures that may never meet up in their separate channels. For some aficionados, a big part of the fun of IRC is the element of fantasy and role playing.

bookmark

For more information on IRC, start at the IRC Help page on the Web (http://www.irchelp.org/).

IRC Lingo

Once you get on IRC, you'll hear a lot of unfamiliar jargon. Table 7.1 provides a quick briefing on some essential IRC jargon.

Expression	Means
nick	A nickname, your name on IRC (not necessarily your username).
channel	An IRC discussion area.
whisper	Send a private message.
channel operator	The person who created the channel (also channel op, chanop).
kick	To throw someone off an IRC channel (must have channel operator privileges to do this).
ban	To kick someone off an IRC more or less permanently.
bot	A program designed to behave like a person on the IRC; a robot.
netsplit	A temporary breakdown in the server network that results in the apparent disappearance of some participants in a conversation. Netsplits usually fix themselves.
motd	Message of the day.
lag	A delay between sending a message and seeing it show up in the channel.
MorF?	Are you male or female? (Asking is considered gauche by some.)
Re	Repeat the above greeting (and, by extension, "hello").

Table 7.1 IRC Jargon

Many of the acronyms popular in e-mail and discussion groups (such as IMHO for "in my humble opinion" and LOL for "laughing out loud") appear as frequently in chat conversations. People will sometimes describe what they (or their imaginary personas) are doing instead of addressing anyone directly.

IRC Server Networks

When you run an IRC client, you have to connect to a server, but the server you choose does not completely limit who you can communicate with. Large numbers of servers are allied in one of two networks. When you connect to a server, you can join any channel created on any of the servers networked to your server. The traditional IRC network is called Efnet. Two newer alternative networks are DALnet and the Undernet. They're all worth visiting. The Undernet touts itself as an alternative to the traditional network.

Most client programs will present you with a list of servers or at least a suggested or default server. Others will leave it up to you to supply a server name. The best servers are the ones that are geographically close to you. Here is a short list of Efnet servers to try if none are suggested by your program:

```
irc.nwlink.com (Washington, Efnet)
irc.sprynet.com (Washington, Efnet)
irc.neosoft.com (Texas, Efnet)
irc.cs.cmu.edu (Pennsylvania, Efnet)
irc.law.emory.edu (Georgia, Efnet)
irc.eng.yale.edu (Connecticut, Efnet) \
irc.mit.edu (Massachusetts, Efnet)
irc.hp.net (Colorado, EuroNet)
irc.aimnet.com (California, EuroNet)
irc.stealth.net (New York, EuroNet)
```

If you're prompted for a port number and none has been suggested, try 6667.

For DALnet, see the http://www.dal.net page on the Web for a list or try one of the following:

```
irc.dal.net (A random DALnet server)
centurion.dal.net (Florida)
```

```
dragon.dal.net (Utah)
dreamscape.dal.net (New York)
farside.dal.net (Texas)
mindijari.dal.net (Sunnyvale)
opus.dal.net (Illinois)
```

For the Undernet, try one of these:

```
us.undernet.org
austin.tx.us.undernet.org
manhattan.ks.us.undernet.org
pittsburgh.pa.us.undernet.org
saltlake.ut.us.undernet.org
sanjose.ca.us.undernet.org
rochester.mi.us.undernet.org
tampa.fl.us.undernet.org
washington.dc.us.undernet.org
```

EXPERT ADVICE

The official Undernet server list is available at http://servers.undernet.org/ serverlist.html. See also http://www.undernet.org. Alternately, to get a list of Undernet servers mailed to you, send a blank message to server-list @servers.undernet.org.

bookmark

For more information on DALnet, see http://www.dal.net. For more information on the Undernet, see http://www.undernet.org:8080/~cs93jtl/ Undernet.html or the Undernet IRC FAQ (http://www.undernet.org:8080/ ~cs93jtl/underfaq/).

If you're outside the U.S. or want to see a more complete list of servers, check the server lists stored at the ftp site (see Chapter 8) http://www.comco.com:80/dougmc/irc-stats/. If you're Usenet-savvy (see Chapter 6), visit the alt.irc newsgroup for an updated list.

EXPERT ADVICE

Your Internet service provider may have an IRC server of its own; for example, Netcom users should try irc.netcom.com.

Participating in an IRC Session

No matter what IRC client program you run, your chat session will work something like this: First you'll run your client. Next you'll connect to a server (this may happen automatically). Then you'll want to see a list of available channels. The most basic way to do this is to type **/list** at the prompt. Channel names all start with the # character, and the list of channels also tells you how many people are currently on the channel (including bots, if any) and what the channel's topic is.

EXPERT ADVICE

Some channels you may want to visit are #newbie (where you can ask IRC-related questions) and #riskybus (where you can practice your IRC skills by playing a trivia game).

Next you'll join a conversation. You do this by typing **/join** *channel-name.* Say hello and start "talking" (that is, typing). To send a private message to someone else, type **/msg** *their-nick your-message.*

Traditionally, all IRC commands start with a slash (/). Some of the new graphical IRC programs offer shortcut menus and buttons as well, but most decent IRC programs recognize all or most of the traditional slash commands. Table 7.2 lists essential slash commands that will work with any standard IRC client program.

Command	What It Does
/away *message*	Tells people you cannot read or respond to the conversation right now. (Type **/away** with no message when you're back.)
/help *command*	Displays information about a command.
/ignore *nick*	Screens unwanted communication from the specified user.
/join *#channel*	Connects you to the specified channel or starts it if it does not currently exist.
/part *#channel*	Disconnects you from the specified channel.
/list	Lists all current channels.
/list -min *x*-max *y*	Lists all current channels with at least *x* participants and no more than *y* participants.
/msg *nick*	Sends a private message to the specified user.
/nick *newnick*	Changes your nickname to a new nickname.
/query *nick*	Starts a private conversation with the specified user.
/quit	Disconnects from the server.
/who	Lists users on the current channel.
/whois *nick*	Gives known information about the specified user.

Table 7.2 Essential IRC Slash Commands

Here's a typical IRC session, using mIRC:

1. Connect to a server. (Decide if you want to connect to Efnet, DALnet, or the Undernet. Beyond that, choose a server geographically near to you.)

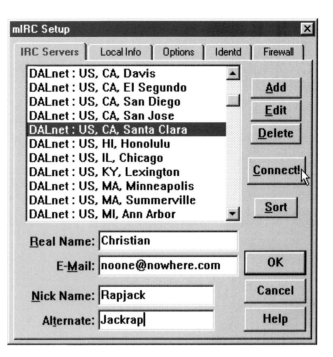

2. List channels. It's often easier to digest the list that shows up if you limit the channels to just those with between, say, three and four users. To do this, you would type **/list -min 3 -max 4**.

3. Join a conversation by typing **/join #channel** or double-clicking the channel name.

4. Chat away. Say hello, read the conversation, and jump in when you have something to say.

Some IRC Client Programs

Although most chat and IRC programs work alike, different programs are best on different platforms. In the next few sections I'll take you through the basics of a few of the more popular IRC clients.

> ## bookmark
>
> Check the DALnet FTP archive site (ftp://ftp.dal.net/dalnet/clients) if you're looking for IRC client software.

Other decent Windows IRC programs include VIRC and PIRCH (PolarGeek's IRC Hack, which you can download from http:// www.bcpl.lib.md.us/ ~frappa/pirch.html). Look to Stroud's IRC list at http://www.stroud.com/ 95irc.html for these and other IRC clients.

For help with downloading software, see Chapter 3.

mIRC for Windows

The most popular Windows IRC client is mIRC. (I asked the author of mIRC, Khaled Mardam-Bey, what the m in mIRC stands for, and he claims not to remember.) It's also free! While it has once or twice frozen up on me (what Windows program doesn't sometimes freeze?), overall it's pretty solid. It has an elegant layout, with each separate task or listing appearing in its own window, all behaving the way normal windows should. It has lots of excellent toolbar shortcuts, and you can right-click many items and choose from pop-up menus appropriate to the context. Try it.

To get a copy of mIRC, start at the mIRC home page (http://www. mirc.co.uk) and scroll down to select the Download link. Choose a site close to you and click the appropriate version (16-bit for Windows 3.1, 32-bit for Windows 95 or Windows NT). If you have trouble connecting, try one of the mirror pages, such as http://www2.axi.net/mirc/get.html.

To install mIRC, simply double-click the downloaded file. Click Install to accept the default options, and mIRC will install itself.

The first time you run the program, type your nick and press ENTER. mIRC comes with some server addresses preloaded.

mIRC32

To run mIRC, Double-click the mIRC32 icon. Close the About mIRC window and then click the Connect icon (the lightning bolt) or select File |

Connect. mIRC will prompt you with a list of popular channels. Either join one of these or use the /list command to get a complete list of channels in a new window. Use the Window menu to switch back and forth between windows. You can join a channel in the usual way (with the /join command) or by double-clicking a channel name.

Then type in the pane at the bottom of the window. The channel conversation will scroll through the large pane just above (see Figure 7.1). You'll notice that some people talk about themselves in the third person. These actions or narrations of a user's own behavior ("Jojo pats sydney99 on the back") are used to give more context or create the illusion of sharing a space together.

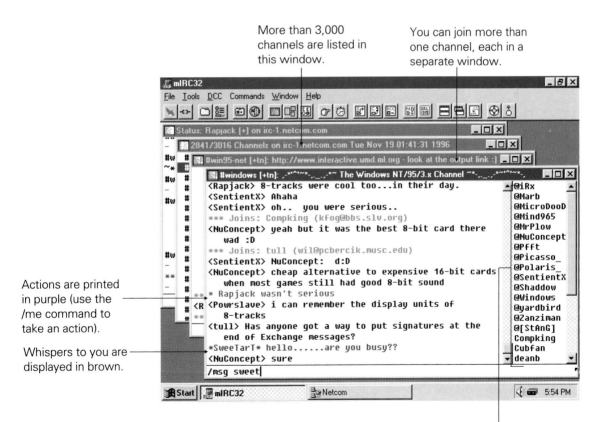

More than 3,000 channels are listed in this window.

You can join more than one channel, each in a separate window.

Actions are printed in purple (use the /me command to take an action).

Whispers to you are displayed in brown.

A list of all the people speaking in the #windows channel

Figure 7.1 Chatting with mIRC on the #windows channel

To leave a channel, just close the window it's in or use the /leave command. Exit the program in the normal way.

mIRC has a toolbar featuring essential commands and a number of options available on a pop-up shortcut menu by right-clicking. There are different shortcut menus for the channel user list, the channel itself, and the channel list window.

IRCle for the Macintosh

The most popular IRC client by far on the Macintosh side is IRCle. To get a copy of IRCle, visit http://www.xs4all.nl/ (or its mirror at http://www2.bridge. net/~ircle/) and click the language that you prefer. This will download a stuffit file for IRCle. You'll need the Stuffit Expander to unpack all of the files. (If you don't have this Macintosh tool, go to Shareware.com, as described in Chapter 3, and download and install it.) Unstuff the downloaded file by double-clicking its icon.

To run IRCle, double-click the IRCle icon. Then select File | Open to open a connection. The version of IRCle that you downloaded will probably have default settings, which you should change (with File | Preferences) once you get your bearings.

To join a conversation, select Command | Join and type a channel name in the dialog box that appears. To leave a conversation, just close the window it appears in. When you're typing your commands, or navigating from the menus, you'll notice your instructions appear in the Inputline box at the bottom of the screen.

Many standard IRC commands are available in the Command menu (List, Who, Query, Invite, WhoIs, Kick, Away, and Message, among others). IRCle also has a shortcuts menu with nine user-defined keystroke sequences, and a windows menu that allows you to tile or stack the windows on your screen, or bring to the foreground whatever window you wish. Figure 7.2 shows a typical IRCle session.

Microsoft Comic Chat

Microsoft's entry into the chat world is the innovative Comic Chat program. Under the skin, it's a fairly typical IRC program, but its display is unique. Instead of showing the running conversation as a script-type dialog, it renders the discussion in the form of a surreal comic book, in the style of (that is, using the licensed art of) underground comix artist Jim Woodring.

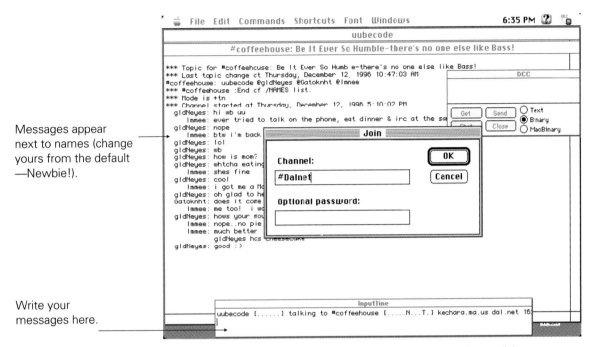

Messages appear next to names (change yours from the default —Newbie!).

Write your messages here.

Figure 7.2 Like a normal Macintosh program, IRCle floats each part of the program in a different window

The surrealism was a good idea (you have a choice of three equally bizarre looking locales) since so much of what passes for conversation on the IRC is non sequiturs anyway.

Comic Chat's home page is http://www.microsoft.com/ie/comichat/, but you can download Comic Chat directly from the Internet Explorer accessories download page at http://www.microsoft.com/ie/download/ieadd.htm—make sure to choose Comic Chat from the drop-down list and then click the Next button.

CAUTION

Microsoft Comic Chat does not recognize standard IRC slash commands— no problem if you never learned them!

One problem with Comic Chat is that there are not enough different character images, so you often can't tell who you're talking to!

Choose a vendor to download from and then double-click the file to install it. Currently, Comic Chat is available only to Windows 95 and Windows NT users.

The first time you use Comic Chat, it will prompt you for a nickname to use. Then you'll have the opportunity to connect to Microsoft's chat server (although you can also connect to any other IRC server). Use the View | Options command to choose a character for yourself and a facial expression to start with. You can also fill in your real name and a profile for other users. Figure 7.3 shows a Comic Chat session.

Spoken words, thoughts, and actions appear in comic book form.

Choose View | Options and click Characters to change your character.

Type here.

Double-click a URL to visit that page.

Change your expression with this emotion wheel.

Figure 7.3 Using Comic Chat

PowWow

PowWow is a program that lets up to seven people chat, send, and receive files and explore the World Wide Web program together. It's primarily text based, but it also includes voice chatting (using Internet Phone technology), a whiteboard program, and sound effects to share with other users.

To use PowWow, download the PowWow software from PowWow's home page (http://www.tribal.com/powwow/download/). Click the appropriate version for your computer and then choose a server that is geographically close to you. Download the software, install it by double-clicking it, and run the program. You'll have to fill in the requested information about yourself. To begin speaking with another user (or users), use the Utilities | White Pages command to list other PowWow users in your browser. Click a person's name to request a chat. Switch back to the PowWow window. Type your text in the upper window, or use the Utilities | Voice Chat command to speak to the other person using a microphone and a sound card. Use the Utilities | Draw command to share a collaborative drawing or use Utilities | Launch Cruise to visit web sites together. You can also play sounds and exchange files.

Web Chat Alternatives

Some other web pages (such as iChat, at http://www.ichat.com) offer their own sort of web chat systems that do not take advantage of the IRC networks. This is technically a different kind of chatting, but users behave about the same way. Some of these pages update the conversation automatically, some start elaborate Java applets that function as chat programs, and some are so rudimentary that you have to reload the web page repeatedly to see any new conversation.

HotWired's Talk.com

HotWired, the popular web site (or is it a network?) spun off from *Wired* magazine, has tried a number of different live chat experiments (such as Club Wired). They recently unveiled Talk.com, a web-based Java chat system based at http://www.talk.com.

You have to be a HotWired member to use Talk.com, but membership is free and not too painful. Click the join link and fill out the information that is requested (see Figure 7.4). Talk.com runs IRC-like Java applets that permit you to chat with other logged-in users.

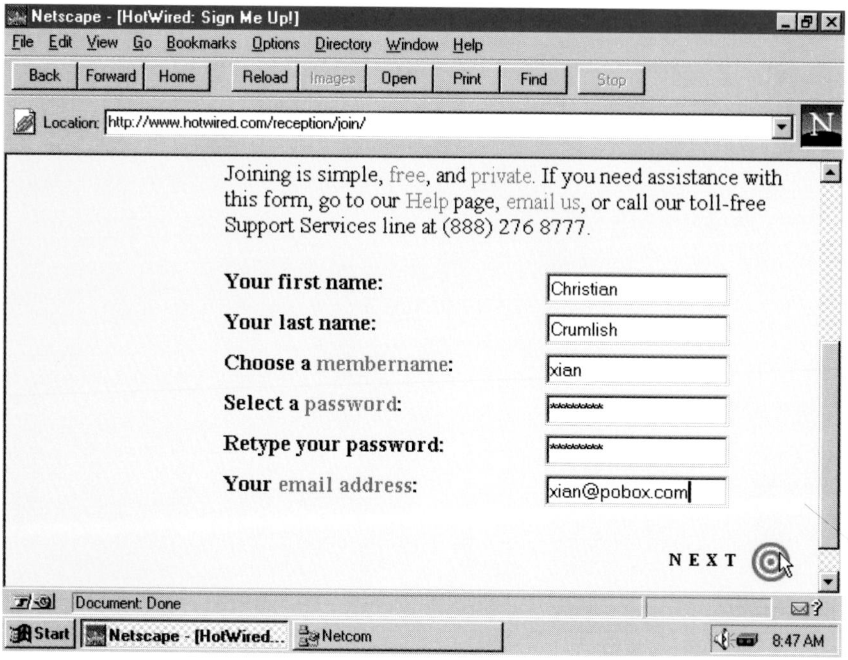

Figure 7.4 Register at the Talk.com home page if you're not already a HotWired member

To connect to Talk.com, start with Netscape or Internet Explorer and go to http://www.talk.com. Click the Enter link (at the upper-left). Sign on with your HotWired user name and Nickname and then follow the procedures in the Step by Step box.

Many, Many Other Web Chat Pages

If you're interested in seeing what other web-based chatting is available, from the simple to the complex, drop by chatting.com (http://www.chatting.com), WebAmerica (http://www.webamerica.com), or the WebChat Broadcasting System at http://www.wbs.net.

STEP BY STEP Use Talk.com

1 Scroll through the List of Rooms
display in the upper right to see the full
list (which is in no particular order).

4 Use the
Options | Logout
command to quit.

3 Type your
text in the main
window. Watch
others talk.

room: Club Wired

Options   Font Size   Input Window

Find It All. BIGYellow

HEALTH FOOD HEALTH CLUBS FITNESS CONSULTANTS DATING SERVICES

List of Rooms

HotWired Lounge
WiredSide Chat
Electronic Frontiers
Packet Chat

Go to room

Electronic Frontiers30

Booth description: The booth for Club Wired live events.

neros [said]: and we make a little
antisoc [said]: thats cool
antisoc [said]: at least you get a taste of everything
neros [said]: true
neros [said]: k
antisoc [said]: whens this interview supposed to start, neros?
neros [said]: we going then?
neros [said]: about now I think
antisoc [said]: umm, ok then, will do
neros [said]: see ya there
carol5 [said]: has anyone see kinko today

Get Info

Squelch

Private Chat

H O T W I R E D   **Club Wired**   Send   Locate User

Unsigned Java Applet Window

Microsoft
Outlook

Start   Netscape - [Talk.com]   room: Club Wired   4:36 PM

2 Click a room that interests
you and then click on the Go to
room button to join.

Adding Voice and Video

For people with microphones and even video cameras plugged into their computers, there are all kinds of new variations on the IRC model for multimedia communication, including Internet Phone (for voice) and CU-SeeMe (for video) and their many competitors.

For more information on Internet Phone (IPhone), go to VocalTec's Internet Phone home page at http://www.vocaltec.com/iphone4/ip4.htm. To get more information on CU-SeeMe, visit the CU-SeeMe Welcome Page at http://cu-seeme.cornell.edu/.

Figure 7.5 shows a conversation with another Internet user through Internet Phone.

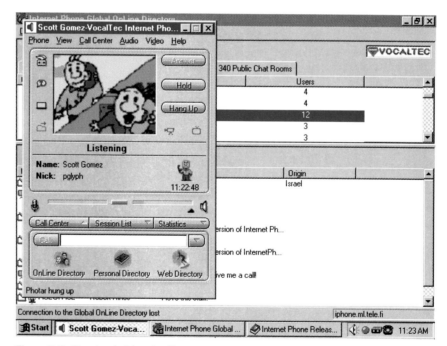

Figure 7.5 Chatting (with voice!) using VocalTec's Internet Phone with Scott

Conferencing and Intranet Chatting

Along lines similar to voice and video chat systems, a new generation of applications is starting to emerge to allow people to collaborate and meet from remote locations. If you've ever participated in a telephone conference call or even a meeting with a participant on a speaker phone, then you realize how hard it can be to communicate among a group of people when they're not all face to face and can't see the same props.

Conferencing programs are designed to enable participants to communicate and demonstrate ideas to each other on whiteboards or even by sharing programs and working on them together. So far, the most popular conferencing programs come from the two web browser biggies: Microsoft and Netscape.

Microsoft's entry in this field is called NetMeeting, and it allows participants to share applications (see Figure 7.6).

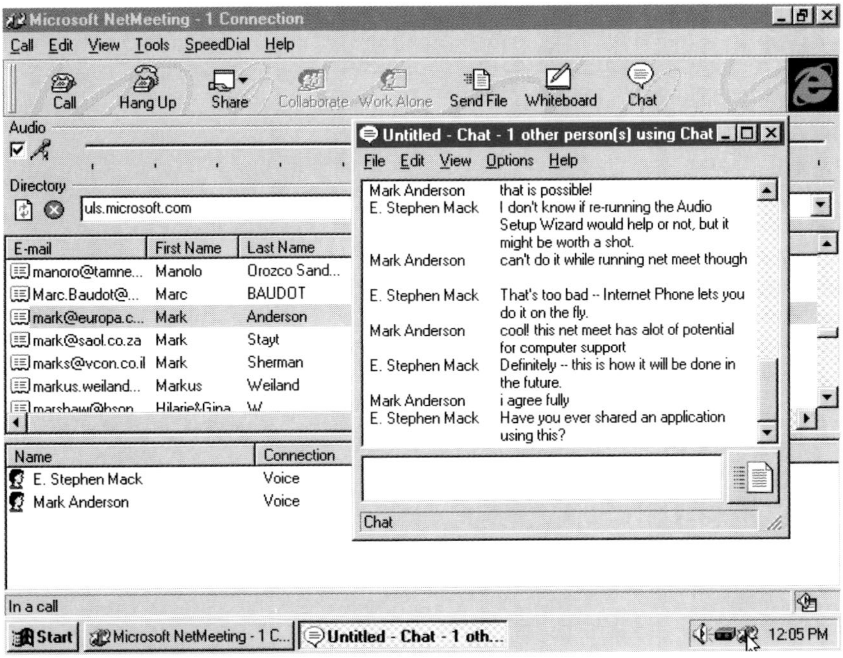

Figure 7.6 A Microsoft NetMeeting conversation, using both voice and chat communication simultaneously

Netscape's program is called CoolTalk and has capabilities very similar to NetMeeting's, although it's not as slick as the Microsoft program.

Pocket Universes

Another new twist on the basic real-time communication model is the idea of a virtual world: a three-dimension imaginary space containing surroundings and objects in which participants can both converse with each other and interact with (or even change) the surrounding space. In these worlds, people are represented by characters called avatars (generally chosen from a menu).

To visit VRML worlds, you first need a VRML-ready web browser. See the http:// www.vrml.org/ web site for an up-to-date list of browsers.

DEFINITION

Avatar: *An imaginary character who represents a participant in a 3D virtual chat world.*

There are currently two different types of 3D virtual worlds: private worlds, run by their own internal standards and open to registered members only; and Virtual Reality Modeling Language (VRML) worlds, designed according to the Internet standard and open to anyone with a VRML browser.

bookmark

For more information on VRML and 3D-world chatting tools, see Hotlinks to Virtual Worlds Industry (http://www.ccon.org/hotlinks/ hotlinks.html).

Worlds Chat is a popular private 3D world (see Figure 7.7). To try it, download the Worlds Chat demo from http://www.worlds.net/ (to do so, click the download demo link or go straight to http://www.worlds.net/wcg/

wcg-download.html). Fill out the registration form and submit it to download and install the Worlds Chat software. Use the arrow keys to move around the gallery. Choose an avatar (an online representation of yourself) by clicking the mouse button and then clicking the avatar you want to be. Enter the Worlds Chat space station. Explore with the mouse or arrow keys. Type text and press ENTER to say something; use the File | Exit command to quit.

Choose someone to whisper to with this menu.

Messages from the server appear here.

Disconnect using the File menu.

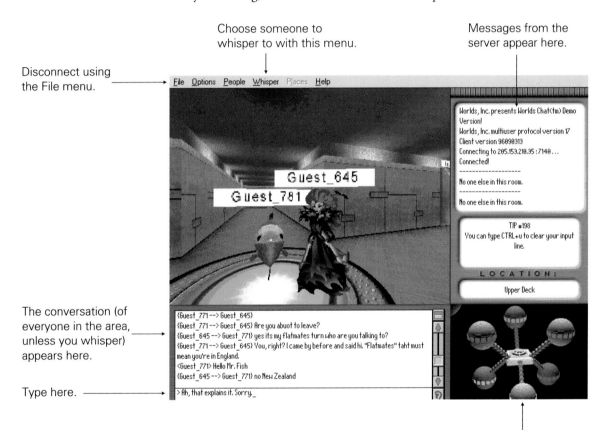

The conversation (of everyone in the area, unless you whisper) appears here.

Type here.

This map shows you where in the Worlds Chat you are.

Figure 7.7 A chance meeting with a bat girl and a fish(?) in futuristic corridors and rooms of Worlds Chat

CHECK POINT

You've now seen just about all the ways people communicate on the Net. If you want to talk to someone *now*, you can do so with any of the real-time chat programs mentioned in this chapter. If you like your conversations slow and comprehensive, then you'll probably stick with e-mail, lists, and Usenet.

The next few chapters will show you how to get around the Internet, connecting to remote computers, and how to search some of the resources that are not so easy to find from the Web.

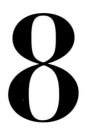

Moving Around the Net with FTP and Telnet

INCLUDES

- Using FTP for Internet file transfers

- Using FTP for intranet file transfers

- Using anonymous FTP

- Using FTP with a web browser

- Choosing an FTP client

- Logging in to remote computers with Telnet

- Choosing a Telnet client

- Plugging your Telnet program into your web browser

FAST FORWARD

Make an FTP Connection
with a Web Browser ➤ pp. 251-254

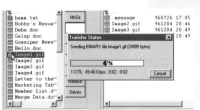

1. Enter an FTP URL (in the form

   ftp://*ftp.site.address/optional/directory/path*).

2. Click folder links to go to subdirectories.

3. Click document links to download files.

Know What to Do if a Site Is Busy ➤ p. 251

Try again later, ideally outside of normal working hours.

FTP Error

Could not login to FTP server

****

Sorry, there are too many off-campus ι
time. Please try again later. There
off-campus users. Before you ask: no,
archive access; and yes, there really

Download and Upload Files with FTP ➤ pp. 253-257

1. Choose a site to connect to.

2. Browse to the desired directory.

3. Point your FTP client at an appropriate folder on your local

   computer.

4. Double-click the file to be transferred and wait for it to be

   downloaded; or drag files from your local folders into the

   destination folder and wait for them to be uploaded.

5. Close the connection.

Connect to a Telnet Site ➤ pp. 258-259

1. Run your Telnet program.
2. Select Connect | Remote System (or the equivalent command).
3. Enter a site name and port number, if necessary, and click OK.
4. Log in, if required.

Plug Your Telnet Program into Your Web Browser ➤ p. 260

1. In Netscape, select Options | General Preferences.
2. In Netscape, click the Apps tab.
3. Click the Telnet Application box.
4. Type the name of your Telnet program (for example, in Windows 95, type **telnet**).
5. Click OK.

As an international network of networks, the Internet features numerous archive sites, repositories of software, data, and informative materials. Before the World Wide Web came along and made it so easy to navigate the Net, there were already ways to get to various storage locations and transfer files from them. These older methods still exist, and web browsers have absorbed many of the capabilities of these earlier, specialized programs.

Working with Remote Sites

Upcoming versions of popular software applications and even operating systems such as Windows 97 and the next MacOS will have FTP capabilities built in. This means that FTP-style access to the Internet as well as to intranets will be integrated into normal file-management interfaces on the desktop and in applications.

So the Internet is not just about sending messages and reading newsgroups and web sites. It's also a way of connecting to other computers: with the file transfer protocol, or FTP, you can send or get files; with Telnet, you can log directly into (some) computers and run programs and edit files directly. To some extent, these programs do away with the differences between different computers and networks, enabling you to visit or control remote computers that run on completely different types of systems from your own.

In this chapter, I'll explain the most efficient way to transfer files: using FTP. Even though Netscape and Internet Explorer both can transfer files with the FTP protocol, there are still advantages to using a separate FTP program. I'll also show you how to use a Telnet program to log in to remote computers.

Transferring Files with FTP

I mentioned in Chapter 4 that you can attach files to e-mail, but except for the occasional, reasonably small file, this is not the most efficient way to transfer files over the Internet. Instead, you can use a protocol developed for sending and receiving files between computers connected to the Net—the file transfer protocol (FTP). FTP is another of the many client-server protocols: individual users run FTP client programs and connect to remote archive sites managed by FTP servers.

DEFINITIONS

Client-server: *A client-server system is a system in which various client programs all connect to a central server to obtain information or to communicate.*

Mirror site: *A site set up as an alternative to a popular address, containing copies of all the files available at the main site and updated regularly.*

Paying for FTP Storage Space

Most Internet service providers throw in some free FTP storage space with a personal (or business) Internet e-mail account. If you don't have that sort of account, you can still pay for space on a commercial server. If you have a web site, then you may not need a separate FTP space, although that depends on what you intend to use the space for (drop box, file archive, back-door to a web site?).

Commercial FTP storage comes free or for a set cost for a certain amount of disk storage space (anything from 5 megabytes up) and a certain budgeted amount of traffic (time the server has to spend sending or receiving files). If you use more disk space or exceed your traffic quota, you'll pay extra. Make sure you know what your rates and limits are.

Using FTP for Intranet File Transfers

Because intranets are private networks run using Internet protocols, any programs designed to work on the Internet, such as FTP programs, should necessarily work on intranets as well. More important, the intranet should make even remote computers seem as accessible as your own computer's hard drive. When intranets work, they're transparent. You don't think about the intranet; you grab the file (even if it's in Tokyo) and get on with your work. As Windows and the MacOS develop native FTP capabilities (such as Unix has always had), intranets should make the process of working with remote computers even more seamless.

Why Do You Need FTP?

Generally speaking, FTP has always been an expert or "power user" protocol, but when will you need to use it nowadays? Probably the most popular use of FTP these days is for the oversight and management of web sites. Though it can be used to connect to any computer on the Internet (and therefore to any site, as long as you have a password), it's perfect for logging in to the protected area of a web site and adding, changing, downloading, or even deleting files at the site. For Unix sites, Telnet programs are also used for this purpose. See Chapter 11 for more on managing web sites.

EXPERT ADVICE

FTP is a more efficient protocol for file transfers than the Web's HTTP protocol. Most web servers or service providers who maintain large sites with software or files to download make the files available by FTP, with ftp://...URLs embedded into the web pages.

After that, FTP is most often used for transferring or sharing files between collaborators. I used to submit chapters to my editors by courier. Recently, I've been sending them as e-mail attachments. Lately, however, I've been experimenting with posting them at my FTP site and asking my editors to download them directly.

Anonymous FTP

There are two ways to use FTP. The first, and less widespread approach, is to log in to an FTP site with a private username and password and then send or download files to or from the site. The more common use of FTP is called anonymous FTP. An anonymous FTP site is one that permits anyone to log in as "anonymous" without having a special account and password. Anonymous FTP sites are public archive sites. It is more common to download files from public sites than to upload files to them, though both are possible, depending on the rules of the specific site.

EXPERT ADVICE

If you have a Unix shell account, you can use FTP to transfer files to and from your home computer and your remote account.

CAUTION

Anonymous FTP is never truly anonymous. Your connection is logged by the FTP server, and the remote site will (theoretically) always know the domain name part of your address. Some sites won't admit you if you don't enter a valid e-mail address as your password.

Public sites usually can accept only a limited number of connections at a time, so you will sometimes fail to connect when a site is busy. Sometimes a busy server will display a list of mirror sites. See if any are near you geographically (to minimize your impact on the Net) and try one.

Once you've connected to a public site, poke around for likely folders containing the files you're looking for. If you find a "pub" directory, that's usually a good place to start. ("Pub" stands for public.)

Using FTP with a Web Browser

Most of the time when you use FTP from within a web browser, you'll do it by simply clicking a link that happens to connect to an FTP site. However, you can enter FTP addresses directly in the location box if you write them in the form of a URL. An FTP URL starts with ftp:// and then lists the Internet address of the FTP site. This may be followed by a directory path as well.

CAUTION

All FTP sites have an upper limit on the number of connections they can handle at once. Whenever possible, try to perform your FTP transactions during off hours.

Type the URL in the location box and press ENTER. If you try to connect to an FTP site during the workday, you may be refused access.

When your browser connects to the FTP site, a special type of page will be displayed, showing a directory listing of the site (and directory) that you're connected to. In Figure 8.1, I've just connected to the FTP archive at ftp.winsite.com in the /pub/pc/win95 directory, from which the various categories of software can be browsed. For example, the FTP client program WS_FTP32 can be downloaded from the netutil directory. (You'd have to scroll down to see it—they're listed alphabetically.)

Click here to go to the next higher directory (in this case, /pub/pc).

Use the Back button to return to this list after clicking a file or directory.

Click here to see the index for all of the files.

Click on this text file to see an overview of the directories.

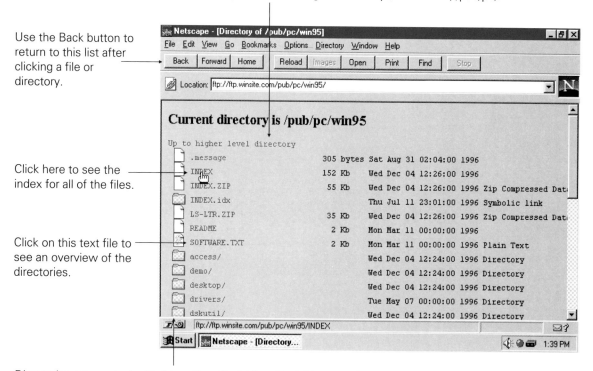

Directories are marked with this yellow file folder; this folder contains disk utilities.

Figure 8.1 Connecting to an FTP site with Netscape

EXPERT ADVICE

To make an FTP connection to a nonpublic site, enter the address in the form ftp://username@usersite.name. You'll be presented with a dialog box for entering your password. Once you connect, you can download files from the remote site.

As you might imagine, folder icons represent directories (folders) on the remote machine, and document icons represent files. The FTP listing should tell you the type of each file, along with its size, and so on. Click a directory name to open the directory. Click a file name to display or download a file.

When you click a file name, your web browser will display text files and any other kind of files that it recognizes and has the ability to display. Some files it will recognize and offer to download. You just have to specify a folder, verify the file name, and click the Save button. If your browser doesn't recognize the file, it will display a dialog box offering you several helpful choices (Pick App to pick an application to open the file with and Save File to save the file to disk) and perhaps some less helpful choices (More Info, Cancel). The safest choice is Save File. You can figure out what to do with the file later.

Save As...		? ☒
Save in:	📁 Download	▼ 🔼 📁 ▦ ▦

🗎 Cchatpack.exe
🗎 Irwin10b7.exe

File name:	ws_ftp32.zip	**Save**
Save as type:	All Files (*.*) ▼	Cancel

EXPERT ADVICE

While your browser is downloading the file, you can continue browsing the Web without interrupting the file transfer.

Your browser will keep you apprised of its progress in downloading the file.

Saving Location	
Location:	ftp://ftp.winsit...til/ws_ftp32.zip
Saving	C:\Download\ws_ftp32.zip
Status:	64K of 468K (at 1.8K/sec)
Time Left:	00:03:47

IIIII   13%

Cancel

A few years ago, web browsers generally weren't able to send (upload) files to FTP sites, partly because the Web is set up as a somewhat passive medium, with browsers downloading files, not sending files. Now, generally, you can upload files by using the File | Upload File command or by dragging files and dropping them into an FTP directory (see Figure 8.2).

Using FTP with an FTP Client Program

So web browsers can do a lot of FTP tricks, but they're still not full-fledged FTP client programs. Why would you need a stand-alone FTP program?

- They often have lists of good FTP sites prebookmarked.
- Some FTP clients can automatically recover aborted downloads (Internet connections *can* be flaky).

Choose the File | Upload File command to select the files to send from a dialog box.

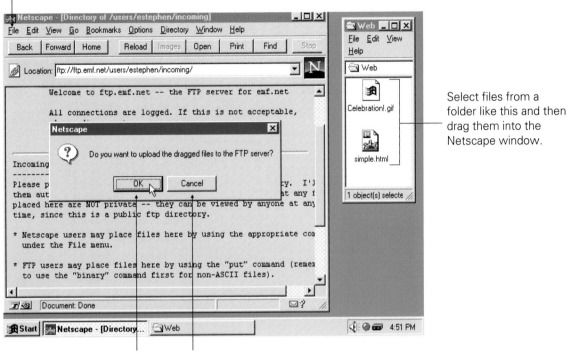

Select files from a folder like this and then drag them into the Netscape window.

Click OK to begin uploading.   Click Cancel to not upload the files—you'll view them in Netscape instead.

Figure 8.2 Dragging files to an FTP site with Netscape

- FTP clients give you the ability to transfer more than one file at a time (and to use wildcards).
- FTP clients let you view, execute, rename, and delete files remotely.
- Most FTP clients let you create, change, and remove directories.
- If you know standard FTP commands, most FTP clients give you more control.

STEP BY STEP Transfer a File with FTP

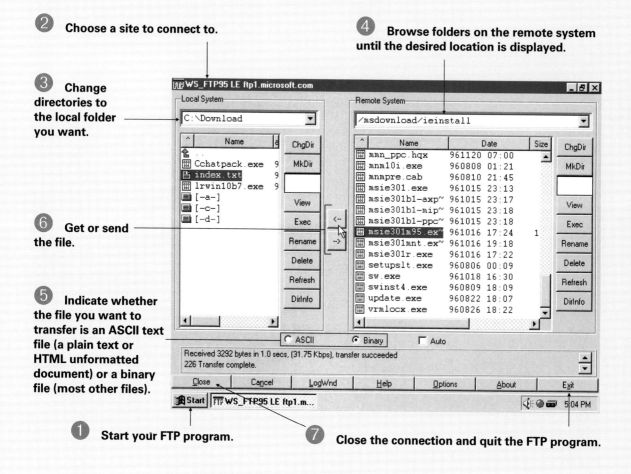

② Choose a site to connect to.

④ Browse folders on the remote system until the desired location is displayed.

③ Change directories to the local folder you want.

⑥ Get or send the file.

⑤ Indicate whether the file you want to transfer is an ASCII text file (a plain text or HTML unformatted document) or a binary file (most other files).

① Start your FTP program.

⑦ Close the connection and quit the FTP program.

Choosing an FTP Tool

Free FTP programs are readily available for both Windows and Macintosh systems. Unix has FTP built in and accessible via the ubiquitous ftp program.

bookmark

You can get WS_FTP (either the free LE version or the commercial Pro version) from http://www.ipswitch.com/pd_wsftp.html. You can get CuteFTP as well as other Windows FTP clients from http://www. tucows.com or from http://www.winsite.com.

A free program, called Ftp.exe, comes with Windows, but it's no easier to use than the character-based Unix program it's modeled on. Your better bet would be WS_FTP or CuteFTP, both shareware products, or WinFTP from Microsoft, which is based on an earlier, licensed version of WS_FTP.

For the Mac, the hands-down favorite FTP program is called Fetch. Another popular program is Anarchie, a combined Archie (FTP-search protocol) and FTP program. You can use it to track down files and then download them directly. The free NCSA Telnet program for the Macintosh also includes built-in FTP capabilities.

bookmark

You can get Fetch and Anarchie from
http://wwwhost.ots.utexas.edu/mac/main.html or
http://www-personal.umich.edu/~sdamask/umich-mirrors/

If you *do* work with Unix machines ever, see if your system has the more advanced ncftp built in. It has more shortcuts and can save you some typing, at least.

To send a file to a remote machine (assuming you have permission—the procedure simply won't work if you don't), the process is about the same. Find the file on your computer and double-click it in the left pane or select the file name and click the right-pointing button. As with downloading, click ASCII first if you're sending a text file (or check Auto to let WS_FTP deal with this setting for you).

Logging In to Other Machines with Telnet

Most machines that permit Telnet logins are Unix machines. (Most of the servers on the Internet are still Unix machines.) However, many, many computers on the Internet are not Unix boxes and don't permit Telnet logins. There *are* other remote login programs for other systems (but they're not nearly as easy to find). There are some good remote-control programs (such as Timbuktu Pro for Windows and Macintosh) that, when installed on both computers, enable someone at one end to control the computer at the other end.

Nevertheless, the only standard Internet remote-login protocol is Telnet, and even more than with FTP, you'll probably use Telnet mainly, if ever, for logging in to a webmaster account to work on or run the files at your web site. See Chapter 11 for more on managing remote web sites.

Figure 8.3 shows a Telnet login screen.

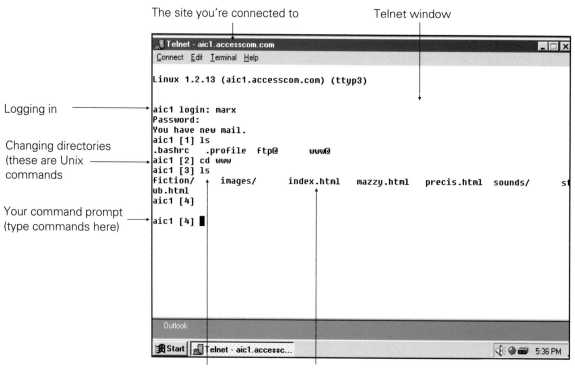

Figure 8.3 Logging in to Telnet

Figure 8.4 shows an updated weather report for San Francisco from the wunderground.com weather telnet site. Another interesting site houses many documents related to the U.S. Federal Government (fedworld.gov).

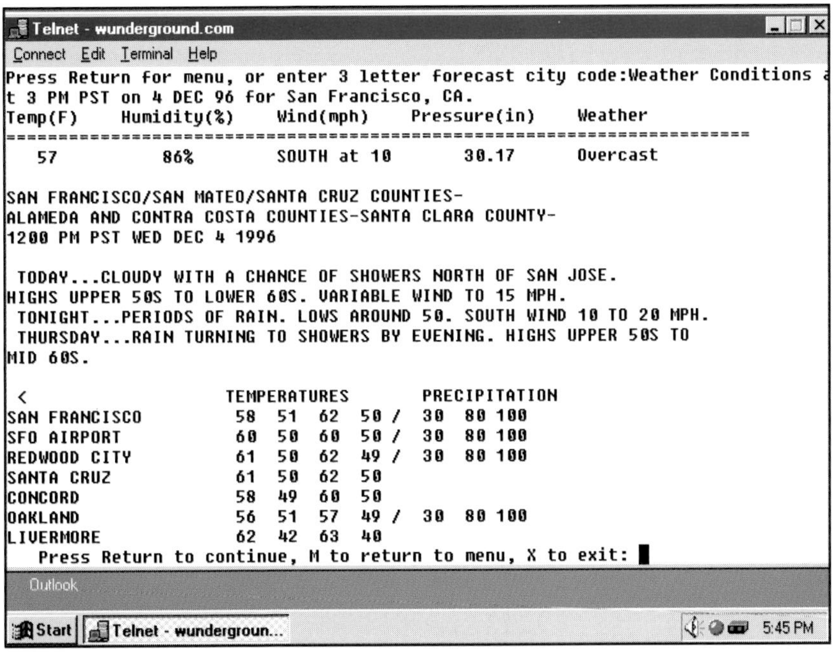

Figure 8.4 Up-to-date weather information via Telnet

If you disconnect from a site from a prompt or if the remote site hangs up on you for any reason, Telnet will let you know that the connection has been lost.

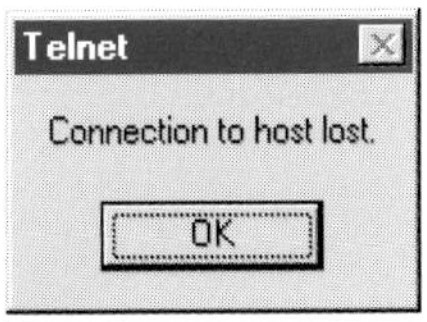

netiquette

It's best to log off from any service you've connected to before closing a Telnet connection, because the site at the other end might spin its wheels for a while before it notices you're no longer there.

Choosing a Telnet Program

Free Telnet programs are also available for both Macintosh and Windows machines. (Unix, the smartypants operating system, has Telnet built in, of course.) For the Mac, NCSA Telnet is free and full-featured (hey, it's an FTP program, too). Windows comes with an adequate Telnet.exe program, and you can get the new version of HyperTerminal (a third-party communications program for Windows that now "does Telnet" too) or other Telnet programs from http://www.tucows.com.

Telnet via the Web

Web browsers don't usually have Telnet capabilities built in, the way they usually do with FTP. Instead, they prefer to just know where your Telnet program is and then start it and point it at the address whenever they encounter a URL that starts with telnet://. Still, you have to tell your browser where the Telnet program is.

STEP BY STEP **Plug Telnet into Your Web Browser**

① In Netscape, select Options | General Preferences.

② In Netscape, click the Apps tab.

③ Click the Telnet Application box.

④ Type the name of your Telnet program (for example, telnet in Windows 95).

⑤ Click OK.

CHECK POINT

With what you've seen in this chapter, you're now among the most well prepared of web wanderers. You have your seven-league boots. In the next chapter, I'll show you how to *scour* the Net for information. Those simple keyword searches of popular web sites are good for the everyday idle browse, but when you're doing research or trying to cover all your bases, you'll need to apply some elbow grease.

Scouring the Net

INCLUDES

- Performing advanced searches with search engines

- Refining a search

- Searching for links to a site

- Finding buried Gopher resources

- Looking for files at FTP archive sites

- Hunting down card catalogs

FAST FORWARD

Focus Your Searches ➤ pp. 266-268

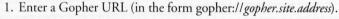

- Enter more keywords to match (by placing + in front of each word).
- Require that words be near each other (by putting them between quotation marks).
- Enter keywords to avoid (by placing - in front of each).

Use Gopher with a Web Browser ➤ pp. 270-274

1. Enter a Gopher URL (in the form gopher://*gopher.site.address*).
2. Click folder links to connect to subordinate Gopher menus.
3. Click search icons to search for keywords.
4. Click document links to display or download files.

Search Gopher Sites with Jughead or Veronica ➤ pp. 272-274

1. Visit a Jughead or Veronica Gopher search site.
2. Enter a keyword in the search box and press ENTER. The search result will be another Gopher page with links to matching Gopher menus and items.

Search FTP Sites with Archie ➤ *pp. 274-276*

1. Point your browser to an Archie gateway.
2. Enter a filename or part of a filename for the program you're looking for.
3. Specify a Case Insensitive and Sub String (or Regular Expression) search unless you know the exact filename.
4. Fill in other search options.
5. Click the Search button.
6. Choose a server from the returned list and click a filename to download the file.

Connect to Telnet Sites with HyTelnet ➤ *pp. 276-277*

1. Point your web browser at a HyTelnet site.
2. Click Library Catalogs.
3. Click to narrow down the geographical location of the university you're looking for.
4. Choose the university or institution.
5. Note the login instructions and click the Telnet link.
6. Log in as instructed and attempt to work with the interface.

Internet Resources via Telnet

HYTELNET 6.9

In Chapter 3, I showed you how to search the Web by entering keywords into search-engine forms. This is by far the easiest way to look for stuff on the Net, but there are additional strategies you can use if your first stabs at hunting something down draw a blank.

Database searching is a branch of computer science, and it can be an infinitely subtle topic. Furthermore, the different search engines often use different commands and even different search principles, so I can only show you so much. I'll give you a grounding in the concepts of advanced searching, and I'll show you a few practical examples with my favorite search engine, Alta Vista.

Another limitation of web-based searching is that not everything on the Internet is visible or well-documented on the Web itself. Sure, you can *reach* most of the Internet via the Web, but that doesn't mean that every file stowed away in an archive, every Telnet-based card catalog, every Gopher menu ever created is indexed in the huge databases you're searching. No, people were searching the Net for resources long before the Web and its directories and search engines came along, and I'll give you a briefing on some of these predecessor search methods for those times when you need to tease out well-hidden material.

Getting the Most Out of Search Engines

A typical rule that can differ from engine to engine is how capitalized keywords are matched. Additionally, some search engines look for pages that contain all of your search terms, while some search engines look for pages that contain any or most of your search terms.

Some search engines do a better job than others of telling you their capabilities. Some have a link to an advanced searching page where you can fill in a more elaborate form. Others offer more-or-less complete documentation of their features. Still others have linked pages of searching tips or hints.

Generally, the way to focus a search is to specify additional keywords and look for certain relationships among them. The most common relationships are those used in Boolean logic: And, Or, and Not. These relationships are symbolized in different ways by different search engines, but the concepts are universal.

Refining a Search

The first step in putting together a focused search is to come up with additional keywords. Putting a single word into the form on a search engine works great for a quick-and-dirty scattershot search, but it won't work if you're trying to be thorough and exhaustive. Try to come up with as many unique words as you can that will help zero in on the information or file you want.

---

bookmark

You can also widen your search by trying to hit multiple search engines with a single query. Besides MetaCrawler (http://www.metacrawler.com), mentioned in Chapter 3, other all-in-one search sites include SavvySearch at http://guaraldi.cs.colostate.edu:2000/, SuperSeek at http://w3.superseek.com/, and a lot more listed by Yahoo! in its All-in-One Search Pages category at http://www.yahoo.com/Computer_and_Internet/Internet/ World_Wide_Web/Searching_the_Web/All_in_One_Search_pages.html.

In most search engines, just putting words one after another, separated by spaces, indicates that you're looking for matches of any of the words. This is an Or type of search (in the Boolean sense): you'll find documents containing *apple* OR *pie* (or both, but that's not required). If you think about this, you'll realize that just stringing words together in this way does not narrow your search; it expands it to include any documents containing the second word as well as all those containing the first word.

To limit the hits that match your list of words, you can specify that each word (or some core set of them) *must* be found or you're not interested. This is the And type of search. In most search engines, you indicate that a word must be found by preceding it with a plus sign. Thus, if you're looking for documents containing both the words *apple* AND *pie*, you usually type

```
+apple +pie
```

The third basic step to take to refine your searches (besides adding additional words and specifying that some *must* be present) is to require that some words be found next to each other (or close to each other, depending on the capabilities of the search engine). This requirement can be handy if you're looking for a specific phrase, or if you just want to make sure of the context of certain ambiguous words. In many search engines, you indicate phrases by surrounding the words in question with quotation marks, like so:

```
"apple pie"
```

Ruling Out Bad Matches

When performing a search, you'll sometimes be surprised by the unexpected matches you get to your keywords, often unintended connotations and coincidences. Fortunately, you can also filter out some responses if you can identify a keyword to be found in all or most of the bogus matches. This brings into play the third common Boolean connector: Not. In many search engines, you indicate that you are searching for phrases containing some words *and not* others by preceding the latter with a minus sign, like so:

```
apple -computer
```

Searching for Links, Hosts, or Applets

Search engines often use special words or commands to search for specific types of information. Alta Vista, for example, allows you to search for web documents that contain links to a specific site. This can be invaluable for "ego surfing" (looking for links to your own web site):

```
link:ezone.org
```

CAUTION

*Alta Vista actually used two entirely different query languages for simple
and advanced searches. All of the "advanced" searches mentioned so far
in this chapter are still variations on the simple searches available on the
main page. Alta Vista has a separate Advanced Search form with different
search commands.*

Click the Help button on the main Alta Vista page or point your browser
directly at http://altavista.digital.com/cgi-bin/query?pg=h to see the entire list of
special prefixes used to search for anchor text, images, titles, URLs, and even Java
applets (see Figure 9.1).

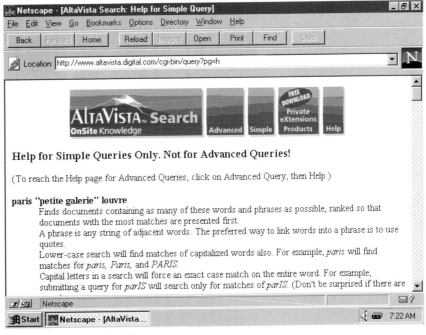

Figure 9.1 Alta Vista's help page

STEP BY STEP Search Alta Vista for Java Applets

① **If you know the name of a Java applet, search for it by typing applet:*name* in this box.**

② **Alta Vista will return pages containing applets by that name.**

③ **Click to visit a page and then use your View Source command to see and copy the applet, if you like.**

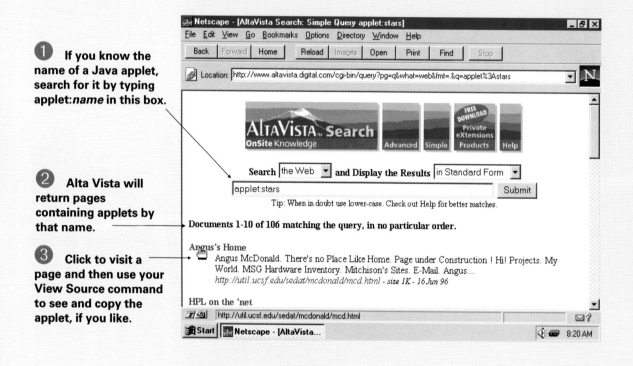

Unearthing the Deep Internet Hoards

Universities and other early adopters of Internet standards put a lot of time, energy, and money into setting up sites before the Web came along. Most of them have not been willing to convert all their existing systems to web servers, even though a lot of this information is essentially invisible to web-search robots. This is gradually changing, and much university information that was only available in the Gopher format in 1994 can now be found on the Web, but there are still tasty nuggets of information buried on Internet computers in the legacy formats of Gopher, FTP, and Telnet.

Gopher Briefly Explained

A newer development of the Gopher protocol is Gopher VR, a graphical (rather than menu-driven) Gopherspace organized with virtual reality technology.

What is this Gopher thing I keep mentioning? Before there was the Web, Gopher was the brave new face of the Internet, and an improvement over FTP as far as beginners were concerned. Gopher organizes connections into menus, or directory listings, with plain-English names, so you can browse the Net just by choosing items from menus. In some ways, it's very similar to the web concept except without all the page formatting and hyperlinks. Just as all the contents and resources of the Internet that can be reached with a web browser can be said to be "on the World Wide Web," all the Internet resources that can be reached with a Gopher client are said to constitute Gopherspace.

For that reason, any web browser makes a perfectly good Gopher client as well. (Yes, Gopher is another client-server protocol.) In contrast to some of the other remaining early Internet tools, such as FTP clients, there are few, if any, advantages to using a real Gopher program these days. To a large extent, the Web has superseded much of the role of Gopherspace, since it can offer menus, just as Gopher does, and additional context as well.

To connect to a Gopher site with a web browser, either click a hyperlink leading to such a site or type the site's URL in your Location window.

Go to: gopher://gopher.uiuc.edu/

Your browser will display a page called Gopher Menu featuring documents, folders, and links to search programs. Figure 9.2 shows the Gopher menu for the University of Illinois at Urbana-Champaign. All of the listed folders contain menus of their own. Text documents will appear in the Gopher window. Other documents can be downloaded.

To see the contents of a folder, click its name. If you click a search link (in Netscape shown as a Binoculars icon), you'll be prompted to enter a keyword and then will be shown a new menu with the results of your search. If you click a file, your browser will offer to download it, unless it's in a format your browser knows how to display or open. If you click a text file, it will be displayed in the browser window.

To continue browsing, click the Back button.

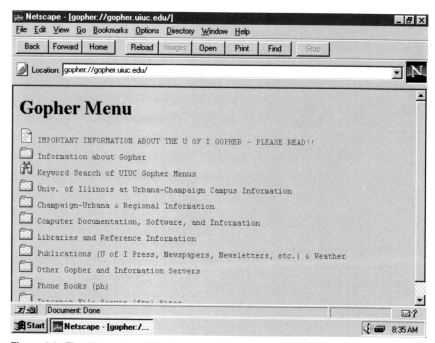

Figure 9.2 The University of Illinois at Urbana-Champaign Gopher menu

bookmark

If you must have a stand-alone Gopher program, try the WSGopher (for Windows) site (http://sageftp.inel.gov/dap/gopher.htm; click Download) or TurboGopher for the Macintosh (http://www.macworld.com/software/Software.503.html; click Download). Unix systems generally have a built-in Gopher program called gopher.

So how do you find things in Gopherspace? You could hunt through menus for days and experience many pleasurable digressions without finding what you're looking for (sound like any other Internet protocol you know?). Fortunately, there are two methods for searching for Gopher items, called Jughead and Veronica.

Each of these appears in the form of searchable Gopher menus. You enter keywords and then visit the Gopher items that are found. The only difference I've ever discerned is that Jughead is limited to top-level Gopher menus (as opposed to those buried several steps down from the initial menu on a server).

EXPERT ADVICE

My technical editor tells me that the difference between Veronica and Jughead is their scope. Jughead is supposed to be used generally within an organization's Gopher server(s), whereas Veronica is for Gopherspace at large.

Table 9.1 lists some URLs for Jughead and Veronica searches.

Gopher Search Type	URL
Veronica list [Washington & Lee University]	gopher://liberty.uc.wlu.edu/11/gophers/veronica
Veronica [Psi Net]	gopher://veronica.psi.net:2347/7
Veronica [NYSERNet]	gopher://empire.nysernet.org:2347/7
Yahoo!'s list of Veronica servers	http://www.yahoo.com/Computers_and_Internet/Internet/Gopher/Searching/Veronica
Jughead list [University of Utah]	gopher://gopher.utah.edu/ click "Search menu titles using jughead" click "Search other institutions using jughead"
Jughead [Washington & Lee University]	gopher://liberty.uc.wlu.edu:3002/7
Jughead [University of California, Irvine]	gopher://gopher-server.cwis.uci.edu:3000/7
Yahoo!'s list of Jughead servers	http://www.yahoo.com/Computers_and_Internet/Internet/Gopher/Searching/Jughead

Table 9-1 URLs for Veronica and Jughead Gopher Searches

STEP BY STEP Search Gopher Archives

1 To find information stored at Gopher sites, visit a Jughead or Veronica Gopher search site.

Netscape - [Gopher Index gopher://veronica.psi.net:2347/7]

File Edit View Go Bookmarks Options Directory Window Help

| Back | Forward | Home | | Reload | Images | Open | Print | Find | | Stop |

Location: gopher://veronica.psi.net:2347/7   N

gopher://veronica.psi.net:2347/7
Gopher Search

This is a searchable Gopher index. Use the search function of your browser to enter search terms.

This is a searchable index. Enter search keywords: Berkeley

2 Enter a keyword in the search box and press ENTER. The search will return another Gopher page with links to matching Gopher menus and items.

Document: Done

Start   Netscape - [Gopher I...   12:46 PM

See Chapter 8 for more on FTP.

Searching FTP Archives with Archie

As one of the fundamental Internet protocols, FTP has been around for quite a while, confounding people looking for specific files without knowing which of the file archive sites on the Net might contain them. It's true that FTP resources have been made available on the Web to a greater extent than some other types have been, and that with sites such as Shareware.com you can now search for files directly from web pages, but even before the Web came along, clever Internet wonks had worked out a solution called Archie.

Archie, supposedly short for "archive," is a system of searchable databases that record what files are stored at which FTP sites, listing them both by name and by type of program, where applicable (so you can search for database applications in general as well as for specific programs).

bookmark

The official Archie home page is http://services.bunyip.com:8000/products/archie/archie.html.

An Archie client program lets you perform a keyword search and then returns the addresses of FTP sites containing files that match your search. There are also some experimental Archie gateways on the Web that enable you to enter your search without having a separate Archie client program (see Figure 9.3).

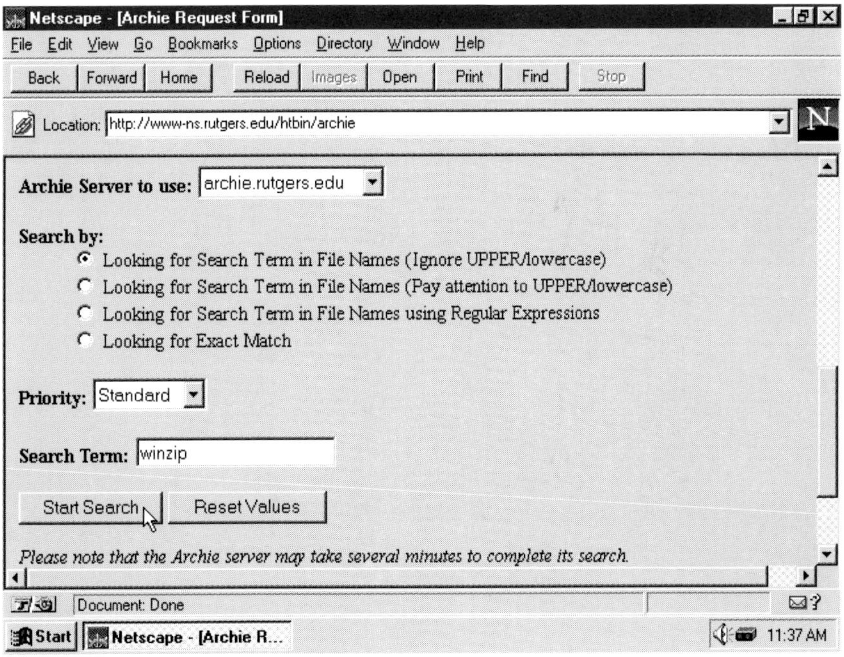

Figure 9.3 An Archie search page on the Web

For more Archie web sites, see Yahoo!'s list at http://yahoo.com/ Computers_and_Internet/Internet/FTP_Sites/Searching/Archie/.

bookmark

Anarchie, for the Macintosh, can be found at http://www.share.com/peterlewis/anarchie/, and WS_Archie can be found at http://dspace.dial.pipex.com/town/square/cc83/wsarchie.htm—or both can be found in the Archie (Windows and Macintosh) sections of TUCOWS (http://www.tucows.com) or Stroud's (http://www.stroud.com).

If you find much use for Archie, you may want to obtain a specific program for your Archie searches. As mentioned in Chapter 8, Anarchie for the Macintosh is an excellent combined Archie and FTP client that enables you to directly download the files you find. For Windows, try WS_Archie. Many Unix systems come with an Archie program called—you guessed it—archie.

Finding HyTelnet Sites

In Chapter 8 you saw how to use Telnet to log in to a remote computer. A lot of early Internet sites were set up as Telnet sites. Instead of connecting to a lush web page or even an easy-to-use Gopher menu, you'd be presented with a login sequence and then a prompt or, if you were lucky, a list of commands to try.

To this day there are still a lot of active Telnet sites, many of which are connected to university library card-catalog databases. A system was set up to make these Telnet sites findable from a central starting point, called HyTelnet (for hyper-Telnet). If you start off connected to a HyTelnet site, you can find just about any card catalog and search it. If not (that is, if you just try poking around on the Web), you're out of luck.

Follow these steps to visit a university card catalog:

1. Point your web browser at a HyTelnet site, such as http://www.nova.edu/Inter-Links/hytelnet.html or http://www.cam.ac.uk/Hytelnet/.

2. Click Library Catalogs.

Make sure to follow the instructions for setting up a Telnet application in Chapter 8 if you're using Netscape.

3. Click to narrow down the geographical location of the university you're looking for (for example, click The Americas, then United States, then Academic, Research and General Libraries).

4. Choose the university or institution.

5. Note the login instructions.

6. Click the Telnet link.

7. Log in as instructed (see figure 9.4) and attempt to work with the interface (click the OPAC link for basic help).

For most systems, you can simply choose a menu item to search for a book; if you're confronted with a command prompt, try to find help by typing h or ? or help.

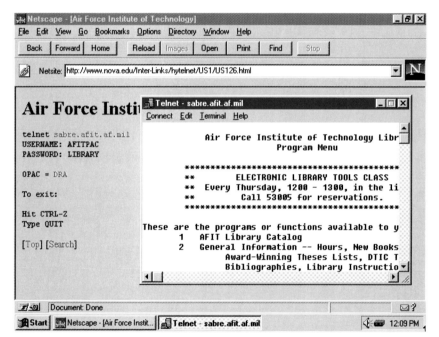

Figure 9.4 Use HyTelnet to find Library catalogs

The Future of Net Searching

Ideally, searching the Internet will continue to become easier and more seamless. You should be able to enter search keywords from almost anywhere to look for resources on the Net. For that matter, searching for items "out there" or on intranets should be as easy as looking for files on your own computer's hard disk (though I realize that's not always as easy as it should be!).

One advance to watch is the development of intelligent agents. In the near future it should be possible to run software and instruct it to keep an eye out for certain types of information or to go out hunting for a specific goal. This kind of agent could work for you without your direct supervision, reporting back when it gets results. There's a lot of research going on in this area, so it's not as science-fiction-y as you might think.

CHECK POINT

With what you've learned in this chapter, you can now burrow deeply into the hidden recesses of the Net and pry out the information or programs that you need. The next two chapters will tell you all about how to create web documents and how to publish them on the World Wide Web or on local intranets.

A Web Design Primer

- Understanding web publishing
- Planning a web site
- Creating web pages
- Editing web pages with Netscape or Word
- Understanding HTML codes
- Formatting web pages
- Inserting hypertext links

FAST FORWARD

WonderWeb

With Links Up the Wazoo!

But first, you'll want to read all of our press releases for the last fifteen years.

Plan a Web Site ➤ pp. 283-284

- Organize your source documents.
- Consider possible interlinks.
- Create a folder hierarchy.
- Design your home page.
- Plan for future growth.

Create HTML Documents ➤ pp. 286-288

All HTML documents

- Start with <HTML>
- Have a head that starts with <HEAD>, which has a title enclosed between <TITLE> and </TITLE>, and ends with </HEAD>
- Have a body that starts with <BODY> and ends with </BODY>
- End with </HTML>

```
sample.html - Notepad
File  Edit  Search  Help
<HTML>
<HEAD>
<TITLE>A Sample HTML Document</TITLE>
</HEAD>
<BODY>

<H1>This is a Sample HTML Document</H1>
```

Featuring Overuse of Formatting!

Yes, that's right, *emphasis* all over the place. Silly stuff. Applied *tackily*, without regard for **GOOD DESIGN**.

This calls for a
clean break
before the next section.

Format a Web Page ➤ pp. 291-292

Insert HTML tags, mostly in pairs surrounding affected text, such as

- <H1></H1> through <H6></H6> for headings
- <P> before new paragraphs
- <B></B>, <I></I>, and <U></U> for bold, italics, and underlining
- <HR> for a horizontal line
-
 for a line break without starting a new paragraph

280

Embed a Hypertext Link ➤ *pp. 293-294*

Insert an HTML anchor tag, usually of the form
<A HREF="*filename*">**active text**</A>.

Create Web Documents
with Netscape Gold ➤ *pp. 295-302*

1. Download Netscape Gold from Netscape's home page.
2. Create a new file with the File | New Document | Blank command.
3. Type (or paste in) text.
4. Format your text with buttons from the toolbars.
5. Insert images and links.
6. Save and publish the document.

Create Web Documents
with Microsoft Word ➤ *pp. 302-306*

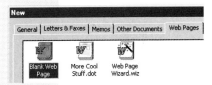

- When working with a version older than Word 97, download and install Internet Assistant from http://www.microsoft.com/word/internet/ia/.
- Start a new web page with the File | New command. Choose the Web Page tab and double-click New Web Page.
- Choose the File | Properties command to assign a title.
- Assign heading levels with the Style drop-down list in the Formatting toolbar.
- Format text with any of the normal formatting buttons that remain on the toolbars.
- Click the Insert Picture button to insert a picture.
- Click the Insert Hyperlink button to insert a hypertext link.

281

Just when you've gotten yourself an e-mail address and begun to explore the World Wide Web, you learn that there's another level of status on the Internet these days—having your own home page. The best-known open secret on the Net is that creating a home page is easy. It's just a matter of putting together a text file and adding a few tags.

Meanwhile everybody and their brother's companies are setting up sites on the Web, ranging from flimsy storefront mail drops to complex interactive worlds. You may be too busy to design and build a complicated web site, but you'd be surprised how easy it is to put together a few simple pages, or make information from your department available to everyone within your company, or promote a project.

An Overview of Web Publishing

Suddenly, the World Wide Web has opened up an entirely new avenue of publishing, one that avoids much of the costly overhead of print publishing and which is open to anyone—or at least anyone with access to a web server. A web server is a program that delivers requested pages to web client programs (browsers).

CAUTION

I can't go into the details of installing and running a web server in this short space. Fortunately, there are a lot of alternatives to maintaining your own server. See Chapter 11 for information on how to publish your pages on the Web (or on an intranet).

A web publication (or site) consists of a home page, all the web pages that are linked from the home page, all the pages linked from *those* pages, and so on. You should always be able to return to a site's home page from any page at the site. Not every page need be linked directly from the home page, but the essence of a well-designed web publication is the organization of the links.

There are two major steps in web publishing: (1) designing and creating the pages and (2) publishing the site. In this chapter, I'll tell you how to go about creating web documents. You don't need to worry at first how to make your pages available to the public (or to your colleagues). Instead, you can build your pages in a staging area—most likely a folder on your own hard disk. Chapter 11 will tell you how to get your pages out there when you've finished creating them (as well as how to maintain them and how to promote your site once it's published).

Planning a Web Site

I'll cover just the basics of web site creation in this chapter—but enough for a busy person!

Here are the steps to follow in designing a web site:

1. Clarify the relationships among documents and organize a structure for the pages at the web site.
2. Design, write, and format the documents in a staging area.
3. Weave together related pages with hyperlinks.
4. Publish the site (go live from the staging area).
5. Promote the web site to its intended audience.
6. Maintain the site with regular updates.

If you are basing a web site on existing documents or a mixture of existing documents and newly created ones, assemble all your source documents and plan a folder hierarchy that reflects their relationships to one other.

EXPERT ADVICE

If you organize your documents with a judicious structure of folders, you'll find it easy to maintain and update the site in the future.

Think carefully about how you want your documents to link to each other. This is likely the part of web design with which you are least familiar. Linking documents in sequence is often a good place to start, but don't overlook the potential for creative and flexible cross-linking of documents. Often a single document will refer to several others. Each of those references can be an active link. You can link to specific parts of documents, too.

Try to plan for potential future growth of your site. The Web is not a static medium. An orphaned site quickly becomes stale and out of date. Think about what areas of the site might end up being expanded upon or replaced. If you anticipate future changes such as updated statistics or newer publications, they'll be much easier to implement when the time comes.

Web Pages Explained

So what exactly is a web page? It's an HTML document, with the extension .html (.htm on some older Windows computers). But what's an HTML document? It's really just a plain text document with special tags, each of which starts and ends with an angle bracket. Look at an HTML file and you'll be <I>surprised</I> how easy it is to read.

A Little HTML Never Hurt Anyone

In most browsers, it's very easy to take a look at the underlying HTML document that's the source for the displayed web page. In Netscape and most other web browsers, the command is View | Document Source (or, for pages with frames, View | Frame Source) or something similar.

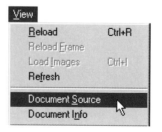

To see the source of a web page in Internet Explorer, right-click an empty part of the document in the window and select View Source from the menu that pops up, or use the View | Source command.

DEFINITION

HTML: *Hypertext markup language; a system of tags used to describe hypertext documents that consist mainly of text, formatting instructions, and hypertext links.*

The HTML source document will appear in a new window (see Figure 10.1). You can select and copy sample HTML from such a window and paste it into a new file.

```
Netscape - [Source of: http://www.berkeley.edu/]

<html>
<head>
<title>UC Berkeley Home Page</title>
</head>
<body>
<img align=top src="/icons/berkeley_960314.gif"><br>
<a href="http://www.urel.berkeley.edu/urel_1/CampusNews/berkeleyan/11-20-96/cybersemest
src="/campusinfo/urel/cybersem/cybersem.gif"></a>

<h4><pre>
<a href="/campusinfo/">Campus Information</a>    <a href="/studentinfo/">Student Inform
<a href="/libraries/">Libraries & Museums</a>    <a
href="/computing/">Computing Resources</a>    <a
href="http://www.uga.berkeley.edu/sas/sohp_txt.html">Student Organization</a></pre></h4:

<p>
Welcome to the UC Berkeley WWW home page.  Click on the
categories above, or scroll below where there is more information
about each category, or use the <a href="/search/">search</a>
page to help you locate a resource.
<hr>
<dl>

<p>
<dt>
```

Figure 10.1 The source HTML file underlying Yahoo's home page

The fastest way to learn about HTML is to look at source files for interesting pages.

How to Create HTML Documents

I'll explain the basics of HTML here, but you don't have to read about HTML if you don't want to. There are more and more tools appearing on the Net that enable users to create web documents without having to know much about the underlying HTML tags. Generally, they let you create and format a document normally and then perform a conversion for you. At the very least, they can automate the insertion of tags and hypertext links.

I'll explain two such tools, Netscape Navigator Gold and Word 97 for Windows, later in this chapter.

HTML Document Layout

All HTML documents must start with <HTML> and end with </HTML>. Between those codes are two sections, the head and the body, marked at start and end by <HEAD></HEAD> and <BODY></BODY>, respectively. The only tag inside the head of the document that you need to know about is the title tag (<TITLE>*the title goes here*</TITLE>). Figure 10.2 shows a diagram of a basic web document.

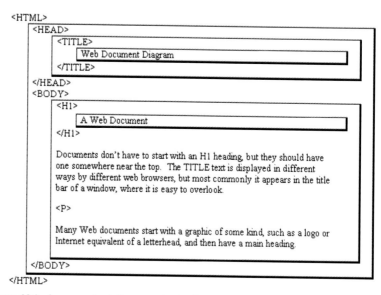

Figure 10.2 A conceptual diagram of a basic web document

EXPERT ADVICE

Since all HTML documents have the same basic tags, there's no need to retype them again and again. Create a template.html document that has the basic tags, along with your name and e-mail address at the bottom. Then you can copy this file and rename it whenever you create a new HTML document.

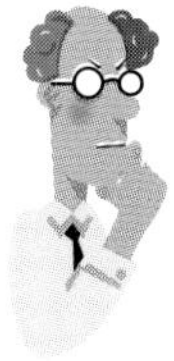

Figure 10.3 shows the document interpreted and displayed by a web browser.

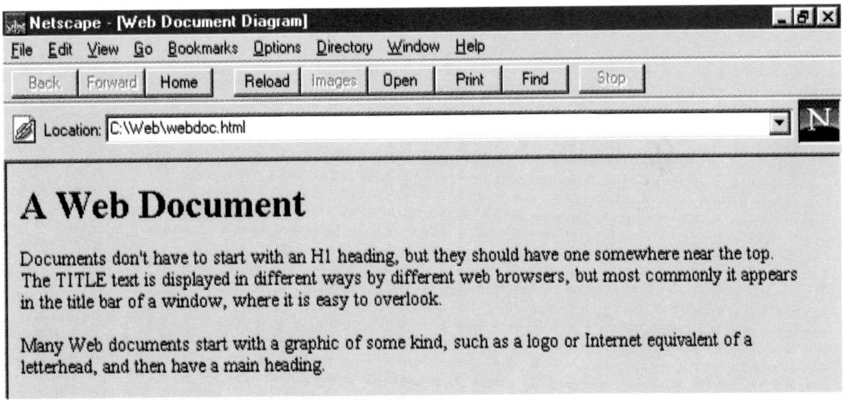

Figure 10.3 The document title (in the title bar), the first-level heading, and the two paragraphs, as displayed in Netscape

Online HTML Reference Material

If you want to learn more about HTML, visit some of the reference sites on the Web shown in Table 10.1.

EXPERT ADVICE

For additional HTML resources, check Yahoo or any of the directories or search engines described in Chapter 3.

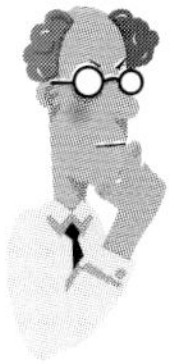

Site Name	Web Address
A Beginner's Guide to HTML	http://www.ncsa.uiuc.edu/General/Internet/WWW/HTMLPrimer.html
Netscape's HTML Reference Guide	http://developer.netscape.com/library/documentation/htmlguid/index.htm
An Example Page That Makes Sense	http://www.dcn.davis.ca.us/~csandvig/ip/example.html
Hypertext Markup Language (HTML)	http://www.w3.org/hypertext/WWW/MarkUp/
HTML Quick Reference	http://kuhttp.cc.ukans.edu/lynx_help/HTML_quick.html
Style Guide for Online Hypertext	http://www.w3.org/hypertext/WWW/Provider/Style/Overview.html
How Do They Do That with HTML?	http://www.nashville.net/~carl/htmlguide/index.html
Yahoo's HTML listing	http://www.yahoo.com/Computers_and_Internet/Software/Data_Formats/HTML
Composing Good HTML	http://www.cs.cmu.edu/~tilt/cgh/

Table 10.1 Online HTML References

Choosing a Web Editing Tool

There are so many different ways to create web documents that it's hard to know where to start. The three broad categories of tools are

- Plain-text editors
- HTML tag editors
- WYSIWYG (what you see is what you get) editors

bookmark

There are many different HTML editors that can help you create a web page. To download software in this category, check the HTML Editors sections at TUCOWS (http://www.tucows.com) and Stroud's (http://www.stroud.com). Anything given five stars (or five cows in the case of TUCOWS) is probably worth downloading.

If you use a plain-text editor, you must type everything yourself, the content *and* the tags. HTML tag editors are similar to plain-text editors but have special commands and shortcuts for inserting the necessary HTML code. They help automate the process and show you what you're working with, but there aren't any tools good enough for me to recommend in this category (except the Mac text editor BB Edit with its special HTML plug-in).

WYSIWYG editors hide the details of the HTML from you and function much like word processors (in fact, some of them are word processors that have learned to speak HTML). I'll explain two useful tools in this chapter, Netscape Navigator Gold and Word 97. Other good web publishing tools include Adobe PageMill and its more advanced sibling, SiteMill (so far Mac-only), and Microsoft FrontPage. Most people new to web publishing use some sort of WYSIWYG editor, but I'll also explain how to type the tags yourself, at least so you know what's going on under the surface.

Creating Web Pages with a Text Editor

This section explains how to create web pages with a simple, raw text editor such as Notepad or WordPad (in Windows) or TeachText, SimpleText, or BB Edit (on the Macintosh).

Converting Old Documents

If you plan to reuse or adapt existing documents, you'll need to save them as text files or as RTF (rich text format) files. If you save them as plain text (ASCII) files, you'll have to insert all the HTML tags manually. If you convert them to RTF, you can then use an RTF to HTML converter to get at least some of the formatting converted to HTML.

EXPERT ADVICE

Whenever possible, try to reuse existing web documents, copying them and rewriting them, to save yourself the tedium of entering the basic tags over and over.

For an RTF converter, point your web browser at http://www.sunpack.com/RTF/, the rtftohtml home page; rtftohtml is a free filter you can download from the Web.

DEFINITION

RTF: *Rich text format; a Microsoft text-based format designed to retain formatting information for file transfers between incompatible systems or formats.*

Writing the Text

A big part of the job, as with the creation of any document, is the writing of the text. Do it in a word processor and save it as a text file with line breaks, or type it in your text editor if you prefer. As with any formal document, do the writing and the formatting in different stages, so that each job is done thoroughly.

EXPERT ADVICE

Because web browsers ignore line breaks in HTML documents, press ENTER *any time you want to make your HTML document clear and easy to read or edit.*

netiquette

To suggest the intention of formatting (to emphasize an item, for instance) instead of the result (such as the use of boldface or italics), use the EM and STRONG tags, which leave the details of emphasis up to each individual browser.

Formatting a Web Page

All the formatting tags you incorporate into your document will go between the <BODY> and </BODY> tags. Most tags go before and after the text they affect, in pairs. Table 10.2 shows a basic set of tags you'll probably want to use. For elaborate documents, consult an HTML designer. Putting together a graceful document is harder than it looks. At the very least, pick up a simple design reference.

EXPERT ADVICE

Numbered and bulleted lists can be nested, one inside of another, to create subordinate list levels, but be careful not to cross the tags.

Purpose	Tag
First- through sixth-level heading	<H1></H1>,...,<H6></H6>
New paragraph	<P>
Line break, same paragraph	
Horizontal line	<HR>
Bold, italics, underlining	<B></B>, <I></I>, <U></U>
Emphasis, strong emphasis	<EM></EM>,<STRONG></STRONG>
Equal-width text (as made by a typewriter)	<TT></TT>
Start or end of numbered list	<OL></OL>
Numbered list item (don't type the number)	<LI>
Start or end of bulleted list	<UL></UL>
Bulleted list item	<LI>
Start or end of definition list	<DL></DL>
Definition term	<DT>
Definition	<DD>

Table 10.2 Some Common Formatting Tags

Figure 10.4 shows a sample web document illustrating the results of various formatting tags, displayed in Netscape.

Netscape - [A Heavily Made-Up Document]

File Edit View Go Bookmarks Options Directory Window Help

Back Forward Home Reload Images Open Print Find Stop

Location: C:\Web\format.html

A Heavily Formatted Document

Featuring Overuse of Formatting!

Yes, that's right, *emphasis* all over the place. <u>Silly stuff.</u> Applied ***tackily***, without regard for **GOOD DESIGN**.

This calls for a
clean break
before the next section.

Here are a few definitions:

Tag
      A code used to mark the start, end, or exact location of a formatting or hypertext feature.
Hypertext
      Text that contains "links" connecting one part of a document with another document or port of

Document: Done

Start Netscape - [A Heavil...   4:11 PM

Figure 10.4 Although no paragon of design, this sample page illustrates some common formatting effects

Inserting Graphic Images

Don't overlook the mixed-media potential of the World Wide Web. A big part of the sudden popularity of the Internet is the Web and the simple fact that web pages can display pictures (on most web browsers). Web sites with illustrations and effective use of graphics are much more inviting and communicative than the text-only world that the Internet has only recently emerged from.

CAUTION

Pictures take longer to download than text and consume more hard-disk space, so use them judiciously. Keep art small and reuse graphical elements so they'll have to be downloaded only once.

The two widely recognized graphics image file formats on the Web are GIF (with the extension .gif, for graphics image file format) and JPEG (with the extension .jpg, the Internet standard promulgated by the Joint Photographics Experts Group). JPEGs can be compressed to much smaller sizes than can GIFs (although there are trade-offs in image quality), and JPEGs are much better suited for photographs and other continuous-tone images. GIFs are perfectly adequate for images with solid blocks of color, and they can also include transparent backgrounds and animation, neither of which can be used with JPEGs. A new file format, PNG (with the extension .png, for portable network graphics format), combines some of the advantages of both other formats, but is still not widely recognized.

The basic tag for inserting a figure is <IMG SRC="*filename*"ALT="*text*">, where *text* is alternative text to be displayed by nongraphical browsers and browsers with image loading turned off. To learn more about the <IMG> tag, view the source of some pages that use illustrations in ways that appeal to you.

Inserting Hypertext Links

The bottom line of the Web is its hypertext nature. The real genius of hypertext is that it hides the baroque Internet addressing protocols that are so clumsy to discuss and learn about. Sure, you still have to type some URLs, but even those are getting easier. (For example, you can visit my web site by just typing syx.com in Netscape or Internet Explorer.) Most of the time, though, navigating the Internet can be as simple as pointing to the name of something you want to see or hear and clicking your mouse.

There's the rub. To make your own web site, it's up to you to plan and insert the hypertext links. The HTML tag used for hypertext links is <A>, the anchor tag; you can use it in any of the ways shown in Table 10.3.

EXPERT ADVICE

Make sure documents are in the same hierarchical relationship where you're creating them as they will be when and if they are moved.

Link Element	Anchor Tag
Clickable hypertext link pointing to another HTML document or other type of file (such as a sound or movie file)	<A HREF="*filename*">*active-text*</A>
Hypertext link pointing to a named anchor in this same document	<A HREF="*#name*">*active-text*</A>
Link pointing to a named anchor in another HTML document	<A HREF="*filename#name*">*active-text*</A>
Named anchor point	<A NAME="*name*">*active-text*</A>
Combined link and anchor	<A HREF="*filename* NAME"="*name*">*active-text*</A>
Clickable image link	<A HREF="*filename*"><IMG SRC="*button-graphic*"></A>

Table 10.3 Hypertext Link Anchor Tags

EXPERT ADVICE

Most web servers will treat a file named index.html as the default file in a directory (meaning the one that is shown if no file is specified). For this reason, the root, or home page, of a site is often named index.html.

Files in the same directory don't have to be identified by a full pathname. In your index.html file, you can link to a file called dogs.html with just the tag <A HREF="dogs.html">*active-text-about-dogs*</A>. If you have subdirectories (a good way of organizing your site), indicate directory levels with a forward slash (as in Unix; not a backslash as in Windows). For example, if you move dogs.html into the pets subdirectory, the tag would be <A HREF="pets/dogs.html">. The parent directory can be indicated with two dots (..), so, for example, the dogs.html file can link back to the index with <A HREF="../index.html">.

These shorter versions of pathnames are called relative addresses; files on a different computer would need to refer to your pages with the full URL, including the path: for example, http://www.yoursystem.com/~yourname/pets/dogs.html.

Finishing the Web Document

When you're finished working on your document (for now), save it with a one-word file name (ending in .html).

File name:	sample.html			Save
Save as type:	All Files (*.*)		▼	Cancel

CAUTION

If you want to save a text file in Windows 95 with an extension besides .txt, you have to reveal file extensions. To do so, choose View | Options in any folder window and uncheck "Hide MS-DOS file extensions for file types that are registered."

Creating Web Pages with Netscape

The first thing you need to do to create and edit web pages with Netscape is to download the Gold version of Navigator (you may recall more or less the same steps from Chapter 2):

As of version 3.0, the web publishing version of Netscape is called Navigator Gold. In the expected 4.0 release of Netscape Communicator, the web publishing module will be called Netscape Composer, but much of the functionality will be similar to what I'm describing here.

1. Click any Netscape Now icon or point your browser at http://home.netscape.com/comprod/mirror/index.html and then click Download Netscape Navigator.
2. Choose items in the online form and click the Click to Display Download Sites button.
3. Scroll down to the list of links that appears.
4. Choose one to download the product. If it fails, click Reload or choose a different link.
5. When you have successfully downloaded the file, double-click it to start the installation process.

With Navigator Gold, you can create a web document in a few simple steps:

1. Create or edit the document.
2. Type or paste in your text, or edit existing text.
3. Format the document.
4. Save the document.
5. Publish the document.

Creating a Web Document from Scratch

If you are creating a file from scratch, you have three choices: you can use Netscape Gold's Page Wizard to help you through the process, you can use a template, or you can start with a blank page. Use the File | New Document command and choose a method.

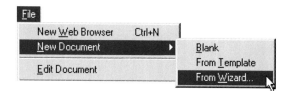

Netscape Gold's Page Wizard

The easiest way to crank out a simple page is with Netscape's Page Wizard. When you start a document based on the Page Wizard, Navigator connects you to a site where you can read some instructions and then start picking and choosing elements for your page. When you've finished filling out the Page Wizard form, the wizard generates your page for you, suitable for downloading.

CAUTION

The Page Wizard is actually stored at the Netscape web site, not on your computer, so the company can change it or improve it at any time. Netscape is changing and improving its templates and Page Wizard all the time, so the illustrations shown here and the step-by-step instructions may no longer precisely match what you'll see online, but the gist of this discussion should remain the same.

From this point on, the procedure is the same as for saving any document from the Web to your local computer for editing with Netscape Editor. The instructions for that procedure follow, in the section "Editing Existing Files with Netscape."

Netscape Templates

Netscape also provides some document templates for specific purposes. These contain recommended layout and structure as well as boilerplate text you can replace with your own specifics. This is a great way to get your documents started; you can edit them into shape later.

To start a web document using a Netscape template, first select File | New Document | From Template. This connects you to the Netscape Web Page Templates page. Read the couple of screenfuls of introductory material at the top of the page. Then read the overview of steps for using a template. Select and click a template name. Navigator will take you to the template.

From there, the procedure is once again the same as for saving any document from the Web to your local computer for editing with Netscape Gold's Editor. The instructions for that procedure follow, in the section "Editing Existing Files with Netscape."

Starting with a Blank Document

It *is* possible to face up to that proverbial blank white page and just write your own web document, without cribbing other people's ideas or boilerplate. To do so, select File | New Document | Blank. Netscape Editor will create a new document named Untitled and let you go at it.

Once you've started a new page, you have to fill it with information, format it, and link it to other pages. The next few sections will help you do just that.

Editing Existing Files with Netscape

If you're editing an existing document on your hard drive, you can just open it normally (with the File | Open File in Editor command).

You can work with any page that's out there on the Web. Just browse until the page (or template or Wizard result) is displayed and then click the Edit button (or use the File | Edit Document command); Netscape will prompt you on how to save the file locally. (Remember that these editing commands are available only in the Gold version of Netscape.) Be sure you're not infringing on anyone's copyrights! (It's best to communicate with anyone whose work you're drawing on heavily.)

To save the page to your computer, follow these steps:

1. Click the Edit button. This brings up the Save Remote Document dialog box.
2. Click the Save button. Netscape will warn you against stealing other people's artwork. (Good advice! Use art you either own or have permission to use. For that matter, hands off anyone else's text without their permission.)
3. Click OK. The Save As dialog box will appear.
4. Select a folder in which to save this document (and maybe your entire site). Type a file name for the document and click OK.

Formatting the Web Page

If you've ever used a word processor or even a text editor, then Netscape Editor should be very easy for you to learn. The idea is about the same: You see what you're typing in the main window and you give commands by choosing them from menus or clicking shortcut buttons. Most of the useful editing and formatting commands are available on the three toolbars at the top of the window: the Character toolbar, the File / Edit toolbar, and the Paragraph toolbar (see Figure 10.5). You can tell what most of the buttons do by their names (just point to a button and a ToolTip appears).

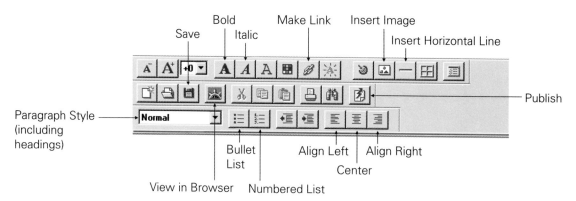

Figure 10.5 The Character, File / Edit, and Paragraph toolbars

You should give your document a new, real title before you save it for the first time. Once you've done that, you can forget about the title. To give your document a title, select Properties | Document to bring up the Document Properties dialog box. Type a title in the Title box and click OK.

You can select text by clicking and dragging. (You can select horizontal rules and images just as easily.) To delete selections, just press the DELETE key. To cut a selection so you can move it elsewhere, click the Cut button (or right-click and select Cut).

Creating headings is easy to do with the Paragraph Style drop-down list box on the Paragraph toolbar. Just select the text you want to make into a heading (or put the insertion point where you want to start typing your new heading), click the Paragraph Style list, and select the heading level you want.

Netscape Editor makes it very easy to format characters and align text in different ways. It's usually just a matter of selecting text and then clicking a button, choosing an item from a drop-down list or menu, or—at its most complicated—selecting an item from a dialog box. To make existing text bold, for example, select the text and then click the Bold button. To type new boldface text, position the insertion point, click the Bold button, and then start typing. The button will appear to be pushed in. When you want to continue typing in regular (unbold) text, click the button again and keep going.

There are a few formatting effects you can apply to entire paragraphs (as well as to headings and other kinds of text). Among them are indentation, alignment, block quotes, and addresses.

When you want to see how your current document will look in the Netscape browser window, save it. Then click the View in Browser button. Netscape will open a new browser window and open your current document in it.

Inserting Graphic Images

Since 1994, a web site has had to include graphics to look state-of-the-art. Graphics on pages are a big part of what has made the Web so popular, humanizing the previously cold, text-oriented Internet. Common types of graphics include custom logos, headlines and banners, buttons (that is, clickable image links), scanned photos, pie charts, and graphs. You can use graphical elements to create a visual "look" and identity for your pages. You can also use them for illustration or visual explanation.

EXPERT ADVICE

Before inserting any pictures into any web document, it's a good idea to first collect all of your graphics files in a single folder. This makes it easier to browse for images and keep track of where things are.

As important as graphics are to the overall effect of a well-designed web page, you should also take care to ensure that your pages will look and function adequately when viewed as text only. Some of your audience may be using a text-only web browser. Even if you expect the majority of your readers to use a graphical browser, such as Netscape Navigator, a lot of people do their browsing, at least initially, with automatic image loading turned off. (Also, some web users are blind and have text-only browsers that read, or rather speak, the content out loud.)

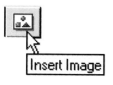

The basic method of inserting an image is to move to the point where the image is to appear and then use the Insert Image button. This assumes that the image already exists; you can create images with a number of different programs, or get (noncopyrighted!) images from public-domain icon and image libraries.

Inserting Hypertext Links

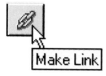

The usual approach to creating hyperlinks is to type the text (or insert the graphics) into the document first and *then* select the salient text (or image) and associate a link with it. With Netscape Editor, inserting hyperlinks is simply a matter of selecting text and then clicking the Make Link button, or dragging a link (or a local document) directly into the web document you're working on.

STEP BY STEP Insert Graphic Images with Netscape Gold

③ If you haven't saved your document yet, Netscape Editor will prompt you to do so.

④ Type the path and file name of the image, if you know it (or click the Browse button to the right of the Image file name box; find the file you want in the Select Image File dialog box and then click the Open button).

② Click the Insert Image button.

① Before inserting a graphic, move the insertion point to where you want the image to appear.

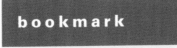

⑤ Put a text description in the Text box in the Alternate representations area and choose any other options.

⑥ Click OK.

bookmark

For information on how to form web addresses (URLs), see Chapter 1 or the official documents at the W3 headquarters (http:www.w3.org/pub/WWW/Addressing).

Once you've filled in the required link information, click OK. The text that activates the link will appear underlined and blue (as is typical of links when displayed in web browsers).

There are two different broad categories of links, by the way, usually referred to as internal and external links. Internal links connect to documents (or objects) located on the same computer (the same server) as the document that contains the link. External links connect to documents (or objects) located somewhere else on the Net. These are also sometimes referred to, respectively, as relative and absolute links, because internal links are referred to relative to the location of the starting document, whereas external links are referred to by complete web addresses (URLs).

Finishing the Web Document

When the document is completed, select File | Save (for now). This will save the file locally on your hard drive. To make it available over the Internet, however, you'll have to publish it. To publish a document means transferring it to your web server and making it accessible for Internet users. Publishing your pages (using Netscape and other methods) is explained in Chapter 11.

Creating Web Pages with Word

Microsoft Word 97 can now convert HTML documents to Word documents and vice versa. It also has a bunch of toolbar items and menu choices useful for web page design. The HTML features may not be installed with your version of Word, though. If you find them missing, you'll need to redo the installation procedure and be sure to check the HTML options.

CAUTION

If you have an earlier version of Word, you'll need to download Internet Assistant to add web editing features. To do so, point your browser at http://www.microsoft.com/word/internet/ia/ and download and install the correct file for your version of Word.

You can also use Word's basic File | Save As command and then simply specify HTML as the file format. Word includes the Save as HTML command directly on the File menu as a shortcut.

If you're using an earlier version of Word (older than Word 97) with Internet Assistant, you won't have the Wizard template.

Converting Old Documents

If you plan to base a web page on an existing document, first open the document. Then select File | Save as HTML. Give the document a one-word name (no spaces).

Creating a Web Document from Scratch

Starting a web document even without a model Word document is also simple. Select File | New. In the Templates dialog box that appears, click the Web Pages tab. You'll see three options: a blank HTML document template, an HTML document-creating wizard (an interactive routine that walks you through the process of creating a generic web page), and a "goodies" template that includes links to additional resources at Microsoft's Word web site.

Formatting the Web Page

Type the text of the document as you normally would. You won't be inserting HTML tags directly. Instead, you'll use Word's normal formatting commands, such as the Bold, Italic, and Underline buttons on the Formatting toolbar, along with special HTML-related commands on the toolbars and styles that are equivalent to HTML tags. You'll notice there is a special web toolbar for navigating the Web; documents you browse are automatically loaded into Word, where they can be edited. Figure 10.6 shows these toolbars.

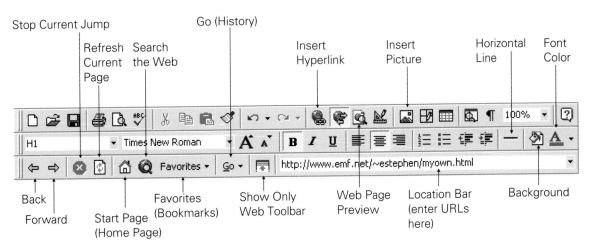

Figure 10.6 Word's toolbars for creating web pages

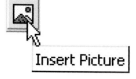

For example, to make a line of text into a first-level heading, select the text and then select the H1 style in the Style drop-down list box on the Formatting toolbar.

Impose HTML formatting for which Word has direct equivalents, such as numbered and bulleted lists, with the normal Word toolbar or menu commands.

This is technically not part of formatting, but to assign the document's title (usually displayed in a web browser's title bar), use the File | Properties command, type a title, and click OK.

Inserting Graphic Images

To insert a picture into a web document, first place all your graphics files in a single folder. Move your cursor to the location where the image should appear. Then click the Picture button and select a picture from the dialog box that appears. Then click Insert.

Inserting Hypertext Links

Word takes the tedium out of inserting links. First, select the word (or graphic) you want to use as the launching point to the linked destination. Then click the Insert Hyperlink button.

This brings up the Insert HyperLink dialog box.

If you want to link to a local document, type it in the "Link to file or URL" box. You can click the top Browse button and choose a file from the dialog box; this box lists both .doc and .html files. If you link to a regular Word file, only people using Word as a web browser will be able to read it.

To link to an address on the Web, click the "Link to file or URL" box. Then type the address in the box or select it from a list of URLs you've visited (see Figure 10.7). Be sure to type URLs exactly to link to another document on the Web (Word will remember all the URLs you type and allow you to reuse them easily).

To link to a specific section of a document, choose the "Named location in file" box and choose a document and bookmark name.

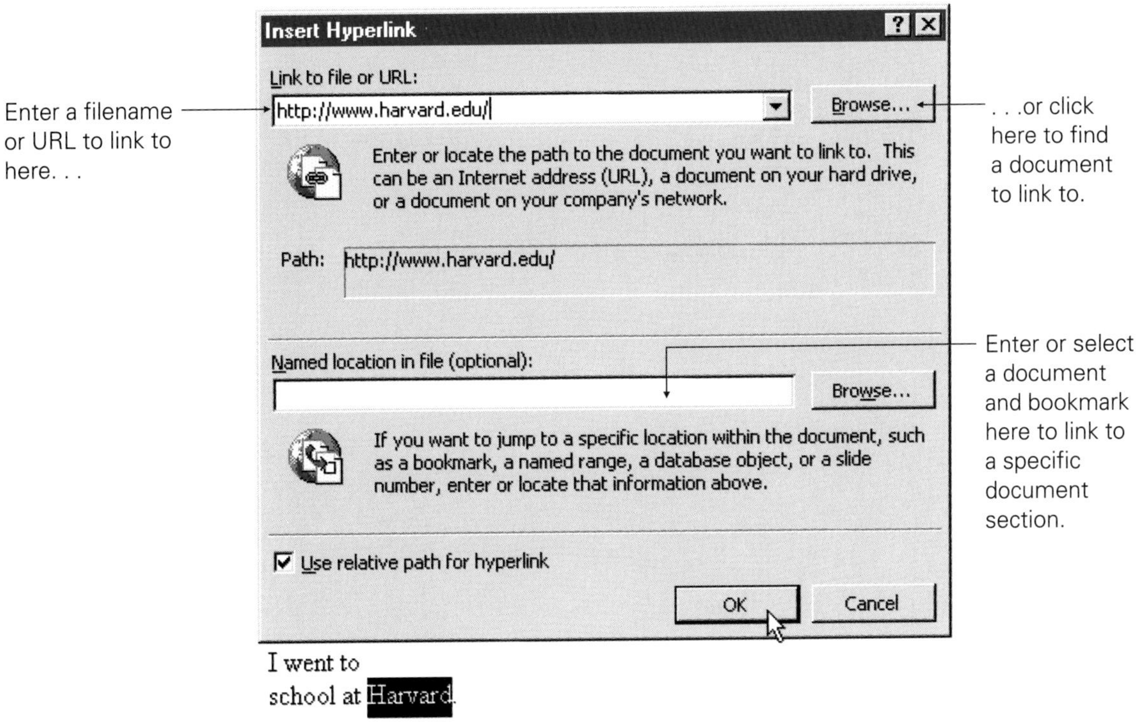

Enter a filename or URL to link to here. . .

. . .or click here to find a document to link to.

Enter or select a document and bookmark here to link to a specific document section.

Insert Hyperlink

Link to file or URL:

http://www.harvard.edu/

Browse...

Enter or locate the path to the document you want to link to. This can be an Internet address (URL), a document on your hard drive, or a document on your company's network.

Path: http://www.harvard.edu/

Named location in file (optional):

Browse...

If you want to jump to a specific location within the document, such as a bookmark, a named range, a database object, or a slide number, enter or locate that information above.

☑ Use relative path for hyperlink

OK   Cancel

I went to school at Harvard.

Figure 10.7 Inserting a link in a Word web document

EXPERT ADVICE

If you plan to link to a bookmark within a document, make sure the bookmark exists (or create it) before you try to link it. (Use the Insert | Bookmark command.)

Then click OK. The text that activates the link will appear underlined and blue (as is typical of links when displayed in web browsers).

Finishing the Web Document

When the document is completed (for now), save it. Word automatically displays the View | Online Layout view, so you can see how the page will look on the Web (more or less). If you want to view your page in a browser, click the Web Page Preview button. You can also test the links from within Word, now that Word doubles as a clunky web browser.

Clicking any link should take you to the linked document or bookmark. Use the Back and Forward buttons on the toolbar to retrace your path.

Advanced Web Design

See Chapter 11 for how to publish web documents on the Web and on intranets, using Word 97 and other methods.

There are more possibilities in web design, although not all of the latest advances have yet been implemented in standard HTML rules or in all or even most browsers. Some advanced elements have become almost commonplace. It's a full-time job keeping up with web design developments, so focus on content first, presentation second, and embellishment last. Here's a list of advanced web design features you might want to explore: alignment commands, tables, border-less figures, gutter space around figures, transparent figure backgrounds, faster-seeming interlaced images, background patterns on pages, background colors on pages, customized text colors, variably sized text, pages that load themselves, style sheets with recommended settings, counters, and frames.

I'll touch on a few of the more standard advanced features (such as tables, frames, and multimedia content) in Chapter 11.

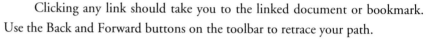

EXPERT ADVICE

When you think you're ready for prime time, ask some friends to beta test your pages to look for typos, broken links, or other potential problems. Try to find people using different browsers or types of computers to test your pages.

CHECK POINT

You're now ready to go beyond passive involvement in the Web. If you have something to say to the world or a product to promote or a report to circulate, you can now create documents in a format that the entire wired world can read. Chapter 11 will tell you how to go about publishing your HTML documents both on the Web and on local intranets.

Going Live on the Web

INCLUDES

- Using advanced web design

- Finding a host for your site

- Setting up your own domain

- Publishing your pages on the Web

- Publishing on an intranet

- Promoting your web site

- Maintaining and updating your web site

FAST FORWARD

Make Your Pages Sizzle ➤ pp. 312-329

- Add custom colors and background graphics to your pages.
- Align elements on your pages with tables.
- Add multimedia events to your site.
- Set up "hip" navigation elements such as image maps and frames.
- Make your pages interactive with forms, scripts, and applets.

Why do you need a site on the World Wide Web?

Publish a Web Document ➤ pp. 329-341

Upload the file to your site via FTP. Then,

- With Navigator Gold, click the Publish button.
- With Word 97, select File | Save As, choose Internet Locations (FTP) in the Save in drop-down list box, and then save the file directly to your site.

Save As

Save in: My Documents
- Desktop
  - My Computer
    - 3½ Floppy (A:)
    - Win95 (C:)
      - My Documents
    - (D:)
  - Network Neighborhood
  - Internet Locations (FTP)

~$myo
myown
Robby.

Promote Your Web Site ➤ pp. 341-345

- Submit announcements to major search engines and directories (listed in Chapter 3).
- Announce your site on mailing lists and Usenet.
- Communicate with the creators of similar or like-minded web sites and offer to exchange hyperlinks.

Add to Yahoo!

This form is for **adding** URLs **only!**

Maintain Your Web Site ➤ pp. 345-346

- Assign someone to regularly monitor traffic to and from the site.
- Make frequent updates and changes to your site
- Consider investing in a site-management program, such as Adobe SiteMill (Macintosh) or Microsoft FrontPage (Windows).

New Sites This Week

ARTS & LITERATURE

310

In the last chapter, I showed you how to create web pages and weave them together with hyper-links. To make your pages available to the public or to the other users of your intranet, you have to post the pages on a server to which your audience has access. This is what is meant by "going live" with your web site. You'll want to take the time to carefully develop and test your site, but when you have done so, it's time to publish.

Once the basic site has been laid down, the hierarchy planned, the central pages created, and the details and art filled in, you have two choices. You can publish the pages immediately and work to improve and jazz them up in later revisions, or you can add embellishments, showing off your mastery of sophisticated web design and interactive features, and *then* publish the pages. Either way, once you've published your site, you must think of it as an ongoing commitment, or it will atrophy and become useless in the long run.

Technically, publishing your pages is easy. It's generally done with FTP—either stand-alone FTP programs or the built-in file-transfer features of web publishing tools (such as PageMill or Netscape Gold). The tricky part is figuring out *where* to publish your site. To publish on the Web, you'll need access to a web server on an Internet host. Publishing on an intranet is relatively easier to arrange, but you'll still need to coordinate with the administrator of the network, who may have a preference about which file server you store your pages on.

If you've been able to create the pages you want to publish from what you learned in Chapter 10, then you can skip directly to "Publishing Your Web Site." If you want to incorporate some more advanced web elements into your documents, you can start with the first section of this chapter, "Advanced Web Design." You can also come back to read that section when you're ready for it.

Advanced Web Design

If you're eager to publish your site, skip ahead to "Publishing Your Web Site," and then come back and read this section at your leisure.

If you've learned all the basic techniques of web publishing (creating, editing and formatting HTML documents, inserting graphic images into web pages, and weaving related pages together into a coherent web site with hyperlinks), and your pages still don't look and feel the way you want them to, then you might want to invest some time (your own) or money (to pay someone else) in adding advanced features to your developing web site.

I'll explain some of the more popular web design tricks, show you some examples, and point you toward a few online sources for additional information if you have time to implement advanced features, including:

If you find that this section just whets your appetite, you might want to read Web Publishing with Netscape for Busy People, *which I co-authored with Malcolm Humes.*

- Colors and background graphics
- Tables
- Multimedia
- Image maps
- Frames
- Forms, scripts, JavaScript, and Java

Colors and Background Graphics

Customizing the colors (text, links, and background colors, that is) or slipping background graphics into your web pages is pretty easy, especially if you're using a web editing tool such as Netscape Gold or Word 97. Even if you're typing your HTML by hand, the tags are fairly straightforward and easy to learn.

In HTML, the way to control general color selections for an entire web page and to insert a background graphic if you wish, is to type the following attributes into the BODY tag:

```
<BODY BACKGROUND="filename.gif/jpg" BGCOLOR="color"
TEXT="color" LINK="color" VLINK="color" ALINK="color">
```

with LINK specifying the color of an unvisited link, VLINK the color of a visited link, and ALINK the color of an active link (a link being clicked). The *color* assignment can be a hexadecimal RGB (red, green, blue) value, such as FF0000 (red, because this value indicates maximum red, minimum green, minimum blue); or it can be one of a limited (but growing) set of named colors, currently including Aqua, Black, Blue, Fuschia, Gray, Green, Lime, Maroon, Navy, Olive, Purple, Red, Silver, Teal, White, and Yellow.

DEFINITION

Hexadecimal: A numbering system that runs from 00 to 09, 0A to 0F, and then 10 to 1F, 20 to 2F, ..., F0 to FF, 100 to 10F, and so on—it's a base-16 system, and I've already told you more than you want to know about it.

EXPERT ADVICE

You can also color any specific stretch of text by preceding it with a <FONT COLOR="color"> tag and following it with </FONT>.

Background patterns have to be the same kinds of files as inline images (that is, GIFs and JPEGs). See Chapter 10 for more on web page graphics.

bookmark

One good online source for background tiles is http://www.meat.com, in a section called Texture Land. Another place to look is the Clip Art section of the http://www.pixelsite.com site.

Both Netscape Gold and Word 97 offer dialog boxes for selecting colors and color combinations and for defining custom colors (by choosing from a color wheel), as well as for inserting background graphics.

Another useful background trick is to create a long, narrow, two-tone tile and use it to create a strip of color across the top or left side of the page. For example, the graphic

when used as a tile, will create a page background like the one shown in Figure 11.1.

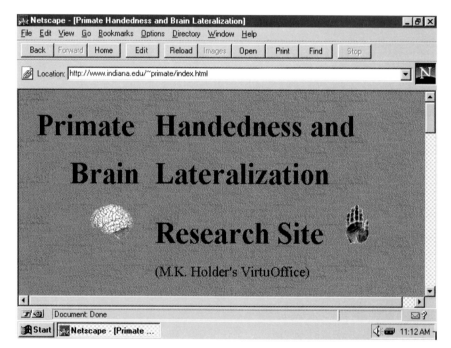

Figure 11.1 This page uses a two-tone tile to create the colored area

Tables

Creating, editing, and formatting tables by hand, unlike color selection, can be very difficult and frustrating. Tables themselves are wonderful and are more often used to structure the layout of a page than as tables of data labeled as such. (This is possible because you can set table borders to zero, hiding the invisible grid underlying your page.) The basic table tags are not too difficult to understand (see Table 11.1), but trying to do anything complicated with them is not so easy.

Notice that there are no HTML tags for columns in a table. Instead, everything is formatted in terms of rows (and the cells within rows).

This Element	Starts With	Ends With
The entire table	<TABLE>	</TABLE>
A row	<TR>	</TR>
A cell	<TD>	</TD>
A header row	<TH>	</TH>

Table 11.1 Basic HTML Table Tags

If you want to include tables in your page designs, I heartily recommend obtaining a good web editing tool, such a Netscape Gold, Word 97, PageMill, or one of the many other decent products. With any of these, inserting and editing tables can be done on the screen in a much more intuitive fashion than wrestling with tags. Figure 11.2 shows a web page that uses a table both to present information and as part of its design.

Multimedia

Because the Web can deliver any type of file to your computer over the Internet, it's not limited to flat web pages and still pictures. In principle, you can embed or link any type of multimedia file (that is, videos, sounds, animation, formatted documents, interactive programs, and even 3D worlds) into a web site to enhance its presentation values. There are a few drawbacks in reality, though.

EXPERT ADVICE

Consider farming out the things you can't do well yourself, especially while you're learning. There's too much to the Web to just be a good-enough generalist.

Cell

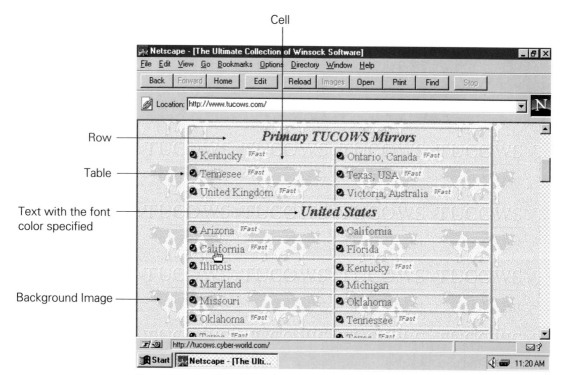

Row

Table

Text with the font color specified

Background Image

Figure 11.2 A table of mirror sites from TUCOWS

One is that the multimedia content takes time and money to develop (whether you teach yourself to do it or hire an expert), and the other is that for most people, the Internet terminates in a fairly slow modem connection, and users will end up waiting all day for your infomercial to download.

CAUTION

Even if you're certain your audience is equipped to appreciate your multimedia presentation, avoid overloading your pages with too many plugged-in bells and whistles.

Be thoughtful about your audience:

- Figure out a maximum practical file size for downloads (see Table 11.2) and stick to it.
- Warn your audience when a link connects to a large file (anything over 50K or so).
- Use extra media elements only when they serve a definite purpose.

CAUTION

You can't assume your readers will have the right type of plug-in to play your multimedia content. To deal with this, you can include links from your pages to web sites from which they can download the tools they need. Bear in mind, however, that many will forego the extra steps necessary and miss out on the extra content.

	Slow Modem (14.4 kilobits per second)	Fast Modem (28.8 kbps)	ISDN or Frame Relay (64 kbps)	T1 (1.544 Mbps)	T3 (44.736Mbps)
Small HTML or Text file (4K)	2+ seconds	1+ seconds	0.5 second	.02 second	.0007 second
400 x 500 compressed JPEG image (15K)	8+ seconds	4+ seconds	2 seconds	.08 second	.003 second
30-page PDF file (100K)	1 minute	0.5 minute	10 seconds	0.5 second	.02 second
4-second sound clip (900K)	8 + minutes	4+ minutes	2 minutes	4.5 seconds	0.16 second
Software (5M)	1+ hours	0.5 hour	11 minutes	30 seconds	1 second

Table 11.2 Approximate Download Times for Different Sizes of Files and Levels of Connection (mileage will vary depending on Internet traffic and server issues)

DEFINITIONS

Kbps: Kilobits per second; a measurement of bandwidth (the number of bits that can be sent through a medium divided by a unit of time). A kilobit is 1,024 bits.

Mbps: Megabits per second; a larger measurement of bandwidth. A megabit is 1,048,576 bits.

The actual techniques for inserting multimedia objects into web pages are simple. You can either link to an object directly (as you would to any document—see Chapter 10 for more on hyperlinks), or you can embed the object either as an image (for some types of animations) or using the new EMBED tag.

Some of the more popular multimedia formats are

- Adobe Portable Document Format (PDF), an efficient way of delivering formatted documents
- Sounds (WAV, au, AIFF, and Real Audio)
- Movies and animations (QuickTime, MPEG, AVI, and GIF89a)

bookmark

For more information about Adobe Acrobat and the PDF format, visit http://www.adobe.com or http://www.projectcool.com/developer/acrobat. RealAudio is at http://www.realaudio.com.

To create your own GIF animations in Windows, download the GIF Construction Set (http://www.mindworkshop.com/alchemy/alchemy.html). For the Macintosh, try GifBuilder (http://www.pascal.com/mirrors/gifbuilder/). For more information, see Royal Frazier's definitive web site on the subject (http://member.aol.com/royalef/gifanim.htm).

- Macromedia Director Shockwave files, small self-running applications that integrate multiple media and can be interactive (with user controls such as buttons and "hot," clickable areas)
- Three-dimensional environments—Virtual Reality Modeling Language (VRML) worlds

EXPERT ADVICE

One environment very well suited for multimedia web content is an intranet, especially one that is not strung out over a large area and reliant on the same sorts of phone lines that the public Internet uses.

Image Maps

Image maps are clickable graphics that send you to different destinations depending on where you click. Most image maps are graphical versions of what you might call a keyword index. They often show some form of illustration with formatted text on top.

CAUTION

Bear in mind that people with nongraphical browsers (or browsing with image loading turned off) will not be able to use most image maps! Be sure to give them some kind of text alternative.

Most of the time, you'll use maps to lead readers to the major categories of pages at your site. The first step then, in the creation of any image map is the production of the artwork. If you want something as basic as plain formatted text or a simple graphic, you can assemble the image yourself. If you want something more sophisticated, you may need to hire a graphic artist.

Here's a simple image map:

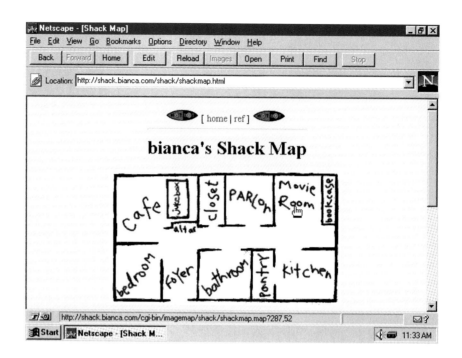

What makes a map work is that different regions of the image are assigned to different URLs. (You usually also assign a default address to go to, in case the reader clicks somewhere on the image but outside any of the "hot" regions.)

There are three types of image maps:

- Traditional server-side maps
- Client-side maps
- Fake image maps

The server-side map requires that you write an image map reference file and post it at your site. Fake image maps are actually separate graphics, displayed seamlessly as one image. I'll give you a brief run-down on client-side image maps, which let the user see where they're going (if they look in the status bar of their browser while pointing the mouse to different regions of the map), and offer text alternatives for non-graphical browsers.

bookmark

If you want to try to make a traditional server-side image map, two good image map tools for Widnows are MapEdit (http://www.boutell.com/mapedit/) and Map THIS (http://galadriel.ecaetc.ohio-state.edu/tc/mt). For the Macintosh, try WebMap (http://www.city.net/cnx/software/webmap.html).

It's silly, really, to go to the server to figure out the meaning of an image map click when the browser can do the job just as well and faster. With client-side image maps, the "thinking" is done on the client, or browser, side of the transaction, instead of on the server end.

A client-side image map has two parts: the description of the map areas (using the new <MAP></MAP> tag), and the image (using a new addition to the <IMG ...> tag, called USEMAP). The MAP description also has to have a NAME description—just like a link to a named target, as explained in Chapter 10.

Inside the MAP tags, you include an <AREA ...> tag for each region of the map. The AREA tag includes the following additional tags:

```
SHAPE="RECT", "CIRCLE", or "POLYGON"
COORDS="x1,y1,x2,y2"
HREF="destination URL"
ALT="alternative text"
```

The MAP description can go anywhere in the document, but to make it actually work, you have to add the USEMAP tag to the IMG tag for the image map, like so:

```
<IMG SRC="navmap.gif" USEMAP="#navmap">
```

Frames

If you've ever worked with a spreadsheet program that allowed the screen to be broken into panes, or if you've ever split the screen of a word processor, then you already have an inkling of what frames look like and do on web pages. Frames are subdivided regions of the screen. Each frame can behave more or less as a separate web document, so a group of frames is not just a fancy type of table. Frames can also contain links that point to other frames, so that clicking in one frame (such as a navigation area across one side of the screen) can result in a change in another frame (perhaps in the large, primary area).

Problems with frames can range from minor to severe. Truth be told, not all browsers recognize them (frames have a built-in way of offering substitute pages to browsers that don't "do" frames). Compounding this problem is the nuisance that the standards are still in flux, with Netscape and Microsoft, typically, tossing around changes. Finally, there are the more fundamental issues of whether frames are worth the bother, or even just plain ugly (not to mention wasteful of precious screen real estate).

Surely, in the long run, some method for keeping fixed navigation tools or other features on the screen while allowing other sections to change will have to be adopted. Frames may just be the answer, but that's not yet perfectly clear.

EXPERT ADVICE

Even if you plan to bring someone else in to code your frames for you, it will help you to understand what's possible so you can mock up or storyboard the frames you want and the way you want them to interact.

The ultimate problem with frames is that the coding can be quite tricky, depending on what behavior you want, and poorly coded frame pages can cause unreadable pages that may even crash a user's browser. With that in mind, we'll give you a quick overview of the essential frame tags and then leave it up to you to decide whether you're too busy to tackle the project yourself.

If you plan to create frames yourself, remember that you can view the document source (for the main page) or the frame source (for any subsidiary frame) to see how frames are put together. If you want to copy any coding literally, cut and paste it from the view windows.

Pages with frames actually consist of several different web documents: a main document containing the frame coding and the alternative coding (for nonframe users); and additional documents, one for each frame.

The master document for such a page, instead of having the usual <BODY> and </BODY> tags surrounding its contents, has <FRAMESET> and </FRAME-SET> tags.

EXPERT ADVICE

Some of the more advanced web design or web site management programs provide automated help with the creation of frames, but not all do. It's sure to be the next feature added to many web design programs, though.

The FRAMESET tag can have either a ROWS or a COLS tag inside, specifying the number of rows or columns and the relative sizes of each. (If you want rows *and* columns, you have to start with one—rows, for example—and then nest additional FRAMESET tags inside the first one to add columns.) The size of a row or column can be expressed as an absolute number of pixels, a percentage of the screen width or height, or a variable (indicated by an asterisk) equivalent to a share of the unassigned space.

Inside the FRAMESET tags, you can include nested FRAMESET tags or FRAME tags. Within the FRAME tag itself, you can nest a number of other tags, of which the following are the most important:

- SRC="*URL of source document for frame*"
- NAME="*named target anchor*" (optional)
- SCROLLING="YES, NO, *or* AUTO" (AUTO means the frame will be able to scroll only if it needs to (that is, if the contents don't fit)
- NORESIZE (to make the frame boundary immovable)

To supply substitute content for browsers that are not frame sensitive, you can enclose normal HTML markup text (created ahead of time, in Netscape Editor if you like) between the <NOFRAMES> and </NOFRAMES> tags and inside the FRAMESET tags.

To make a hyperlink bring up a page in a specific frame, add the attribute TARGET="*named target anchor*" to the standard <A HREF="*URL*"> tag.

Figure 11.3 shows a complicated frame layout designed by web maestro Malcolm Humes.

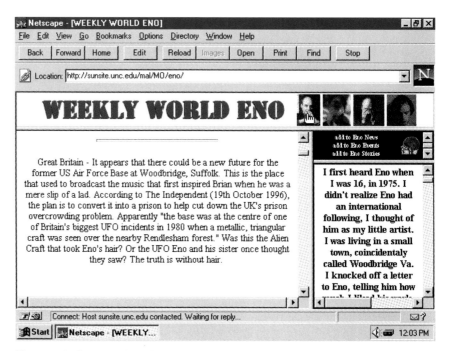

Figure 11.3 Frames at http://sunsite.unc.edu/mal/MO/eno/

Interactive Forms

To really make your site grab your reader, you should include interactive pages— pages that either request input or involvement from the user or that change or respond to the user's actions. However, livening up web documents in this way is no cup of tea. It requires at least some basic scripting abilities, and depending on your ambitions, it can require full-fledged programming work.

The most basic kind of interactive page is a form. If you've bought anything on the web or even downloaded any shareware, you've already filled out a form. Remember typing your name and maybe your VISA information and then clicking a Submit button? That's a form.

It's one thing to learn the coding that makes forms look good on the screen. Although it's a little tedious, it's not too hard, and if you've become accustomed to working with dialog boxes, then you'll recognize the different types of doo-dads that make up a form. However, it's another thing entirely to get the forms working on the back-end (the server side) so that when your reader fills out a form, something actually happens. That part requires scripts written, tested, and saved on your server. Finally, it's yet another matter to actually entice any of your visitors to fill out the form. This last part, however, is an issue for the marketers and psychologists.

EXPERT ADVICE

An alternative to mail forms (which require CGI scripts) is the mailto: URL. This can be combined with options to force specific headers to conform to a preset format. For instance, to enable you to send me mail, I could insert the following into a web document: <A HREF="mailto:xian@syx.com? Subject=Busy">Send mail to Christian about the <CITE>Busy People</CITE> book</A>.

(More advanced forms of interaction come from JavaScript routines embedded in HTML pages and full-fledged Java applets that your browser downloads and then runs.)

If you want a form, you may have to enter the tags by hand.

1. Start with <FORM METHOD=GET *or* PUT ACTION="*URL of script for form*">.
2. Put buttons at the bottom of your form with <INPUT TYPE="submit" VALUE="*optional text, instead of 'Submit'*"> and <INPUT TYPE="reset"VALUE="*optional text, instead of 'Reset'*">.
3. To insert text-entry areas, insert <TEXTAREA NAME="*name*" ROWS=*x* COLS=*y*> *optional suggested default text*</TEXTAREA>.
4. For other types of input, use <INPUT NAME="*name*" TYPE="*text, password, check box, radio, int, hidden, submit, reset*" VALUE="*default value, if any*" SIZE="*optional size*" MAXLENGTH="*optional maximum length*">.

Some (but not all) web editing tools can create forms. (For example, Netscape Gold can't and Word 97 can.)

5. For a drop-down list with several entries to choose from,

- start with <SELECT NAME="*name*" SIZE="*optional number of items to be shown at a time*">
- include <OPTION>*option text* for each option you want to appear in the drop-down list
- end with </SELECT>

6. End with </FORM>.

7. Find and install a script to make the form work (that's the catch) or find someone to do it for you.

bookmark

A good general reference for forms (and CGI scripts) is An Instantaneous Introduction to CGI Scripts and HTML Forms (http://kuhttp.cc.ukans. edu/info/forms/forms-intro.html).

Programming the Web

If you want your web pages to do more than just lay there waiting for someone to read every word and click every link, then you've learned all the web design you need to accomplish your goals. If, on the other hand, you want to develop a truly interactive web site that offers a different experience to each user, depending on how the visitor responds and behaves at the site, then you'll need to do some scripting or some program-development to get "things to happen" either on the server end (where your site is stored) or on the client side (inside your reader's browser).

CGI and Other Server-Side Controls

Both traditional server-side image maps and forms require the cooperation of a server to function properly. The ingredient that tells the server what to do, how to do it, and when to do it is the CGI script. (There are other methods of server-side scripting, such as server-side includes, Denali, and HTMLScript.)

If you've ever worked with macros in a program such as WordPerfect or Word, then you have some idea of what a script does. You may also know that the devil is in the details, and understanding what to do in principle is a far cry from writing a script with no bugs in it, putting it in the right place on a server, and getting it to work.

DEFINITIONS

CGI: Common gateway interface; a standard set of commands for passing information back and forth between a web server application and the computer it's running on, including other software running on the same computer or network.

Script: A small-scale program consisting of instructions designed to respond to varying circumstances with different actions and results.

Another common type of script is the sort that negotiates between a simple form and a mail server, enabling people to send replies in a consistent format. Another is the type that keeps track of how many visitors have come to a page — "You are visitor number XXXX since our hit-count script last broke down!" A more sophisticated type of script, coupled with a regularly updated index of a site, can enable your readers to search your site by entering keywords into a simple form.

bookmark

For archives of existing scripts, try Matt's Script Archive (http://worldwidemart.com/scripts/).

For more on CGI scripting, try Introductin to CGI Programming (http://www.usi.utak.edu/cgi-programming), the CGI Book—Links (http://www.cgibook.com/links.html), or Mike's Guru Page (http://www.cs.unc.edu/wwwc/public/capps/guru.html).

Java, ActiveX, and Other Client-Side Controls

The cutting edge of web development involves the development of small modular web-based programs that web browsers actually download from the server site and then run, on the user's host computer. This distribution of computing time and resources is much more efficient than enabling each user who hits the site to spin the wheels there.

The two competing approaches to web development are Java and ActiveX. By no means mutually exclusive (ActiveX incorporates Java controls and Java programs can initiate ActiveX events), the two represent fundamentally different philosophies of the desktop and the Web.

Java, developed by Sun Microsystems and embraced by a wide consortium of industry heavyweights, is an open system that can be used to develop object-oriented program modules (called applets) which, in theory, should be able to run equally well on any type of computer platform. ActiveX, by contrast, is Microsoft's baby, a program language for controlling applications and file systems, fine-tuned for Windows computers.

Either way, unless you're a programmer, you'll need to hire one to develop programs and routines in either of these languages. Other methods for "hopping up" web pages include developing multimedia content designed for special browser plug-ins, but these necessarily narrow your audience to only those intrepid enough to install the plug-ins.

The final way to jazz up web documents—one that's within reach of a normal busy person—is to incorporate scripts into your web document. As with the more advanced programming languages, there are two major competing scripting languages, JavaScript and Visual Basic.

JavaScript is not the same thing as Java itself, nor is it the same thing as the CGI scripts described in the previous section. Java is a much more fully functional programming language. CGI scripts run on the server side. JavaScript is interpreted by the browser (on the client side). Microsoft's Visual Basic, naturally, works best with Microsoft applications and operating systems.

DEFINITIONS

JavaScript: A set of programming instructions that can be inserted into a web document and interpreted by a browser to produce interactive or variable effects.

Java: A platform-independent object-oriented programming language used to write programs that can be downloaded by web browsers and played on any computer.

As with CGI scripting, it's not really possible to casually learn the ins and outs of JavaScript. However, there are a number of useful existing JavaScript routines that you can borrow and adapt for your own pages, the same way you might borrow and adapt someone else's HTML code.

Examples of popular, simple JavaScript routines include a scrolling (possibly annoying to some) marquee message in the browser's status bar, and a script using a command called onMouse Over that puts explanatory text instead of the destination URL in the status bar when the user positions the mouse pointer over a link.

bookmark

More JavaScript information can be found online at the JavaScript Index (http://www.c2.org/~andreww/javascript/), the Unofficial JavaScript Resource Center (http://www.ce.net/users/ryan/java), the JavaScript Tip of the Week (http://www.webreference.com/javascript) or Netscape's own JavaScript page (http://home.netscape.com/comprod/products/ navigator/ version_2.0/script/script_info/index.html).
An organization that calls itself the Bandwidth Conservation Society (http://www.infohiway.com/faster/index.html) has a nice archive of cut-and-paste JavaScript examples (http://www.infohiway.com/javascript/).

Unless you're a programmer, you have no business messing with Java itself. Howver, if you have need of a full-fledged application that you can serve up to any web browser who wants to run it, then you should consider hiring a programmer to develop your software in Java. HotWired's Talk.com chat web site uses Java for the specialized dialog boxes that appear once you join the system and connect (see Chapter 7).

Publishing Your Web Site

When your site is ready for prime time, you need to find a place for it to live (a server) and then transfer all the files from your staging area (see Chapter 10) to the server. If you plan to publish your site on the World Wide Web at large, you can either set up and maintain your own server or post your pages on someone else's server. If your site has been designed for an intranet, then you can publish it to any local file server that everyone else on the intranet has access to.

Finding a Server

There are two ways to publish your web site on an Internet server. One is to set up and run your own server on a machine connected to the Net. The other is to pay a provider to host your site for you on an existing server. Depending on the size of your organization and your budget, either solution may work for you.

If you rent space on a provider's server (or web farm), you generally lack security and control of your site. It may be difficult or cumbersome to update your site, and you may not be able to install the software you want there (such as a RealAudio server). On the other hand, the site will probably be faster to access and cheaper to maintain. Cost issues are subtle and have to be considered with the bandwidth you're getting.

DEFINITION

Web farm: A large Internet web server site that hosts many smaller web sites, either because the owner or primary tenant has a huge surplus of resources, or because the owner is in the business of providing web presence.

Maintaining your own site can be expensive when you take into account all the labor, equipment, lines, servers, and so on. You also won't be able to have the fastest type of connection (a T3). On the positive side, you can integrate your web presence with your other Internet servers, such as e-mail, and you'll have total control over the site.

Running Your Own Server

Running your own server can mean setting up a 386 PC clone running the free Linux operating system and free Unix web server software, such as Apache or httpd, over a round-the-clock ISDN link. It can also mean being given access to a directory on a server already set up for your organization or setting up and maintaining a network with a fast, dedicated gateway to the Internet on a high-end Pentium Pro workstation running Windows NT and Netscape, Microsoft, or other server software.

No matter what solution you choose—and you should solicit as much advice as possible for your specific circumstances—you must be prepared to maintain a 24-hours-a-day, 7-days-a-week Internet presence if you intend to run your own server. Decide on what sort of computer you are going to run your server. Do you have a spare PC? Ideally, you shouldn't share your server machine with other processor-intensive tasks, such as database management.

The type of server software you choose depends primarily on what sort of computer you plan to run it on. I'll tell you about the most popular servers on the most common platforms. More importantly, I'll tell you how to keep up to date as these facts change. New developments emerge on the Net all the time, so you'd do well to know how to keep abreast of the news.

EXPERT ADVICE

If you choose one of the more popular servers, then you'll more likely be able to find working examples of useful scripts. With up-and-coming servers, you may have to do more script development yourself.

Other considerations that will help you decide among servers are cost (some are free, some are cheap, some are expensive), available support, whether the server is commercial (can handle transactions, whether you need this capability now or in the future), and the speed or efficiency (throughput) of the server.

bookmark

Keep up with web server developments at Serverwatch (http://serverwatch. iworld.com/ or http://www.serverwatch.com/). Another site that compares servers is WebCompare (http://webcompare.iworld.com/) Yahoo!'s server page is http://www.yahoo.com/Computers_and_Internet/ Internet/ World_ Wide_Web/HTTP/Servers/, and there's a subpage just for Macintosh.

Servers for Windows

Most Windows web servers are designed to run on the 32-bit versions of Windows (NT and Windows 95), although a few do run on the earlier 16-bit versions (Windows 3.11 and Windows for Workgroups). Windows is a bit of a latecomer to the server game, but Windows NT already threatens to become a dominant platform. Netscape's two servers are the most popular, but Microsoft is aggressively pushing the Internet Information Server as the best solution for integrating the back-end of a web server with Microsoft Office software. O'Reilly's WebSite is also a bit of a sleeper, with positive critical reviews (see Table 11.3).

Unix Servers

At one time, all the sites (or nearly all) on the Web were Unix sites. Many of the large service providers still rely heavily on Unix machines, and most scripts and other add-ins for web sites are still first developed in Unix, before being ported to Macintosh and Windows platforms.

The first web server was CERN httpd. This was succeeded by NCSA httpd, which is still in circulation. An update of the NCSA server, called Apache, is currently the most popular Unix-based solution (see Table 11.4).

EXPERT ADVICE

It is also possible to install the freeware Linux operating system (a Unix clone) on PCs, from the 386 up to the Pentium Pro, and then run one of these Unix web servers on a PC.

Vendor	Product Name	Price	Download Site	Remarks
Microsoft (**www.microsof. com**)	Internet Information Server (**http://www. microsoft.com/ InfoServ/**)	Free	**http://www. microsoft.com/ infoserv/iisinfo.htm**	Part of NT Server, no remote administration, some security
Netscape (**home.netscape. com**)	FastTrack; formerly Communications Server (**http:// www.netscape. com/comprod/ server_central/ product/fast_track/**)	$295	http://cgi.netscape. com/cgi-bin/123 server.cgi (60-day evaluation copy)	Most popular, not secure for commerce
	Enterprise Server; formerly Commerce Server (**http://www. netscape.com/comprod/ server_central/product/ enterprise/**)	$995	**http://home.netscape. com/comprod/ mirror/server_ download.html** (60-day evaluation copy)	Most popular, secure for commerce
O'Reilly & Associates (**www.ora.com**)	WebSite	$249	**http://software.ora. com/download/** (evaluation copy)	Fast, easy, sophisticated
	WebSite Pro	$499	**http://software.ora. com/download/** (evaluation copy)	Commercial (secure)

Table 11.3 Windows Web Servers

Macintosh Servers

While the makers of other web server software always promise that a Macintosh version is on the way—*real soon now*—it seems that for the time being, the field of Mac servers is not crowded. Your choice is essentially between StarNine's WebStar, the free MacHTTP product from which WebStar evolved, and a new integrated server product (it does FTP and gopher, too) called InterServer Publisher (see Table 11.5).

Vendor	Product Name	Price	Download Site	Remarks
Apache Group (http://www.apache.org)	Apache	Free	http://www.apache.org/dist/	Based on NCSA httpd, most popular server
NCSA (http://hoohoo.ncsa.uiuc.edu/)	httpd		http://hoohoo.ncsa.uiuc.edu/docs/setup/Download.html *or* http://hoohoo.ncsa.uiuc.edu/docs/setup/OneStep.html	No official support
Netscape (home.netscape.com)	FastTrack; formerly Communications Server (http://www.netscape.com/comprod/server_central/product/fast_track/)	$295	http://cgi.netscape.com/cgi-bin/123server.cgi (60-day evaluation copy)	Not secure for commerce
	Enterprise Server; formerly Commerce Server (http://www.netscape.com/comprod/server_central/product/enterprise	$995	http://home.netscape.com/comprod/mirror/server_download.html (60-day evaluation copy)	Most popular, secure for commerce

Table 11.4 Unix Web Servers

Finding a Host for Your Site

The alternative to maintaining your own server is to hire out the hosting and a good deal of the day-to-day site maintenance (also known as the webmastery) to a service provider.

Vendor	Product Name	Price	Download Site	Remarks
InterCon (http://www.intercon.com)	InterServer Publisher	Not set yet	http://www.intercon.com/products/interserverp.html	
StarNine (http://www.starnine.com)	WebStar; formerly MacHTTP	$499	ftp://ftp.starnine.com/pub/evals/webstar/webstar.sea.hqx	Most popular Macintosh server
	MacHTTP	$65 (educational), $95 (others)	http://www.starnine.com/machttp/machttpsoft.html (30-day evaluation copy)	Predecessor to WebStar

Table 11.5 Macintosh Web Servers

It may be possible or preferable to get your web site hosted by your e-mail or Internet access provider, but it's not necessary. You don't even have to limit yourself to providers with local-access phone numbers. As long as you have some sort of Internet access already, you can negotiate a separate hosting arrangement with any provider on the Net.

EXPERT ADVICE

To get the best network connection, you may not want to limit yourself to local providers. Many Japanese companies, for example, hire providers on the West Coast of the U.S. to provide web mirroring to U.S. customers and, in some cases, to host their primary Internet presence.

Service providers can also offer domain name service, providing a domain name for your company (www.yournamehere.com) either for a separate fee or as part of your company account package. See "Establishing Your Internet Presence" (the next section) for more on domain names.

If you are creating a site for a small division of a large company or organization and the publishing space available to you is on the server of a bigger part of the company, then your relationship with the administrator of the site will be much like that between a customer and a commercial service provider's administrator.

The best place online to hunt for service providers is The List (both http://www.thelist.com and http://thelist.iworld.com).

When negotiating with a potential host for your site, here are some issues to consider and questions to ask:

- Can I make updates to the site directly myself or will I have to send changes to a webmaster and wait for them to be posted?
- What type of machine houses the site and what web server software runs on that machine (see the previous section for more on server software)?
- How much traffic does the server handle now? What are the quotas (included in the base charge) for disk storage space and server traffic?
- Will I be permitted to run CGI scripts from the server?
- Is an existing library of common scripts already available at the server?
- Are any supplementary servers or facilities available for building a web presence (such as mailing list software, hypernews or other discussion group tools, and so on)?
- What provisions, if any, are there for password protection, secure commercial transactions, and other privacy and security needs?
- How dependable is the server? What provisions are in place for backing up the server in case of failure?

See Appendix A for more about establishing an Internet connection.

Establishing Your Internet Presence

Beyond setting up a web site, to establish a full-fledged Internet presence, you'll probably want to establish your own domain name (that is, if you or your organization has not already done so). Primarily, this has cosmetic advantages. A short URL focused on your company name is more memorable and attractive than a longer one where your company name hangs off the end of your provider's address.

EXPERT ADVICE

Perhaps the best advantage of having your own domain name is that it's completely portable. You can change your host provider or move a site to different machines and keep the address exactly the same.

As with servers, you can either register and maintain your own domain name or you can have your provider do it for you. To maintain your own domain, you'll need access to at least two computers on the Internet that are running name-service software (this is why it's often easier for providers or other centralized entities to do this, rather than individuals), and you'll need to fill out the appropriate paperwork for InterNIC (http://www.internic.net) and pay $100 for two years of service.

Most providers offer domain-name service as part of a package (particularly for business accounts) or as a separate billable service. This can mean the difference between a nice short URL like http://www.*yourcompany*.com, or something along the lines of http://www.*providername*.com/*yourcompany*/ or, worse yet, http://www.*providername*.com/~*yourcompany*/. Then again, some providers offer a quick-and-dirty method in which your home page URL is not at the root of a server but in a subdirectory, something like http://www.*yourcompany*.com/*your company*. This is not as good, since anyone entering just the www...com part will actually end up at your provider's home page instead of yours. The site redirection option (which gives you your own root address) may cost more, but it's worth it.

Browsers are getting smarter about guessing URLs, with Netscape leading the way. An address such as http:// www.yourcompany.com will be found even if a user simply types yourcompany *in the Netscape address box.*

Transferring Files and Posting Pages

Whether you maintain your own server or contract for someone else to host you, you'll have to deal with sending (also called publishing or uploading) your web documents and related media files to the server. Traditionally, this was done using either file transfer protocol (FTP) to transfer the files or Telnet (remote login) to log in directly to the remote site and create the file there. You can still work this way or, if you have a web editing tool, you can usually post your pages directly from within the program.

Publishing a Site via FTP

Generally, any site running a web server will also maintain an FTP server so that the owner or owners of the content on the site can log in (using passwords) and change or add to files. The FTP connection is therefore a sort of back entrance or backstage area to which the public does not have access.

Chapter 9 explained how to use FTP programs (or how to use your web browser to transfer files with FTP). All you need to know to apply these techniques to publishing web pages is a username and password for logging in to the site and the pathname (the folder and subfolders) to which you should transfer your files. Whoever has given you access to the site should be able to give you this information. If you run the server yourself, then this information will depend on how you initially set up the site!

Word 97 has integrated FTP (and web) access directly into its normal operations. This means you can post a page to a web site with the normal Save As dialog box.

STEP BY STEP Save Your Pages to a Site with Word

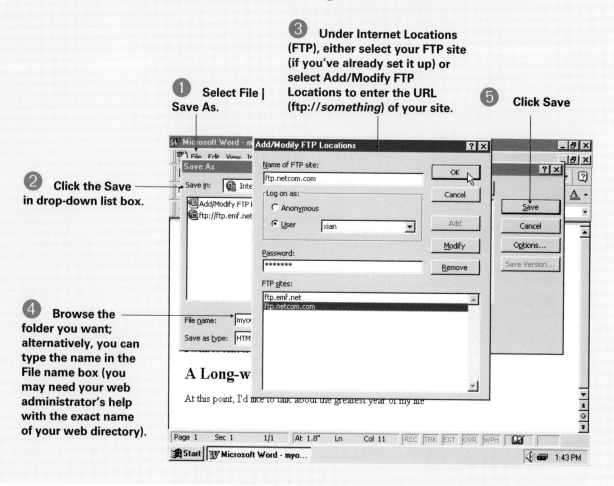

*If you haven't saved your
most recent changes to the
document, Netscape Editor
will prompt you to do so.*

Netscape Gold's "One-Button" Publishing

When the time comes to publish a document to your server, start by clicking the Publish button.

This will bring up the Publish Files dialog box (see Figure 11.4), where you specify the location of the file you want to publish The first time this appears, the Publishing location area of the dialog box will be blank, but in the future, it will contain your previous entries, and you'll be able to reuse them if you want to.

If you just want to publish the current document, you can ignore the upper half of the dialog box.

If there are any graphic images in the file, the Images in the document radio button will be selected, and all graphics will be sent. To prevent transmission of a graphic, click Select None and then reselect only the graphics that you *do* want to send.

If you want to include additional documents, graphics, or other files in this single upload, click the All files in document's folder radio button and then select the specific files you want.

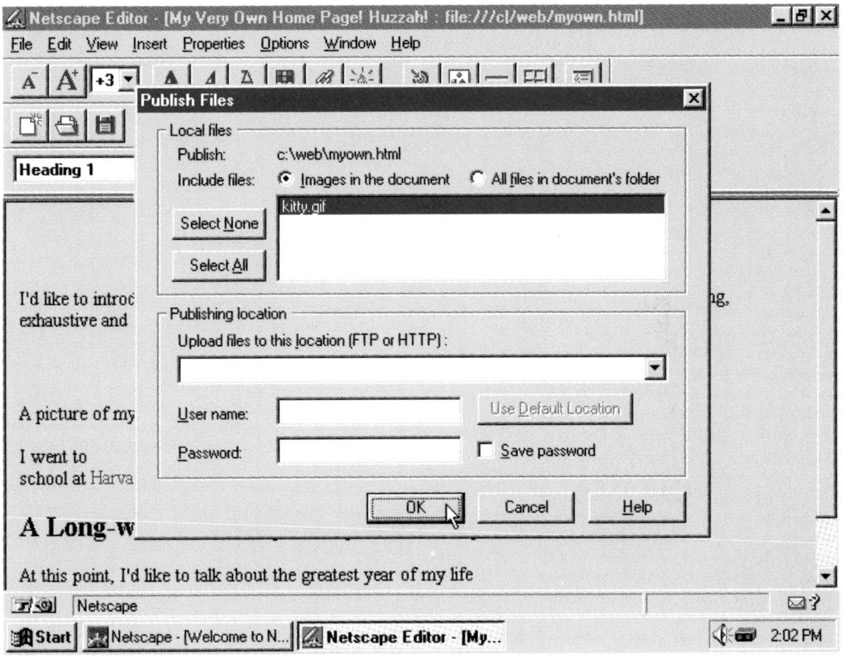

Figure 11.4 The Publish Files dialog box

In the Publishing Location area of the dialog box, click the Upload files to this location box and enter the FTP address. FTP addresses start with ftp:// and usually include more directory information than the corresponding HTTP address. For example, to place a file called path.html at the address http://ezone.org/ez/e8/path.html, you'd have to send it to ftp://ezone.org/./ public_html/ez/e8/. (The single dot between the slashes indicates the home directory that you're logging in to. Many Unix web servers are set up so that user's web pages are located in a subdirectory called public_html.)

After entering the URL to publish to, press TAB and then type the username for the account associated with the web server (which may be a personal account, corporate account, or special webmaster account). Press TAB again and type the password. Check Save password if you want to avoid typing it again in the future. Then click OK. Netscape will switch to a browser window to make the connection and will then send the file. If you've made an error in the address, username, or password, Netscape will tell you. Click OK and try again.

CAUTION

If you tell Netscape Editor to save your password, then anyone using your computer will be able to publish files to your web server, so be careful.

If everything is in order, Netscape will send the file or files to the server and inform you that it's doing so.

CAUTION

*On some Unix web servers, your page still won't be visible until you set its mode to world readable. To do this, you'll either have to use Telnet to go to your site and then issue the command **chmod o+r filename**, or ask your system administrator to do so for you. (See Chapter 9 for more on Telnet.)*

Netscape Gold publishing is called one-button publishing because it provides a handy Publish button on the toolbar, but publishing always requires at least two buttons! Next time you need to send a page to the same location, you can

can click the Publish button and then just click OK to publish the document (see, two buttons).

It's also possible to browse to your server using its FTP address and then just drag files from the folder windows directly onto the Navigator screen. First, though, you have to set up a default publishing location. To do so,

1. Select Options | Editor Preferences.
2. Select the Publish tab of the Editor Preferences dialog box.
3. Enter the address you want to publish to in the Publish to box.
4. Enter the public URL (the http:// address) of the site in the Browse to box.
5. Enter the username and password information for the publish-to address.

Any time you want to jump directly to the site to which you've been publishing, select Go | Default Publish Location in the Netscape browser window.

EXPERT ADVICE

Once you've set up a default publishing location, you can click the Use Default Location button in the Publish Files dialog box to select it in when publishing in the future.

Promoting Your Web Site

What if you built a storefront and no one came? It can happen on the Web, where sure, you can set up shop on prime real estate, directly across from Time/Warner's mega-website, but you'll have no visitors unless you promote your site. Without promotion, a public web site is a lonely voice, crying alone in the wilderness.

To start, if there are web sites for related issues or interests, send their webmasters e-mail and offer to exchange links. As for Usenet newsgroups and mailing lists that deal with subjects related to the topic of your site, feel free to send brief announcements to them when your site is first published and whenever you make major changes or updates to it. For example, if you have compiled a list of writing resources, you could post a brief announcement describing your page to misc.writing and/or to comp.internet.net-happenings.

Then visit all the directory and search engine sites mentioned in Chapter 3 and submit the URL of your web site to each one. (They all have pages where you can fill out forms to submit web addresses.)

netiquette

Don't spam (send multiple or unwelcome messages to) mailing lists or newsgroups to promote your site. Be careful to keep commercial messages out of noncommercial areas.

Once you get past the wonder of it all—the fact that you can set up a tidy little web site just "down the road" from CNN, the White House, and Sony—you realize the catch: how will anyone ever find you? The Internet and the Web get more complicated and crowded every day. There's no space to run out of, but you still have to work to make sure that people who might be interested in your site can find it—so publishing is one thing, but findability is the key.

There are really two ways to publicize your site online. The first is to submit the URL of your site to every directory and search engine you can find (excluding perhaps the uncategorized "What's New" pages out there). This is easy, but tedious. The second way is more subtle and is more in line with the traditional meaning of the word "networking." To make a site visible from the many avenues on the Internet, you have to communicate with other people who publish on the Net or participate in discussion groups. You have to tell them, by e-mail or in public posts, about your site and trade hyperlinks with sites that have common themes or interests.

EXPERT ADVICE

Don't underestimate the importance of promoting your site in the "real world." Be sure to put your URL on business cards and letterhead and mention it in advertising or marketing campaigns to promote your site's address.

To prevent robots from adding some of your pages to their indexes, see http:// info.webcrawler.com/mak/ projects/robots/norobots.html.

Submitting Announcements

All directory and search engine sites send robotic indexing programs around to browse the Web, follow links, and add sites to their databases. But why wait until they find you when you can go directly to the source?

The first step is to write an announcement describing your site, what makes it unique, and its intended audience. If your announcement is long (more than a few paragraphs), create a companion, condensed version of it, since many of the sites allow only short statements. (Many of them won't even use your text, for that matter.)

CAUTION

There are a lot of freelance operators who offer to submit announcements to sites all over the Net. Most of them just drop by the Submit It! site (we'll cover that in a moment), and many don't follow up to make sure that the URL has shown up at all the sites. You're better off doing this task (or supervising it) yourself.

After that, just repeat the following process as many times as you can stand:

1. Browse to a search, directory, or "what's new" site (see the list in Table 11.6).
2. Choose the Submit URL or an equivalent option.
3. Enter your site's web address and as much of your announcement as the form permits.
4. Submit the information.
5. Check back after a week (or whatever lead time the site recommends) to make sure that your site is now listed.

Table 11.6 lists the major sites to which you should consider submitting your URL. New search sites appear all the time, so to make sure you haven't missed any, visit some of the centralized search sites such as Netscape's Internet Search page (http://home.netscape.com/home/internet-search.html) or clnet's Search.com (http://www.search.com) and scan the sites, adding any new ones to your list.

Site Name	URL
100 Hot Web Sites	http://www.100hot.com
AltaVista	http://altavista.digital.com
Excite	http://www.excite.com
G.O.D.	http://www.god.co.uk
HotBot	http://www.hotbot.com
InfoSeek Guide	http://guide.infoseek.com/
Internet Resource Meta-Index	http://www.ncsa.uiuc.edu/SDG/Software/ Mosaic/MetaIndex.html
Lycos	http://www.lycos.com
Magellan	http://www.mckinley.com
OpenText	http://www.opentext.com/omw/f-omw.html
Point	http://www.pointcom.com
Submit It!	http://www.submit-it.com
W3 Web Servers	http://www.w3.org/pub/DataSources/WWW/ Servers.html
WebCrawler	http://www.webcrawler.com
WWW Virtual Library	http://www.w3.org/hypertext/DataSources/ bySubject/Overview.html
Yahoo!	http://www.yahoo.com

Table 11.6 Sites for Submitting Your URL

Your first stop should be Submit It! (http://www.submit-it.com), since that page contains links to most of the other relevant sites. Submit It! is a sort of mega-form that you can use to submit to multiple search and directory places. It's not quite as easy as it sounds since you still have to submit to each individual site, one after another, but at least many of them are all in one place.

Networking and Trading Links

To really have a presence on the Net, you have to spend time communicating with people one-to-one via e-mail and one-to-many via discussion groups. You need to go beyond just responding to e-mail from visitors to your site; you need to also put the URL of your site in your e-mail signature so that anyone who gets mail from you gets at least a minimal, classified-ad type plug for the site. Here's my signature to give you an idea:

```
--
Christian Crumlish              http://www.pobox.com/~xian
Internet Systems Experts (SYX)  http://www.syx.com
Enterzone                       http://ezone.org/ez
```

Also, you have to be on the lookout for organizations and groups of people on the Net, and other web sites, that deal with topics similar or related to your own. For a business site, this may mean tracking down other vendors, suppliers, and so on whose products and services relate to your own. As long as they're not your competitors, there's no reason why they shouldn't want to trade links with you.

CAUTION

Don't send announcements to every single list, group, or private e-mail address you can find! This is known as spamming and will create more enemies than customers. Make sure that when you post information about your site, especially if your site is a commercial one, you do so only in forums whose members will appreciate the information.

Webmastery: Maintaining a Living, Breathing Web Site

Even after you've finished creating your site, published it to the Net, and worked day and night promoting it, your job is not necessarily done. There's a distinction between designing (and building) a site and webmastery. Every site needs a webmaster in the same sense that every mail server needs a postmaster. Someone has to fix things that go wrong, respond to basic e-mail, keep the server running, and—perhaps most important—post updates and changes to the site as they occur.

You must ask, "Who will do this job? Me? My service provider? An assistant?" If you hire web designers to create or enhance your site, don't assume that they will also take over the webmaster chores unless it's written into the agreement.

If it falls to you to oversee a site, you may want to invest in a site management program such as Adobe SiteMill (on the Macintosh side) or Microsoft FrontPage (on the Windows side). These programs, at the very least, make it easier to keep all your internal links up to date if and when you make changes to the overall structure of the site.

bookmark

ServerWatch (bookmarked earlier) maintains an up-to-date list of site development and management tools . Yahoo! also has a good section on this subject (http://www.yahoo.com/Computers_and_Internet/Internet/World_Wide_Web/HTTP/Servers/Log_Analysis_Tools/).

Webmastery also involves analyzing the access logs that most servers generate. If you pay a service provider to host your site, ask to receive your access statistics on a regular basis. (They may just point you to a page at the site that can generate reports for you.)

A web site will wither away if you don't revisit it often to improve its appearance, content, and organization and to add up-to-date information to it. To avoid chaos, you need to establish a clear, simple system for making updates. Only one person should have the final say regarding what gets posted, and all changes should be made in some safe staging area and tested before being posted to the public site.

CHECK POINT

By now you are one of the masters of the Internet! If you've made it this far, you've not only learned how to communicate with people around the globe and download information and files from archives near and far, but also how to create, publish, and maintain your own little corner of cyberspace on the World Wide Web. In fact, with what you've leearned so far, you have more than adequate opportunities to learn more about the Internet directly from the Net itself.

Welcome to the Net!

No matter what degree of participation you choose or how much information you help yourself to, you're now part of a global community, vital and growing. There's no reason why the Internet has to eat up all your time and energy. You now know enough to make productive use of the Net, avail yourself of its vast resources, and avoid entangling yourself in technical distractions.

For a shortcut to all of the web pages referred to in this book, be sure to visit the Busy Persons Links (http://syx.com/busy/bookmarks/). See you on the Net!

Get on the Net

A

If you're poking around back here in this part of the book, then you're probably confused about something. No problem. I'm here to help.

First of all, you may already be connected to the Internet to some degree. If you are, your first step is to identify the type of modem connection you have. If you don't yet have an Internet connection, I can help you figure out what kind of connection you want and how to find a service provider offering that kind of hook-up.

Even if you have direct access to the Internet at work, you may still want to dial up your network from home or connect to a private Internet service provider (ISP), perhaps to make personal or business use of the Internet that might not be appropriate over your work connection.

DEFINITIONS

Dial up (v.): To connect to a network over phone lines using a modem and a computer.

Dial-up (adj.): A description of the type of account one accesses by dialing up a network.

Direct access means working on a computer that is either directly connected to the Internet or connected to a smaller network that is itself directly connected to the Internet. An ISP is a private company that specializes in providing Internet access, especially dial-up access for individuals.

A direct network connection to the Internet is usually the fastest, but if your access comes by virtue of your employment at a company or membership in a department or organization, then your participation in the Internet may be limited by your capacity as a representative of your organization. Many companies consider it improper for you to conduct personal business over a company Internet connection, although personal e-mail is usually permitted, within reason, to the same extent that personal phone calls are.

Once you've found some ISPs, grilled them thoroughly, and compared their services and prices, you'll still have to get your computer set up, so I'll cover those details as well.

One final disclaimer: Yes, this stuff is boring. That's why we stuck it in the back of the book. I won't pretty anything up—I'll just tell you the details and move on.

Am I Already Connected to the Internet?

What does "on the Internet" mean? It depends. If all you're mainly interested in is e-mail, then any type of e-mail system that can send mail to and receive mail from Internet addresses is "on the Internet." If you want to be able to browse the Web, then you'll need either a direct network connection to the Internet or a dial-up connection.

Are You on a Network at Work, School, Prison?

If you use or have access to a computer that's part of a network and that network is connected in some way to the Internet, then you may be able to run a web browser, for example, and your network will provide the Internet connection. This is often true at universities and at medium-sized and larger corporations.

You may have to ask whoever maintains your network. If you don't have direct access to the Internet from a local network, jump ahead to "How Can I Get Connected to the Internet?"

Do You Subscribe to an Online Service (AOL, MSN)?

If you have an account at an online service such as America Online or the recently relaunched Microsoft Network, then you already have fairly complete access to the Internet, though you may have to learn some specific rules and methods that are particular to your service. These all offer technical support, although some are occasionally swamped with calls.

If your online service allows you to run a program such as Netscape when connected, then you most likely can run all the other programs discussed in this book, also while connected. You may be more comfortable, however, with the interface provided by your service.

What Kind of Connection Do I Have?

If you have a network connection (that is, you're on a network, and the network is connected to the Internet), then you shouldn't have to set up anything yourself (aside from specific programs, as explained throughout the book). Enjoy your network connection. If you want to dial up to connect to your network and run graphical programs from a modem, then you'll be using a PPP (or, possibly, SLIP). This requires configuring some software and possibly putting together a dial-up script. Windows 3.1 requires the most helper software and massaging to get going. Windows 95, Windows NT, and Macintosh are pretty easy to set up for PPP (or SLIP). You should be able to get technical support to do this.

By the way, PPP stands for point-to-point protocol, and it's the preferable method for handling Internet traffic over a modem. SLIP stands for serial line Internet protocol and is nearly as good a method for the same thing (but not quite as well supported by Windows 95). PPP is faster and more efficient than SLIP.

If you subscribe to an online service, make sure that you're getting full Internet access. You shouldn't have to do any setup beyond installing the service's software. Here's the key question: Ask if you have full PPP (or SLIP) access. If they say yes, then you can run any of the software mentioned in this book.

If you already have an ISP, then you either have a PPP or SLIP account perfectly suited for all the instructions in this book, or you have a dial-up Unix shell account. If the latter is the case, then you'll be using mostly different software than that described in this book (mainly a terminal/communications program on your personal computer and then a number of Unix programs at the other end, all in a character-only interface).

How Can I Get Connected to the Internet?

Okay, now say you don't yet have Internet access. That means you need to find an ISP, which is a company that specializes in hooking up individuals to the Internet. If there is more than one in the local area, so much the better. Competition does wonders for Internet rates. You shouldn't have to spend more than $30 a month for a reasonable amount of Internet access, and you can spend closer to

$20 in larger metropolitan areas. Many providers offer a range of accounts, each with its own pricing plan, such as

- A flat-rated, unlimited access account (for $20 to $30 per month)
- A basic-rate account with per-minute charges and (often 40) free hours (for $10 to $20 per month plus $1 to $2 per minute over the allotted free time)
- A low-rate, light-usage account with (sometimes high) per-minute charges and few (perhaps 10) or no free hours (for $5 to $10 per month plus $2 to $2.50 per minute)

Shopping for a Service Provider

Shop around before choosing a provider. Compare the rates of direct-access Internet service providers (ISPs) such as Netcom, Hooked, Portal, Pipeline, Crl, and so on to those of online services such as CompuServe, AOL, and MSN. See if there is a Free-Net in your area (a public access network) or if any local universities are offering access. In some areas, newspapers, libraries, and other civic entities are evolving into service providers as well.

If you have to compromise more than you want on price for a provider, you can get an additional forwarding address with an e-mail forwarding company such as pobox.com (e-mail info@pobox.com or http://pobox.com on the Web) and give out the pobox address. Then you can move your provider when a better deal becomes available and not have to inform everyone you know or do business with that your address has changed. The pobox service costs $15 for three years.

Some people prefer to start exploring the Net through the more controlled environment of an online service. The big online services are sometimes more expensive than ISPs, but they do offer additional content of their own and, in most regions, their prices are now competitive. They also offer more hand-holding and all-in-one interfaces that can be easier to use, but limited.

If you can get or borrow web access, visit The List (http://www.thelist.com). You can enter your area code there and search for service providers who offer local-call access in your area. Local access is essential to keeping your costs down. (Another list of providers, for comparison's sake, can be found at http://www.

tagsys.com/Providers/index.html.) Look in local newspapers and computer periodicals for other listings of providers.

What Questions to Ask

When you call up a service provider and say that you're looking for access to the Internet, here are some specific questions to ask:

- Will I have a PPP (or SLIP) connection?
- Will I be able to browse the Web (and see pictures), send and receive e-mail, subscribe to Usenet newsgroups, and so on?
- Is there flat-rate access (a rate for unlimited time)?
- How busy are your modems? Will I ever have trouble getting through? When are the peak usage hours?
- Does the service provider include a disk of useful software (such as connection software, a web browser, an FTP program, a mail reader, and so on) with the service?
- Does the service provider also offer a manual? Free training classes? Technical support?
- Will the service be easy to set up? Will the provider or installation software do all the geek work (such as IP configuration)?
- What is the top dial-in modem speed? The top dial-in modem speed should be at least as fast as your modem—the slower modem in a connection controls the speed. Today, the fastest modems are 57.6 Kbps (kilobits per second) but very few (if any) ISPs have modems that fast. With compression, the fastest practical modems are 33.6 Kbps, but 28.8 Kbps modems are still standard. (Another, faster, more expensive alternative is ISDN.)
- Is there a local dial-up number? Are there nationwide numbers for when I'm traveling? Is there an 800 number, and if so, how much does it cost?
- Are there any hidden or extra charges?
- Are there any quotas or limits on disk storage, e-mail, or other Internet traffic?

- Does the provider offer space on the World Wide Web as part of the account?
- What's the file-transfer allowance (100 megabytes per month? 500?)?

Also, if you encounter people on the Internet with the domain name of a provider you're considering, ask them (by mail) what they think of the service.

What Kinds of Connections Do I Want?

Your best bet is a direct (PPP or SLIP) account, or some other sort of account that is equivalent (such as online service accounts, which amount to full PPP access).

Your next best choice would be a Unix shell account, but you'd want to obtain and install an emulator program, such as SLiRP or TIA, that will enable you to run most PPP/SLIP-type software. You can run a mail program such as Eudora on a shell account without any special arrangements. I discuss TIA and SLiRP in more detail in the upcoming section, "Setting up Different Types of Connections," under "Dial-up PPP or SLIP?"

Lastly, an online service with partial Internet access or a service provider with its own unique interface (one that does not permit you to plug in standard programs) would be an adequate first step toward full Internet access.

Setting Up Different Types of Connections

Here are the essentials of setting up an Internet connection. You'll need to get specific details from your service provider, but most likely they'll offer the information and may possibly set up your software for you, saving you the trouble. If you get stuck anywhere, your provider can walk you through the problem and get you set up (some charge a premium for this service).

A Network with an Internet Gateway

Your network system administrator should be able to tell you either that you can simply go ahead and run Internet software such as Netscape and send Internet e-mail out from your network e-mail program, or that you'll have to set up a TCP/IP network connection or, for Windows 3.1, obtain a Winsock driver to enable Internet software to run. A Winsock driver enables a PC not connected to a network to send and receive TCP/IP packets. (Windows 95 comes with a Winsock driver.)

Setting up TCP/IP will mainly entail typing certain numerical Internet addresses (your system administrator can give you the addresses) into specific boxes, to indicate specific gateways and servers (see Figure A.1).

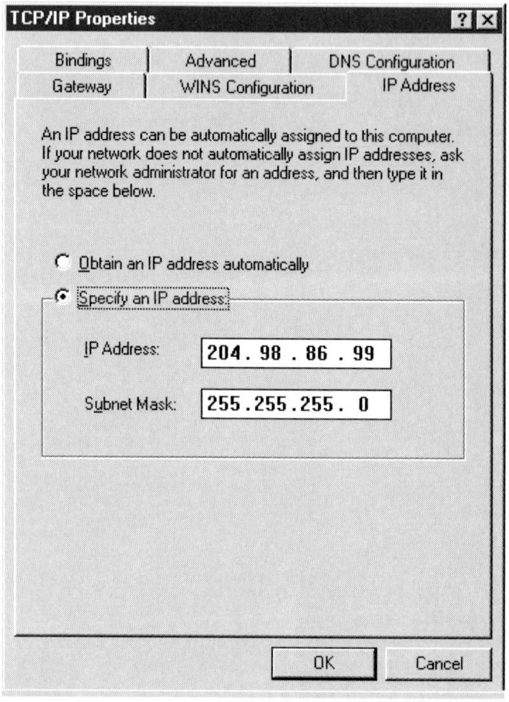

Figure A.1 In Windows 3.1, on a Macintosh, or on another type of computer, the specific program and dialog box may look different, but the type of information you have to supply remains the same.

If you need to find a copy of Winsock to download, see the Winsock FAQ (http://papa.indstate.edu:8888/winsock-faq.html). Windows 95 comes with Winsock.

On a Macintosh, if you have system 7.5 or later, then you have the MacTCP control panel already installed on your computer. You'll have to purchase MacTCP from Apple for earlier versions of the Macintosh.

CAUTION

Windows 3.1 Winsocks such as Trumpet are 16-bit, whereas Windows 95's Winsock is 32-bit. You can't run 16-bit Internet software over a 32-bit Winsock, nor vice versa.

Dial-up PPP or SLIP

To get a PPP or SLIP connection going, you need to have the same software and settings in place as are needed for a network connection. (That is, you'll need TCP/IP software running, and on Windows machines, you'll need Winsock.) You'll also need a PPP or SLIP dial-up program to make and maintain your phone connection to the Internet. Windows 95 has built-in software for PPP (and you can get the SLIP driver from http://www.microsoft.com). Also, Windows 95's Plus! Pack comes with a dial-up networking scripting tool for putting together a simple dial-up script, so you won't have to log in by hand every time.

For a Mac, you'll need InterSLIP (http://www.intercon.com/) or MacPPP (http://www.compumedia.com:80/pub/Software/mac/MacPPP.sit.bin. For Windows 3.1, you'll need a third-party PPP or SLIP program, such as Chameleon Netmanage (http://www.netmanage.com) or Trumpet (http://www.trumpet. com.au/wsk/winsock.htm).

No matter what conglomeration of programs you're using to maintain your PPP (or SLIP) connection, you'll need to tell it the correct modem settings and numerical Internet addresses for nameservers, e-mail, and news.

So, for example, to set up a PPP account on Windows 95, first double-click the Make New Connection icon in the Dial-Up Networking folder. Type your provider's name, select your modem, and click Next. Enter the phone number and click Next again. Then click Finish. (That's the easy part.) Next, right-click the new connection icon, which appears in the Dial-Up Networking folder, and select Properties.

In the dialog box that appears, click the Server Types tab. Make sure PPP is chosen as the connection type. Click the TCP/IP Settings button. If your provider assigns you a new address every time you connect (you can ask this), make sure

"Server assigned IP address" is checked. Otherwise, your provider should give you primary and secondary name-server addresses, and you should enter them in the boxes provided in this dialog box. Then click OK repeatedly to close the windows.

ISDN versus Modems

Integrated Services Digital Network (ISDN) accounts require a special kind of modem and a special kind of phone line coming into the house or office, but they are faster than any other type of dial-up modem connection. (They connect at a minimum of 57.6 Kbps and in some circumstances can go at 128 Kbps—more than four times as fast as a 28.8 Kbps modem.)

ISDN modems are faster than analog modems and can make voice *and* data connections at the same time, but they're more expensive (they have higher setup fees, higher monthly fees, and per-minute phone usage charges) and more difficult to set up. ISDN service is still unavailable in many areas, and ISDN might become obsolete when cable modem technology comes along, any year now. (Another alternative to standard modem connections are direct satellite—yes, satellite—Internet hookups, such as the service available from DirectPC.)

That should be enough to get you up and running.

For bigger-budget, higher-demand corporate solutions, try comparing frame relay and dedicated lines for costs, dependability, and speed.

B

Top Busy People Picks and Essential Links

The Internet changes fast, so it's difficult to single out specific sites you definitely should visit. Nevertheless, I've put together a small set of addresses you might find interesting. Perhaps more importantly, I've also collected all the URLs from every chapter in this book and assembled them at the web site for this book (http://syx.com/busy/) so I can keep them up-to-date for you.

CAUTION

The Web changes rapidly. Some of these sites may have moved by the time you get to them. If you can't find a listed site, try searching for it by name (see Chapter 3), or visit the Busy Person's Bookmarks page at http://syx.com/busy/bookmarks/, which will stay up to date.

Shopping

Resource	Address
Amazon.com Bookstore	http://www.amazon.com/
Branch Mall	http://www.branchmall.com/
CD Now	http://cdnow.com/
FTD	http://www.ftd.com/
McDonald's	http://www.mcdonalds.com/
DigiCash Ecash	http://www.digicash.com/
FirstVirtual	http://www.firstvirtual.com/

Recreation and Gossip

Resource	Address
Firefly (music and movie community)	http://www.ffly.com/
Mr. Showbiz	http://www.mrshowbiz.com/
Entertainment Weekly	http://www.pathfinder.com/ew/
The Ultimate TV List	http://www.tvnet.com/UTVL/utvl.html
Comedy Central	http://www.comcentral.com/
The Discovery Channel Online	http://www.discovery.com/
ESPNET Chatterbox	http://espnet.sportzone.com/editors/talk/chatter.html

News

Resource	Address
Newspaper and Current Periodical Room	http://lcweb.loc.gov/global/ncp/ncp.html
Mercury Center	http://www.sjmercury.com/
New York Times (CyberTimes)	http://nytimes.com/
NandO.net	http://www.nando.net/
The Gate	http://www.sfgate.com/

Business and Finance

Resource	Address
FinanceNet	http://www.financenet.gov/
Investor Web	http://www.investorweb.com/
Taxing Times	http://www.scubed.com/tax/tax.html
SEC Edgar Database	http://www.sec.gov/edgarhp.htm
Electronic Credit Repair Kit	http://www.primenet.com/~kielsky/credit.html
America's Job Bank	http://www.ajb.dni.us/
The Wall Street Journal Money and Investing	http://update.wsj.com/
Small Business Resource Center	http://www.webcom.com/~seaquest/

U.S. Government

Resource	Address
The White House	http://www.whitehouse.gov/
Thomas	http://thomas.loc.gov/
Library of Congress	http://loc.gov/

Entertainment and Complete Wastes of Time

Resource	Address
Internet Movie Database	http://www.imdb.com/
50 Greatest Conspiracies	http://www.conspire.com/
biancaTroll productions	http://bianca.com/
Useless WWW Page	http://www.go2net.com/internet/useless/
The Net Legends FAQ	gopher://dixie.aiss.uiuc.edu:6969/11/urban.legends/net.legends.FAQ
	http://rampages.onramp.net/~jaffo/nl/
The Urban Legends Archive	http://www.urbanlegends.com/
Anagram Generator	http://csugrad.cs.vt.edu/~eburke/anagrams.html

Internet

The following table offers some Internet information sites.

Resource	Address
Internet Society	http://www.isoc.org/
EFF's Guide to the Internet	http://www.eff.org/papers/eegtti/
Zen and the Art of the Internet	http://www.cs.indiana.edu/docproject/zen/zen-1.0_toc.html
Stroud's Consummate Winsock Apps List	http://www.stroud.com/
The Windows 95 TCP/IP Setup FAQ	http://www.aa.net/~pcd/slp95faq.html
DUNCE (dial-up networking connection enhancement)	http://www.cjnetworks.com/~vecdev/vector/index.html
Cache Master	http://www.neosoft.com/~osl/cm.htm
Hot Sheet	http://www.tstimpreso.com/hotsheet/
NetWatch	http://www.pulver.com/netwatch/
Busy Person's Bookmarks	http://syx.com/busy/bookmarks/

Keeping Up with Joneses.Com

Resource	Address
Java	http://www.javasoft.com
Personal Agents	http://www.yourcommand.com/
Netsurfer Digest	http://www.netsurf.com/nsd/
clnet	http://www.cnet.com
News.com	http://www.news.com
Tech Talk	http://www.ttalk.com

Index

:-) smileys, 136

Browse the Web—Companion CD Offers Special Trial Offer of 50 Free Hours from America Online®!

The enclosed CD-ROM features AOL 3.0 for Windows, AOL for Windows 95, and Netscape Navigator. AOL for Windows 95 is equipped with Microsoft's Internet Explorer, enabling you to explore the World Wide Web with enhanced speed and ease. With its custom version of WINSOCK.DLL, you can use third-party Internet applications such as Netscape, Real Audio, Internet Phone, Shockwave, and Virtual Places over your AOL connection. This Winsock is automatically installed when you begin an AOL session, and removed when you sign off. AOL Branded Netscape can be downloaded through AOL by simply going to Keyword: Netscape, or it can be installed as a separate application from this CD-ROM.

Installation

1. Insert the America Online CD-ROM into your CD-ROM drive.
2. Click on the File Menu of your Windows Program Manager (or the Start menu on Windows 95) and select Run.
3. Type **d:\setup** (where "d" is the letter that corresponds to your CD-ROM drive). Press ENTER.
4. Follow the simple step-by-step instructions and when prompted, enter the special registration number and password found on the card beneath the CD-ROM.

Questions About Connecting? Need a Floppy Disk?
Need a Replacement CD-ROM?

For any questions about the CD-ROM, call America Online at 1-800-827-6364.

Free 50-Hour Trial

You must be 18 years of age or older. Use of America Online requires a major credit card or a checking account. Limit one free trial per individual. Use of America Online is conditioned upon acceptance of the terms of service. The free trial must be used within 30 days of your initial sign on. To avoid being charged your first monthly fee, simply cancel your membership before your free trial period ends. Members outside the continental U.S. and Hawaii and Alaska may pay communication surcharges, even during trial time. Members outside America Online's extensive selection of local access calling areas may incur charges applied to their telephone bill, even during trial time. See online registration information for complete details. America Online is a registered service mark of America Online, Inc. Windows is a trademark of Microsoft Corp. Other names are trademarks or service marks of their respective holders. 1996 America Online, Inc.

Licensing Agreement